Good Now

Ascension Messages from Sanhia: Volume II

Good Now

Ascension Messages from Sanhia: Volume II

Michael Hersey
with Sanhia

www.lightspira.com

Other books by Michael Hersey:

Ascension Numerology, 2016
God Blesses You, 2017

Published by: LightSpira, Sweden
www.lightspira.com

ISBN: 978-91-86613-41-9
First edition, 2022

Author: Michael Hersey
Word Whisperer: Ulla Lindgren
Book & Cover design: Marie Örnesved
Editing: Stella Hansen
Ascension Guidance: Sanhia

"Many are called but few are chosen" should be. "All are called but few choose to listen".

A Course in Miracles: Text.3.IV.7.12

It takes great learning to understand that all things, events, encounters and circumstances are helpful.

A Course in Miracles: Manual for Teachers.4.1.A.4.5

Content

Michael's Introduction

I have been channeling Sanhia for over thirty years. If you want to know that story, you can read about it in *Ascension Numerology: A Love Letter from Your Higher Self.* The significant thing for you to know now is that I am a conscious channel. I am fully aware of everything that comes through me from Sanhia. That means it is possible for me to block things that are uncomfortable or haven't yet been integrated into my own life. Therefore, as my spiritual development has progressed, the channeling has become clearer and stronger. I could say that I am now fearless in allowing Sanhia's full intention to shine through.

For years I wanted to find a way to share in print the wonderful things Sanhia was saying, but the time was not ripe. In 2009 Sanhia encouraged me to start channeling a short monthly message to be emailed to people who were interested. In 2014 we began posting them on our website: www.channelswithoutborders.com. Over time the messages became longer and deeper. In 2017 Sanhia let me know it was time to publish the then existing messages. That book was titled *God Blesses You: Ascension Messages from Sanhia.*

Let me explain a little about the co-creation process that gives birth to these messages. The procedure starts with my partner Ulla making a recorded interview with Sanhia, which I then transcribe. While typing I am guided to make significant changes in Sanhia's wording. For those of you who haven't heard Sanhia directly, it is quite an experience. He is spontaneous and dramatic, often repeating things for emphasis. Much of the communication is through the energy of his voice. This doesn't come through well when the words are read from print. Our job became one of not just transcribing, but of interpreting Sanhia's intent into a prose form. Sanhia also wants us to bring more of a sense of timelessness to the messages. He says to tell you that he is always pleased with the final result.

Sanhia's Introduction: Why not now?

Why not now? Do you look at your awakening process, your ascension, or your spiritual path and think that someday you hope to wake up? Do you assume that, sooner or later, you will drop your ego? If those are your thoughts I guarantee you that you are right. Someday it will happen, but it will not be today. And guess what kids, today is the only day you have. No matter how much you might wish it to be tomorrow, or even yesterday, it is always today. To say "someday" is to say "never". It will never be someday. It will only be the *eternal now*. Why not now? The choice is now or never (fortunately in the *eternal now* you can always re-choose). Those are the choices you have. There is no tomorrow. There is no next year or next lifetime. There is only the *eternal now*. Everything else belongs to the ego. If you wish to release the ego, the only thing you can do is to be 100% in this moment.

There is a wonderful English term called procrastination, which means "putting things off". This is not considered to be an admirable quality by the mass consciousness. The popular saying is, "never put off until tomorrow what you can do today". My suggestion to people has always been the reverse, "Never do today what you can put off until tomorrow". Today is for what is really important. If there isn't a significant reason for action, such as inner guidance or a strong desire, why give it time in your present? Put it on the back burner until it is time for action, if ever. Is waking up really important? If it isn't important enough to give your full focus to it today, admit that and stop playing games with yourself. Acknowledge if it is not so important to you to ascend, even though it might be a fun game to play around with. Be honest with yourself and say that you are not choosing to awaken at this time. On the other hand, you may realize that you really do want to drop your ego, but you don't know how to do it, so you wonder how it could be today. If the latter represents your thinking, you are at the right place at the right time. The purpose of this message is to explain to you what the *eternal now* means and how to always be here.

The *eternal now* means "this very moment". Nothing else matters. If you can successfully stay in the *eternal now*, you will awaken. So, you commit yourself to waking up, to remaining in the *eternal now*. Nothing is of greater importance. With everything else you can procrastinate, except this – if you want to awaken. There is no "should" about this. It cannot come from guilt; it must come from a deep desire or even from total desperation. This is not a comfortable process to go through. It is easy for the ego to find a way for you to skip out on it. If, however, you are aware of the pain and suffering that the ego always brings and you wish to drop it forever; if you want to let go of the specialness, the victimhood, the neediness, the emotional swings, the grief, and of feeling unloved and unlovable, and you realize there is no other way, then go for it. You do that by being vigilant with every thought and feeling you experience. If you sense or recognize that the thought or feeling is ego driven, ask the hard questions. Is this really true? If it isn't really true, what changes does that bring to what you do and feel?

Being committed to the *eternal now* and to awakening means that you embrace and welcome absolutely everything that comes into your life. You don't reject anything; you don't push anything away. You don't say to yourself that this isn't what you want. You don't judge anything that happens as wrong or bad. You stop pretending that you are in control and that you know how your life should be. You realize that if you knew how to awaken, you would be awake. How silly would it be to know and yet to stay asleep. Obviously, you don't have a clue what is good for you. Admit it. You have expressed to Spirit your wish to awaken, your wish to understand and live the truth, your wish to leave your ego. Therefore Spirit brings to you that opportunity in every moment. Are you embracing these gifts? If not, why not? Those are the questions to ask yourself. Is this the place where you think you know better than God, that *you* realize what would wake you up?

To awaken is to be enormously humble, the humility that comes from realizing that you don't know anything. You don't even comprehend what is good for you. In that humility, a place of trust is allowed. Everything that happens is for your greater good, no exceptions. Is it required that you understand the meaning of your gift? If it is for your good, does understanding really matter? It is acceptance, not understanding, that you seek. If it is for your greater good to understand, then explanations will be provided. It is that simple. If acceptance is hard, you have directions for your task for today. You believe something to be true that is not true. What is it? This moment is the time to do this work, not tomorrow, next week, or..... The alternative is to face the fact that you don't really want to wake up that much; you only want a fun game. You will be able to enjoy the ego illusion more if you don't pretend that you want to leave it behind. In that case, you will have a constant, lingering sense of failure, of not being good enough. You will have another reason to beat yourself up. That is the ego's game. If you are honest about it being a game, you can possibly have fun, win or lose (but of course you will lose). In Spirit's game, Spirit takes your hand and asks: "Why not now?" Tell me one good, true reason why you cannot awaken right now, one excuse for why you have to stay attached to the ego illusion and to take it seriously. Give me one proof why things have to be a certain way in order for you to be okay. Why not now?

An important awareness to have is whether or not you are presently in the *eternal now*. If you are thinking about something that happened in the past, no matter how recent or far back, you are not in the *eternal now*. Your job is to notice that your mind is traveling in the past and be aware of how that affects you at this moment. Are you angry? Do you feel victimized? Are you guilty, blaming yourself for past choices or actions? There is no way to be living in the past and also to be in the *eternal now*, awake, and free of the ego. One choice is to ask Spirit to help you let go of the past and to bring your focus back to the present. Maybe there is something you are holding on to that you believe about the past that it is time to release, to change that belief. For example, you might think that because your father treated you in a certain way you are left emotionally vulnerable. Is your father there in the room with you in this moment? Probably not. Maybe he is not even in a body anymore. Yet, are you inviting him into your present to control your life? Why do you choose to do that? In truth, what power can a memory of another person have on you in the present moment? The answer is *none*. You are doing this to yourself. How crazy is that? An idea has been planted in your mind about yourself that is not true and you are still repeating it to yourself. Look at this thought, this untruth. Whatever it is, it isn't true. Look at it until you understand that and then choose your thoughts. If you are in the *eternal now*, nothing matters except what is in this moment. Your job is to do whatever it takes to release the past. Change your mind. When you realize, accept, and trust that everything that happens to you is perfect, that includes the past. It was absolutely perfect that you had the father you had. Spirit could not have done better. It was precisely what you needed for your spiritual growth. Your job is to feel gratitude for that, to feel love for all that your father did for you. Your vision widens when you see through Spirit's eyes. Ego looks at the past and sees self as a victim. Spirit points out where your eyes were closed and helps you to open them to see the truth of what really happened. It doesn't matter whether you opened them then or you do it today. Time isn't real. The *eternal now* is real. What you see in this moment is true for all time. You can choose to carry your pain with you through all time or release it. The past is an enormous venue of not being here now. You can't be two places at once.

Then, of course, there is the future. What if this happens? Am I prepared for that? All the fear that you feel over what you should be doing to create your best possible future takes you out of the *eternal now*. And what about all of the things you believe you have no control over: accidents, disease, death, world events? This is all ego insanity. There is no future; there is just the *eternal now*. If you are taking care of the present, you are taking care of the only place you will ever be. All happens in the *eternal now*. Anything that comes into your experience is perfect. Remind yourself that you have no conscious awareness of what that perfect is. All you can do is receive what comes with humility and gratitude. When you notice you have a fear about the future, your only job is to look at the truth of that belief. It is never your job to change the world. Your only task is to change your mind, to release untruths. If you are fully in the *eternal now* you will have no time for tomorrow. This moment will keep your hands and mind full. One of these days you will notice that all of those old fears about the future are gone. That day will be the one where you finally find yourself firmly rooted in the *eternal now*.

It is an enormous habit to be in the past or the future, rather than to be in the *eternal now*. It requires willingness, an intention, and finally a discipline to be here. Ask Spirit for support. Ask to be gently reminded when you are drifting. There may be work for you to do concerning your beliefs about the past and the future. The work you do with them is in this moment. If you are in the past or the future, you can be sure that you are not dealing with truth. Leave your little confused ego mind and go sit with us above the battlefield. Look down at your silly little you with loving acceptance. Enjoy the humor of your running around with your head cut off. Each moment you are a little more in the *eternal now*. You are willing to be shown the next step. That step is being shown to you at this very moment. In the scope of time, this challenge seems enormous. In the *eternal now* it is just one step. To return to the beginning, your only job is to be present. If you are not there, do whatever it takes to release time. Thoughts of hopelessness or helplessness are not in the *eternal now*. Neither of them is true. If the thought comes that someday, probably, everybody, including yourself, will wake up, my question is "Why not now?" Why do you want to put it off? You feel incapable of doing it right now. Why? Why stop yourself with an ego lie? Don't give up on yourself. Why not now?

Good Now

Sunhia

Reading Instructions

Here are a few suggestions for how to use this book. Of course you are free to do whatever you are guided to do, but simply reading through from cover to cover in a few days is not likely to bring you the greatest benefit. The following are a few ideas you can keep in mind:

1. Read just one message at a time. Over the following days, contemplate, reread, and meditate upon the message. See if there is any action you are guided to take. The messages are arranged chronologically as they were channeled, but it isn't necessary for you to follow them in that order. However, some concepts are introduced and then further developed in later messages. Sometimes when that occurs there is a reference to look back to the earlier message.

2. On page 15 is a listing of themes. You might wish to scan it to see if there are any topics that particularly attract your attention. Under each theme is a listing of the messages that deal with that topic. You will find each message listed under multiple themes.

3. Each message is written for mass consumption rather than aimed at you, the individual reader. Everything in the message you are reading may not be for you today. Find what part speaks to you.

4. Directions for the *five-step process* are included on page 282.

5. The purpose of every message is to encourage you to realize your Divine nature and to experience your ascension.

Bon Voyage!

Themes

Messages are not organized in any particular fashion and each one might deal with a variety of different themes, while it answers a specific question. On these pages are all of the themes, each with a chronological listing of related messages for your deeper exploration. I can't stress enough that repeated reading, accompanied by reflection and contemplation will assist you in integrating these concepts into your being.

Acceptance
Letting what is be okay

21. Can we create heaven on earth?
23. Am I really supposed to accept everything that happens to me?
24. What is meant by pure non-duality?
38. How can I deal with my feelings of hopelessness?
39. What is the difference between judgment and discernment?
46. How can I let go of grief?
51. Is there a difference between awakening and ascension?
52. Will you speak to us again about the Coronavirus?

Ascension
The reason you are here, realizing your Divinity, your Oneness with God

Sanhia's Introduction: Why not now?
3. When am I finally going to experience my ascension?
4. Do I need to transform all of my fears before I can ascend?
6. What if my "old stories" are good ones?
8. What is the difference between a special and a holy relationship?
10. What spiritual practices should I be doing? (Part 1)
11. What spiritual practices should I be doing? (Part 2)
12. How can I see the Divinity in other people?

Attachment

*The false belief that you need something or
someone in order to be happy*

Awakening

*Letting go of the ego, being aware that illusion
is an illusion*

12. How can I see the Divinity in other people?

13. How do you define yourself?

14. How can we deal with the world immigration problem?

15. Why is it so hard for me to forgive?

16. What do you mean when you call the world an illusion?

17. Are other people a part of the illusion?

19. Do we have free will?

20. What if this was the last day of your life?

21. Can we create heaven on earth?

22. Do you confuse cause and effect?

23. Am I really supposed to accept everything that happens to me?

24. What is meant by pure non-duality?

26. Is it part of my purpose to help heal others?

27. How do I give it to Spirit?

28. How can we not see children as innocent victims?

29. How can I be a better parent?

31. How can I become One with God?

32. What is the meaning of the Coronavirus?

33. How long will the Coronavirus last?

34. Is the ego part of me or is it separate?

35. What is the nature of power?

36. Is compassion an important tool for awakening?

37. What part, if any, should prayer play in my spiritual path?

38. How can I deal with my feelings of hopelessness?

40. How do I deal with my fear of death?

41. Do I have to surrender my personal identity in order to ascend?

42. Are love and hate opposites?

43. If the world is an illusion, why does it feel so real?

44. If the world is an illusion, why does it matter what I do?

47. How can I get control over my ego?

51. Is there a difference between awakening and ascension?

Dream

The illusion, the movie, the ego world

Duality

The "reality" of the illusion; there are two sides to everything, opposites; the gold standard for untruth

Ego

A terrified voice you listen to that thinks you are separate from God and doesn't believe in your Divinity

23. Am I really supposed to accept everything that happens to me?
24. What is meant by pure non-duality?
25. Do I have to be perfect to ascend?
26. Is it part of my purpose to help heal others?
27. How do I give it to Spirit?
29. How can I be a better parent?
30. Why is it so difficult to let go of the illusion of the world?
31. How can I become One with God?
32. What is the meaning of the Coronavirus?
33. How long will the Coronavirus last?
34. Is the ego part of me or is it separate?
35. What is the nature of power?
37. What part, if any, should prayer play in my spiritual path?
38. How can I deal with my feelings of hopelessness?
39. What is the difference between judgment and discernment?
41. Do I have to surrender my personal identity in order to ascend?
42. Are love and hate opposites?
43. If the world is an illusion, why does it feel so real?
44. If the world is an illusion, why does it matter what I do?
47. How can I get control over my ego?
49. Can you give a few more hints on how to go about finding the truth?
50. Should we still be doing the forgiveness process?
51. Is there a difference between awakening and ascension?
52. Will you speak to us again about the Coronavirus?

Fear

*An insane response to a non-existent threat, the cause
of all suffering*

43. If the world is an illusion, why does it feel so real?
45. Can you explain more about others being my mirror?
50. Should we still be doing the forgiveness process?

Gift

*Realizing that everything that comes into your life is a
present for you to assist in realizing your Divine nature*

Sanhia's Introduction: Why not now?
3. When am I finally going to experience my ascension?
6. What if my "old stories" are good ones?
13. How do you define yourself?
32. What is the meaning of the Coronavirus?
38. How can I deal with my feelings of hopelessness?
52. Will you speak to us again about the Coronavirus?

Grace

*The support of God, unearnable,
because the time has come*

3. When am I finally going to experience my ascension?
4. Do I need to transform all of my fears before I can ascend?
20. What if this was the last day of your life?
24. What is meant by pure non-duality?
43. If the world is an illusion, why does it feel so real?
52. Will you speak to us again about the Coronavirus?

Gratitude

*Feeling thankful for everything that happens to
you, gratefulness for everything God has given you*

12. How can I see the Divinity in other people?
13. How do you define yourself?
21. Can we create heaven on earth?
32. What is the meaning of the Coronavirus?
33. How long will the Coronavirus last?

13. How do you define yourself?
26. Is it part of my purpose to help heal others?
30. Why is it so difficult to let go of the illusion of the world?
31. How can I become One with God?
32. What is the meaning of the Coronavirus?
34. Is the ego part of me or is it separate?
40. How do I deal with my fear of death?
41. Do I have to surrender my personal identity in order to ascend?
51. Is there a difference between awakening and ascension?

12. How can I see the Divinity in other people?
24. What is meant by pure non-duality?
25. Do I have to be perfect to ascend?
26. Is it part of my purpose to help heal others?
33. How long will the Coronavirus last?
35. What is the nature of power?
38. How can I deal with my feelings of hopelessness?
39. What is the difference between judgment and discernment?
40. How do I deal with my fear of death?
44. If the world is an illusion, why does it matter what I do?
45. Can you explain more about others being my mirror?
50. Should we still be doing the forgiveness process?

Intention

*What you decide you will do, communicating
to Spirit what you wish to manifest*

4. Do I need to transform all of my fears before I can ascend?
20. What if this was the last day of your life?
23. Am I really supposed to accept everything that happens to me?
45. Can you explain more about others being my mirror?
49. Can you give a few more hints on how to go about finding the truth?

Judgment

*Believing there is such a thing as right and
wrong, deciding what and who fits in each category*

Sanhia's Introduction: Why not now?
5. #Me Too?
8. What is the difference between a special and a holy relationship?
9. When should I share my spiritual perspective with others?
12. How can I see the Divinity in other people?
15. Why is it so hard for me to forgive?
16. What do you mean when you call the world an illusion?
17. Are other people a part of the illusion?
21. Can we create heaven on earth?
24. What is meant by pure non-duality?
25. Do I have to be perfect to ascend?
26. Is it part of my purpose to help heal others?
28. How can we not see children as innocent victims?
29. How can I be a better parent?
30. Why is it so difficult to let go of the illusion of the world?
31. How can I become One with God?
33. How long will the Coronavirus last?
39. What is the difference between judgment and discernment?
42. Are love and hate opposites?
45. Can you explain more about others being my mirror?
50. Should we still be doing the forgiveness process?

Mirror

Wherever you look, there you are

11. What spiritual practices should I be doing? (Part 2)
17. Are other people a part of the illusion?
26. Is it part of my purpose to help heal others?
32. What is the meaning of the Coronavirus?
33. How long will the Coronavirus last?
36. Is compassion an important tool for awakening?
42. Are love and hate opposites?
44. If the world is an illusion, why does it matter what I do?
45. Can you explain more about others being my mirror?

Movie

Life is just a picture show, it's your movie

13. How do you define yourself?
23. Am I really supposed to accept everything that happens to me?
38. How can I deal with my feelings of hopelessness?
45. Can you explain more about others being my mirror?

Oneness

Another definition of truth, all is one, you are One with God

3. When am I finally going to experience my ascension?
26. Is it part of my purpose to help heal others?
30. Why is it so difficult to let go of the illusion of the world?
31. How can I become One with God?
32. What is the meaning of the Coronavirus?
34. Is the ego part of me or is it separate?
35. What is the nature of power?
36. Is compassion an important tool for awakening?
37. What part, if any, should prayer play in my spiritual path?
40. How do I deal with my fear of death?
48. Sanhia, how can we trust that the things you are telling us are true?
51. Is there a difference between awakening and ascension?

Projection

*Pretending that what is going on with you is
actually going on with somebody else, scapegoating*

14. How can we deal with the world immigration problem?
17. Are other people a part of the illusion?
23. Am I really supposed to accept everything that happens to me?
25. Do I have to be perfect to ascend?
28. How can we not see children as innocent victims?
29. How can I be a better parent?
30. Why is it so difficult to let go of the illusion of the world?
31. How can I become One with God?
33. How long will the Coronavirus last?
36. Is compassion an important tool for awakening?
39. What is the difference between judgment and discernment?
41. Do I have to surrender my personal identity in order to ascend?
45. Can you explain more about others being my mirror?

Purpose

What you are here to do

3. When am I finally going to experience my ascension?
20. What if this was the last day of your life?
35. What is the nature of power?
51. Is there a difference between awakening and ascension?

30. Why is it so difficult to let go of the illusion of the world?
49. Can you give a few more hints on how to go about finding the truth?

Responsibility
Not just a good idea, it is the law

2. What do you mean when you say to give it to Spirit?
8. What is the difference between a special and a holy relationship?
14. How can we deal with the world immigration problem?
18. Is there any place for fun on the ascension path?
22. Do you confuse cause and effect?
28. How can we not see children as innocent victims?
29. How can I be a better parent?
41. Do I have to surrender my personal identity in order to ascend?
42. Are love and hate opposites?

Right and wrong
Belief in this is the original sin

1. If the body is an illusion, why do I have one?
9. When should I share my spiritual perspective with others?
11. What spiritual practices should I be doing? (Part 2)
15. Why is it so hard for me to forgive?
18. Is there any place for fun on the ascension path?
21. Can we create heaven on earth?
24. What is meant by pure non-duality?
26. Is it part of my purpose to help heal others?
39. What is the difference between judgment and discernment?
50. Should we still be doing the forgiveness process?

1. If the body is an illusion, why do I have one?

4. Do I need to transform all of my fears before I can ascend?

7. Can you tell more about being in *the now*?

8. What is the difference between a special and a holy relationship?

11. What spiritual practices should I be doing? (Part 2)

13. How do you define yourself?

14. How can we deal with the world immigration problem?

16. What do you mean when you call the world an illusion?

19. Do we have free will?

21. Can we create heaven on earth?

23. Am I really supposed to accept everything that happens to me?

24. What is meant by pure non-duality?

25. Do I have to be perfect to ascend?

26. Is it part of my purpose to help heal others?

27. How do I give it to Spirit?

28. How can we not see children as innocent victims?

30. Why is it so difficult to let go of the illusion of the world?

31. How can I become One with God?

34. Is the ego part of me or is it separate?

35. What is the nature of power?

37. What part, if any, should prayer play in my spiritual path?

38. How can I deal with my feelings of hopelessness?

39. What is the difference between judgment and discernment?

40. How do I deal with my fear of death?

41. Do I have to surrender my personal identity in order to ascend?

42. Are love and hate opposites?

43. If the world is an illusion, why does it feel so real?

44. If the world is an illusion, why does it matter what I do?

45. Can you explain more about others being my mirror?

47. How can I get control over my ego?

50. Should we still be doing the forgiveness process?
51. Is there a difference between awakening and ascension?

Specialness
*Wanting to appear better than others so God
will choose you; this can also be projected upon another*

6. What if my "old stories" are good ones?
8. What is the difference between a special and a holy relationship?
26. Is it part of my purpose to help heal others?
30. Why is it so difficult to let go of the illusion of the world?
31. How can I become One with God?
36. Is compassion an important tool for awakening?

Story
Personal "belief" that creates your reality

6. What if my "old stories" are good ones?
12. How can I see the Divinity in other people?
13. How do you define yourself?

Trust and faith
*The bridge between the human and the
Divine*

2. What do you mean when you say to give it to Spirit?
10. What spiritual practices should I be doing? (Part 1)
11. What spiritual practices should I be doing? (Part 2)
23. Am I really supposed to accept everything that happens to me?

5. #Me Too?

14. How can we deal with the world immigration problem?

32. What is the meaning of the Coronavirus?

33. How long will the Coronavirus last?

48. Sanhia, how can we trust that the things you are telling us are true?

52. Will you speak to us again about the Coronavirus?

If the body is an illusion, why do I have one?

I have mentioned many times that the body, along with all physical manifestation, is an illusion. It is not real. It is not the truth of who you are. Sometimes people ask me, "Why do we even have a body? What is it all about? The body certainly seems real. If you pinch me it hurts. It seems like I have a body. If I run up against the wall, it feels solid. It's there. If I go under water, I can only stay so long. What do you mean this is an illusion?" These are all very good points. The ego does an excellent job in asking good questions.

What is there to do is to find the source. When you have conflict in the world, one person making a response to another's action, it is in reaction. This can go back and forth endlessly. Where is the source of all of that contention? Where does it begin? It is one of those chicken and egg questions. When you speak of reincarnation, you may say that you have something happening now because of something you did in a previous life. Why did you do it then? Well, you had a life previous to that, and so back it goes. Where is the source? If we go far enough back, you arrive at the first man and the first woman. Is that the source? The Bible will tell you its creation story. There were Adam and Eve. They were in paradise and everything was perfect. Then she tempted him. Actually, she was first tempted herself by the serpent. Who was this snake? The serpent encourages her to just eat of this apple. God said not to eat of the apple or there will be severe consequences. That's the Bible story.

What is the real story? The serpent is the ego. The fruit was of the tree of the knowledge of good and evil. Upon eating the apple, good and bad appeared. That was the original illusion. They are not real, as the ego is not real. The god that kicks you out of heaven is not the real God. It is your guilt. All of that is part of the illusion that began then. You allowed this voice that was separate from God to have power over you. You decided that maybe truth was being spoken. The ego said to believe in good and bad. Spirit said this will separate you from God; more correctly, create the illusion of separation. Spirit didn't threaten punishment, It warned of the illusion you would thereby be creating. This was what Christianity calls "original sin". The sin is the belief in good and evil. It separates you from God. Out of this whole separation story, you, who were in truth One with God, created this illusion of physicalness, created a world that seemed real, but is fueled by the opposing energies of good and evil, or duality. You manifested bodies and disappeared into them to hide from God, forgetting your Divinity, believing that your body was the truth of who you were. You believed that this body that feels pain when you pinch it, and this wall that you can't walk through, and this water which seems impossible to breathe in are very real.

Before we talk about what to do with these bodies on this earth, in this physicalness, the first thing to understand is that they absolutely are illusions. They are not real. You are real, but your body is not. God is real. The physical universe is not. If something does not last forever, it is not real. If it has a birth and a death; it is an illusion. All that is real is eternal. It is good news is that the world is an illusion. I say good news because most of you aren't having such a great time in it. The news of its unreality should be welcome to you. Time is not real either. God is timeless. You don't have to worry about how long this hell is going to go on because time doesn't exist.

We come back to the original question. Why even have these bodies? The answer is that in order to fully realize your Divine nature and Oneness with God, you need to do it in a body in the physical world. In a sense, you have locked yourself into this world and only you can let yourself out. When you use up one body, because they are quite expendable, you eventually choose to create another. If you don't realize the truth in that body, you create another, and another. You have already created countless ones.

The body is not something to be honored or revered. Though it is not Divine or real, it is a tool, a vehicle. You respect and take care of it because it is a required part of realizing your Divinity. You do it in a body. If you deny the body or fight the bodily desires, through severe fasting, defying sexual desire, eliminating music and dance, or even gouging out your eyes so as not to be distracted by physical beauty, you are giving power to the physical. You are saying that it has such control over you that you have to go to war with it in order to ascend. It would be more aligned with truth to hold the physical as neutral. It has no meaning one way or the other. But now you are in a body believing it is real, which all of you do even though you might have some awareness through reading things here or from other studies, such as *A Course in Miracles*. You haven't had the full experience of your Divinity. If you had, you would no longer be with your body. While you still believe your body is real you can't pretend that it doesn't exist. That won't work for you, so you take care of it. Otherwise, you will just have to trade it in for another. The body is a tool, and you take care of your tools or they are of less use. You created your illusion of separation by creating the illusion that you were a body, so you create the end of the illusion through a body. It is that simple.

In the eyes of God, none of this ever happened. Or, we could say it happened in the wink of an eye. The ego says there have been billions of years of evolution, so many lifetimes, and so much trouble and pain. But, it is just a blink of the eye of God. As you created the illusion, God created the solution. He made the Holy Spirit. As the ego dispenses confusion and falseness in one ear, Spirit whispers truth in the other. At some point, you will choose to begin shutting out the ego and listening to Spirit. At some point this transition will become complete, and you give your life fully to Spirit. You let go of judgment, separation, and fear. You fully realize the truth. Then time begins to disappear along with the universe. We call that ascension. You do it while you are in a body. That is the only reason you have a body. There is no necessity for you to suffer in the body while you are completing this process. Suffering only comes from listening to the ego. God would have you enjoy every moment. As you are transforming fear into love you will experience less and less pain on all planes.

Begin by acknowledging the body is not you, is not real. Do this even if you don't fully understand or believe it. Accept that everything the ego tells you is a lie (Book I: Message 77: *How do I discern Spirit from ego?*). Give intention to turn your mind over to Spirit. Ask It to keep you focused on the truth until that is all that is there for you. The ego will always give value to things in the physical world and have goals. You will have goals. Don't put any value in them beyond holding them as tools for your ascension. Nothing of the world has any other value. Any additional importance you place on the physical will bring you pain and separation from God. Spirit will provide you with all your physical needs as you are realizing your Divinity. It *is* that easy.

Good Now

Sanhia

What do you mean
when you say to give it to Spirit?

People have a variety of reactions when I suggest they give something to Spirit. Some are upset at the thought and express that it feels like I want them to give their power away. Does that mean they don't trust themselves? Others are willing but don't know how to go about giving something to Spirit. Still others make the attempt but wonder how they can tell what Spirit's response is. In reality, you have but two choices. You can give something to Spirit or you can give it to the ego. That's it. You may think it is you alone making the decision, but if you haven't given it to Spirit, "your decision" is really made by the ego.

You are not expected to be sure what it means to give it to Spirit or how what Spirit decides is different than what the ego might choose. It can be very confusing. The ego has been running your life, and your lives, for what feels like an eternity to you. The place to truly begin in meeting God and finding your Divinity is to accept that you don't know anything. Whatever you think you know is probably wrong. Even if you are right, you are still just guessing. And you probably won't guess right the next time, nor have any certainty of knowing when you have made a lucky stab at truth. You won't be able to take advantage of being right, because you will follow it up with so many wrong choices. If you knew how to realize your Divinity you would have done it long ago. But here you are, in confusion, in pain. Even if you have managed to minimize some of that discomfort, you are still here, not experiencing your Divinity. The question is, "How do you get there?" Your answer is (let's see who has been paying attention), "Sanhia, I don't know". When you know that you don't know, you know a lot. You know more than most people. If you also know that when you don't know, you give it to Spirit — you know more than almost everyone.

When you give it to Spirit, you let go of it, whatever "it" is, whatever the confusion is, whatever the choice is, whatever the weakness is, whatever the pain is. You let go of it and give it to Spirit. You don't think about it anymore. You stop worrying. If you notice yourself doing either of those two things, give it to Spirit. Again! It is no longer your responsibility. Keep giving it to Spirit until you have let go of it. Don't tell Spirit when it has to give you an answer or how it should look. Have no expectation of the form or the means. You don't know what it will look like. You don't know what Spirit is going to do. Remember, you don't know anything. All you do is trust. Whatever comes into your life next is Spirit's response. What do you do if what comes into your life doesn't look right, if you have a hard time receiving it? You give it to Spirit. That's all you do. In between giving it to Spirit and feeling clear about the response, you remain a "happy idiot". You don't know anything, but you don't care. Whether or not the guidance you receive makes happy sense to you, follow it. Do your best to trust. If that is hard to do — I'm waiting for the drum roll — give it to Spirit. How much simpler can it be?

That's what we mean by saying "Give it to Spirit". It is an acknowledgement that the ego is never going to get you there. Never! Its suggestions will be endless. Do this. Do that. Meditate every day. Change your diet. Give up everything you enjoy. It has all kinds of ideas for how to realize your ascension, all of them guaranteed not to work because the ego does not believe that such a goal is attainable. If they worked, the ego would be out of a job, in fact out of existence. This is a great challenge for you because you believe so strongly that it is your effort, your will power, your determination, your spiritual wisdom, your good deeds...something from you that will lift you out of this hell. But it isn't and it won't. None of it! All that you can do is give it up to Spirit. That is all you can do.

Your mind is absolutely helpless in getting you out of the grasp of the ego. The greatest pronouncements of the ego appear to come from the "outside". The whole world agrees that death is certain and unavoidable. Who are you to fly in the face of that? It doesn't matter how close to unanimity those around you are. If the choice is not what your heart most desires, give it to Spirit. That is the job for your mind, to learn to give everything to Spirit. Let go of everything else.

When you give it Spirit there is always a response. When It gives you an answer it is always for *the now*. Spirit may suggest something different tomorrow. Ego tends to give rigid orders. It tells you that there is only one way to do something and you should always do it that way. This becomes an idea of what to do. That is why spiritual practices don't work. Spiritual practices are not from Spirit. They are always ideas from the ego. Rituals don't work either. The ego embeds "should-ism" and guilt for non-performance. Even those of you who are working with *A Course in Miracles* might consider this. Jesus has no expectation that you be loyal to the *Course* every day. If you are having difficulty doing the *Course* one day, give it to Spirit. The proof of this discipline is not in its regular repetition, but in how you take it to heart in every moment. If you are doing that, you will find yourself constantly giving everything to Spirit. Enjoy the *Course* or give it to Spirit.

The goal is for you not to carry anything around with you. You are empty, light, and free. If this is not your experience, give whatever is weighing you down to Spirit. Say, "Spirit please handle this for me. Thank you." It's like having your own personal assistant. You all have special needs, so give them to your personal "spiritual" assistant. And let go. Be free.

Good Now

Sanhia

When am I finally going to experience my ascension?

The basic topic of all my messages is ascension, the realizing of your Divinity. For some of you, this is a rather new concept or one that you haven't explored deeply. If that is the case for you, I suggest that you go back and read some of the earlier messages that deal with this subject, either on the website (channelswithoutborders.com) or in the first book (*God Blesses You: Ascension Messages from Sanhia*). Some of you who have been working with ascension for some time have the questions "When am I finally going to realize my Divinity? How long is this going to take?" For those of you who read the message last month, the short answer to those questions is to give them to Spirit, as you give everything to Spirit. You give it to Spirit in the spirit of ignorance. You don't know anything about the timing or importance of the realization of your ascension. If you are looking at it from the ego standpoint, your ascension is about you. "When do I get mine? I don't give a crap about anybody else! When am I going to get out of this hellhole, get rid all of this shit in my life, stop being born again to parents who - well you know how parents are - and bring an end to teachers, police, governments, war, and rape? When do I get out of all of this?" Even though you might deny that you look on your ascension in quite that light, if you are honest with yourself you really do. You might not word things in quite that way, because you want to convince God that you are such a saint, but there is ego selfishness and separation involved in any desire to experience your Divinity now. When you feel that urgency, you can never experience your Divine perfection, because you are not coming from the truth of you.

We started with the short answer, now it is time for the medium depth and length response. You absolutely need to give the timing to Spirit and give up all attachment to when you will realize your Divinity. This is not your decision. That belongs to Spirit. If it *were* up to you, the choice would really belong to the ego. But, the ego can never choose Oneness. Its existence is based on separation. Ascension is about realizing Oneness. To demand something from Spirit is an act of separation. This keeps you stuck where you are. You can't possibly realize your ascension until you don't care whether you experience it or not. You are absolutely unattached. Some of you have said to me that you really want to heal some problem. Perhaps it is with a health issue or finances or relationships. When these desires are expressed, I look you in the eye (as much as I am capable of doing that) and say, "What do you want more; to realize your ascension or to heal that issue?" If you choose the worldly desire, I encourage you to ask Spirit for support, but remind you that you will continue to live in hell, no matter what Spirit does. Until your desire for ascension is the number one thing in your life, it will not occur. You will continue to cycle through incarnations until your priorities shift. There is no judgment of you involved. You are welcome to take as long as you wish. On the other hand, if you are one who has chosen ascension, and you have surrendered everything else to Spirit, it is time to surrender your desire for ascension also. The realization of your Divinity will happen at the perfect moment. Your only job is to be present, to listen to and follow Spirit.

Now let's move on to the more fully developed answer to this ascension timing question. Spirit has a master plan for you and for every other human. You can choose to play your role in that master plan or you can listen to ego. To fully play your role you give everything to Spirit. You are then told what to do and you do it. Your ego fear is that relinquishing direction to Spirit will leave you forced to go against your own will. Actually, your will and Spirit's are One, but you are only partially aware of what yours truly is. There may be significant things for you to do in a body in order to support others in bodies in following their part of the Divine plan. If you were to realize your ascension today, to leave behind this physicalness, you would be unable to carry out this part of the plan. You couldn't fully play your role. You could work as I do, but that is not what Spirit has set up for you right now or you would be doing it. Your task is to listen to Spirit to find out what your present purpose is and then do it. In previous messages we have called this Right Livelihood. It is doing what you came here to do, absolutely and with full integrity. The only way that you can do this is to acknowledge that you have no idea what you are here to do. Whatever you think it is, that is at best only a piece of it. Let Spirit guide you. Spirit will present you with what you are here to do and what to say. You have a gift to offer to the other Divine beings around you. It is the same gift that Spirit is offering you. First you receive it from Spirit; then you give it others. In fact you don't fully receive it until you do share it with others. The giving and the receiving are One, as are you and the others, along with Spirit and God. Spirit will let you know when It is through with you, and you have completed your function on earth. It is on Spirit's time, not yours. You don't have a say in this. Your say would be from the ego.

Many of you believe that your ascension is something that you earn, perhaps through good works. Your ascension is not earned. It is extended to you through the grace of God. When you fully receive the grace of God, which comes when you let go of everything else; you realize your Divinity. The grace of God is with you now, and has always been with you. But you are not receiving it. It is this process of surrendering to Spirit that allows you to open to the grace of God. It comes to you through the messages and guidance of Spirit. As you share with others what Spirit has given, you begin to realize this grace, not as a learning, but as a knowing. How much sharing will it take until you know? Give that to Spirit. It is none of your business. That is the question of the ego, which only wants to know the answer so it can throw a monkey wrench into the gears to slow down the process. The true appearance of God is the disappearance of the ego. It is not for you to know. It is not for you even to wonder. Your ascension is part of a Divine plan. It will come at the perfect time for the ascension of all. Nobody's ascension is complete until everybody's ascension is realized. It is not just about you. We are all One. If you are still in a body, that is Spirit's purpose. If you are concerned about the status of your body – your health or your aging process - give that to Spirit. You can't choose to leave your body in order to experience your Divinity, because there is nothing real for you to leave. The body is an illusion. You can't leave something that is not there. When your desire can only be fulfilled by ascension, you have given the body an importance that it doesn't have. You have created an impossible situation. If you are ascended you would have no desire to be ascended, because that is all that you are and have always been. The desire proves that you are in illusion.

The only way to make the jump is to let go of every part of the illusion and give it to Spirit. Receive back whatever Spirit sends you. When the next confusion is felt, give it to Spirit. And on and on until there is nothing remaining to let go of and Spirit is fully directing your life. When the time comes where the Oneness benefits by you no longer being in a body, you will realize your ascension. In the meantime, just let go and enjoy the ride.

Good Now

Sanhia

Do I need to transform all of my fears before I can ascend?

We will continue in this message with the theme of ascension. Many of you are doing a wonderful work here, facing your fears and perhaps dealing with them through the *five-step process*. When the energy in your body is transformed from fear to love, the transition is permanent. This does not mean that you may not create more fear in the future, but if you have the intention of aligning with and giving everything to Spirit you are not as likely to manifest new fear energy in your body. There is, however the residual old fear that you are still carrying with you.

While I do not wish in any way to discourage you from continuing to work with the process to transform any fear that you become aware of, I do want to give you the following warning. You may believe in an "incremental" approach to ascension. You may have the idea that if you chisel away at your fear a little bit at a time there will eventually be nothing left and you will realize your ascension. I want to give you a different way to visualize this. Those of you who have studied math in the past may remember the image to the right, or perhaps it will just trigger your math phobia. There is a function in geometry which generates an asymptote. This is a straight line that is approached by a curved line. The curved line gets closer and closer to the asymptote without ever touching it. The distance between the curve and the asymptote continues to be cut in half, but, in infinity, the curved line never reaches the asymptote. Close, oh so close, but no cigar. Cutting the distance in half will never fully eliminate it.

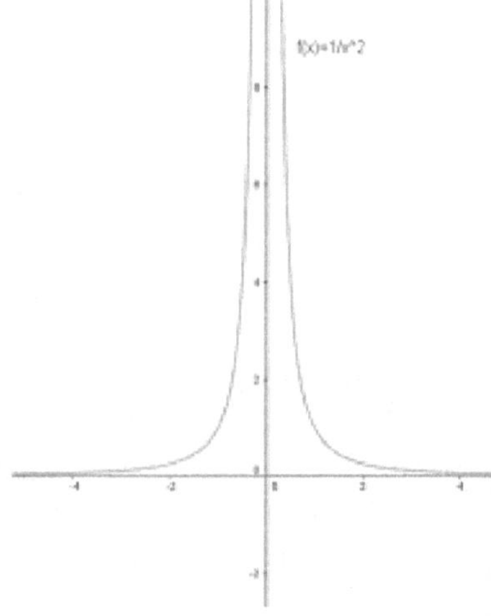

Let's look at how this relates to your ascension process. Though there is a finite amount of negative fear energy carried in your body, the *five-step process* also transforms it geometrically. You may think that if you keep chiseling away it will all disappear, but this is like the asymptote. It represents your ascension, while the curved line measures the fear you are continuing to transform. You keep getting closer and closer to realizing your Divine self, but never fully realize it. The upside is that as you approach the awareness of your Divine self, you experience more joy and less pain in your life. You likely find yourself providing more of your Divine service for others. Your ego is less of an irritant. But you don't fully realize your Divinity.

Again, I am not suggesting that you stop working with your stuff. If you feel pain or fear, by all means reduce the pressure. Transform it into love. This leaves you much more capable of hearing Spirit and following Its direction. What I would encourage you to let go of is the thought that facing your fears is enough. It is not by your work that you realize your ascension; it is by the grace of God. If it is not about eliminating all of your fear, what is it about? It is about giving everything to Spirit. In *A Course in Miracles* Jesus speaks of the *sacred moment*. This is when you absolutely experience the Oneness with God. It is not something that can be forced into being. It happens when you give up all intention and become One with whatever Spirit is presenting. This realization does not require that you be free of all fear. You do not need to work and work until every last drop of fear is squeezed from your body. As we explained above, that is not going to happen. You can only approach that point, but can never reach it. There is no magic point on your curved line where you suddenly jump over to the line of infinity (Divinity). There is no order. I can't look at each of you and measure how close you stand to realizing your Divinity. Your position on the curved line measures nothing about the timing of your ascension. It is only about surrendering to the *sacred moment,* about being open to Spirit and to the grace of God.

But Sanhia, you may be thinking, you are beginning to sound like a broken record. Give it to Spirit. Give it to Spirit. Is there anything else? Of course! If you are in pain, do the process. There is no reason for you to suffer. If you are pain free, but wondering what to do next - you give that thought to Spirit. There is nothing for you to do. Anything that you might choose to do would only get in your way. Your only job is to get out of the way. That may sound like a double-edged sword; the thing to do is not to do. How can you think about not doing? That seems crazy. Of course it is. Your entire creation is crazy. It is insane. Your mind can never think its way out of it. Enjoy your insanity, and give it to Spirit. There is nothing else to do, nothing to worry about. Any attempt to realize your ascension comes from the ego. It comes from the assumption that you are not who you are. It assumes that you are separate from God, when you are not. Only the ego can have that thought. The truth of you knows your Divinity. The good news is that you are off the hook. There is nothing you have to do, nothing you have to worry about. Listen to Spirit. That Voice will remind you of the truth. You are already ascended.

Good Now

Sanhia

#Me Too?

Today I would like to make some comments on world events, the things going on around you right now. One of the biggest current happenings, or what Ulla's Divine guidance calls "cosmic wind", is around the energy that has acquired the label "#MeToo". There are those points in time where there is a shift in mass consciousness. They are unpredictable and always come as a surprise. To those who have wanted the change, it has been much too long in coming. However, then it arrives with such a speed and power that it kind of takes the breath away.

I can give you a partial list of such "cosmic winds" in recent history. First was the civil rights movement in the United States. After centuries of being held down, suddenly those of African descent had the right to vote, to attend integrated schools, to hold higher paying better jobs, and to live in better neighborhoods. Not by any stretch of the imagination were the issues of prejudice, segregation, and inequality solved, but there was an enormous leap. Shortly after that another great leap occurred, this time for women's rights in many parts of the world. For the first time in history, doors began to swing open to allow women to hold jobs in all fields and to rise to positions of power. This allowed them to have more financial independence and control of their lives, besides making it possible to pursue their dreams. This did not immediately create a level playing field in pay and opportunity, but the change was exponential. Much more recently, there came a rapid change in the acceptance of those who prefer same sex relationships. Less than seventy years ago, such actions not only caused one to be shunned in western society, but were grounds for imprisonment. Now, in many places, the right to marry, or at least to enjoy the same legal benefits, is afforded to same sex couples. Again, has all prejudice dissipated? Of course not, but in all three of these cases the mass consciousness quickly shifted. What had not been possible or legal was now protected by law and could happen.

Now we are on the threshold of another "cosmic wind". Throughout much of history there was little legal or societal consequence for men who sexually mistreated women. This is not to say that there were not convictions for rape or assault, but they were the exception rather than the rule, and there was little to halt harassment. More likely to happen was that if a woman came forward with accusations, she became the "evil one" and her reputation suffered - not to speak of receiving retribution relating to her financial/career prospects - while the man denied everything. Now the tables have turned. It is hard to look at the news in the U.S. without seeing the story of the latest kingpin to be the recipient of multiple accusations of sexual abuse. Women feel empowered to speak up. Many who were afraid to speak out are now coming forward. Men are losing their positions and their reputations. This will make it far more difficult in the future for a man to get away with such behavior. The likelihood of prosecution will deter many from taking such actions. Laws are created to guide the behavior of those who are motivated by fear rather than love. Most people would not choose to do things that would bring harm to another. For the others, the threat of legal problems and of social rejection is necessary. That is what is in the process of occurring. Are women now fully protected? Of course not, but it is likely that safety will continue to expand. A leap has occurred.

Now let's look at all of this from a spiritual perspective. For you as an individual to progress spiritually, it is absolutely necessary for you to listen to and honor your feminine side. This will guide you to a place of love and safety, a place where you can hear Spirit. The same is true for a culture. A society that cannot respect the feminine energy is doomed to spiritual frustration. The mass consciousness is not a happy one. The old saying "Happy wife, happy life" is apt. If a society serves the feminine, its spirituality and love will bloom. Remember that "feminine" and "female" are not synonyms. All people possess feminine and masculine energy.

There is another side to this coin. Before this "cosmic wind" blew through, the prevailing belief was that women are victims to men. Masculine energy cannot be trusted. If women feel empowered now to speak up so that they can fight the evil power of masculinity, it will be a long battle, one they will be fighting for the rest of their lives. Not all women have experienced "#MeToo". They have not all experienced physical abuse. Think about what we have said in the past about victimhood and being the power in your life (go to *Sanhia Messages* on the website and choose *victimization* or go to Book I and look for messages under the theme *victimization*). Some women hesitated to speak out in the past because they felt guilty. It was not that they consciously welcomed the abuse, but the male energy defined it for them in that way. Some women felt guilty for being unable to say no. Above all they feared that the only way to get ahead or to support themselves and their children was to surrender to this male power. They felt guilty because they had given their power away. Some women, however, refused to give away their power, or did it once and learned from the experience. We would encourage the "#MeToo" energy to be not just, "I have been abused", but more importantly "Me too! I will take the power in my life. I will not be a victim. There is nothing that I need to do, that I do not want to do, in order to create what I wish to have in my life." This is not an either/or situation. You do not need to sacrifice yourself to receive what you want. Work with your fears with the *five-step process*. Give it to Spirit. Ask for the peace you want in your life.

This "cosmic wind" is supporting the release of a great deal of anger, vindictiveness, and judgment toward these male perpetrators. We recognize the pain you are feeling. There is no judgment about it. Feel free to express it and allow it to move. Then let it go. If you hold on to the anger, your blame will eat away at you. If you seek revenge, then as you sow so shall you reap. If you have the awareness that your judgment is always ultimately of yourself, perhaps it will be easier to forgive. The forgiveness is infinitely important. It is not a question of wrong or right. If you hold the energy of judgment, you will be held victim to it. The cycle continues. It does not serve you. You can also work with *Ho'oponopono* (Book I: Message 8: *Why is forgiveness important?*)

We want to remind you that this is an illusion. This physical world, full of drama and stories, is not real. They will become nothing when you leave your body. They are nothing now. Your job is to realize your Divinity. Here. Now. God would never ask you to sacrifice your Divinity for any reason. The fear of being controlled by the masculine energy is really the fear of God. God is neither male, controlling, nor vindictive. That is only a projection of your fear. God knows only unconditional love, has no judgment, asks nothing of you, and offers everything. Choose love over fear. Come home.

Good Now

Sanhia

What if my "old stories" are good ones?

We have talked many times about changing your "old sto-ries", taking responsibility for the things that trigger pain and suffering in your life, and facing the fears connected to those stories using the *five-step process*. Many of you have done won-derful work in transforming these fears and experiencing more love and peace in your lives. This message is for you. If you have not yet chosen to take responsibility for your "old sto-ries" (Book I: Message 64: *What do you mean by my "old story?*), doing so may be the next step for you. For the rest of you, please read on.

It is not only the fear-based "old stories" that keep you stuck. All of your stories keep you mired. What do you mean by that Sanhia? There are stories that give you a positive feeling, stories like: "My intelligence is a great asset", "I am good at healing my body", "People like me and I get along well with others", "I am beautiful (handsome)", or "I have a wonderful primary relationship". These are things that others might look on with envy. You may look at them and say that even though you have pain and crap in your life, you have this to feel good about. All of these feelings stand in the way of realizing your ascension.

We have talked some before about special relationships (Book I: Message 36: *How do my relationships fit into my ascen-sion path?*). It is not our purpose to go into that subject today, though we intend to cover it more fully in a future message. When you like things about yourself, as we have just described, or are happy about how things are working out in your life, it is like having a special relationship with yourself. You are seeing yourself as special. As with the sad stories, there is a basis of comparison. With the painful stories there is a sense that others are faring better than you are. With the success stories or positive qualities there is a comparison with those who have less. What you are creating is a sense of being special or different, whether that difference is felt as a positive or a negative. Behind all of this is a desire for God to notice how special you are. You are so special that God doesn't have to punish you now. Either you are so good that God will want to reward you, or you are so bad that you are already punishing yourself (or is it God who is already punishing you?). These are just two sides of the same coin. The special relationship is the same as the un-special relationship. Neither is holy. They are either especially good or especially bad. But the holy relationship is Divine and perfect as it is. You are perfect as you are.

You can thank Spirit for gifting you with whatever seems positive so that you can use it to realize your Divinity, as you can also give thanks for whatever seems to bring you fear and pain, so that you can use it to realize the truth of who you are. The truth of you has nothing to do with your positive attributes or with your perceived weaknesses. You are absolutely Divine and perfect as you are. Anything that seems to differentiate you from another is simply a gift from Spirit to support you in the realizing of your Divinity and to offer as a gift to others in realizing their Divinity. It is not that you can help others because you are so evolved; rather you thank Spirit for what is given you, knowing that the receiving is always connected with the giving to others. If you accepted the fullness of God's love, you would give it to others. If you allowed yourself to receive the fullness of God's love, you would realize your ascension. We do call you ascended now, because this love is always coming to you, at every moment of every day. It is only a question of your willingness to receive it.

When you hold yourself as special, you are holding yourself separate from others and from God. You are unable to receive the fullness of God's love. You may feel that you don't deserve it or you might think you are so good that you don't need God. That is what got you here in the first place. That is the oldest story. It is even older than the story that you are not worthy and God is going to punish you. It is the story that you don't need God. It is the crazy idea that you can create on your own, separate from God. That is the ego's voice. When you have stories of being good at something, you are listening to the ego's story. It is the ego saying you don't need God.

As you let go of this story that you are so smart and competent, you don't replace it with being so dumb and helpless. That is the ego, too. The Holy Spirit simply says *I Am*. And that's it. Nothing else is the truth of you. Or, if you wish, "I am love" or "I am loved". Anything else is there to separate you from others and from God, and you are guaranteed to stay in hell until you let there be only God.

Good Now

Sanhia

Can you tell more about being in the now?

There is a lot of talk in spiritual circles about *the now*, such as "living in the now" or "be here now". I hear confusion expressed about just what it really means to "be here now". Where else could you possibly be? I am going to follow a few different threads in talking about time. It is always a confusing thing to discuss because the truth is that there is no time. So, we are talking about something that doesn't exist, using words that can never express the truth. We have quite a dance to perform today, but then it usually is so with these messages. The truth of you, who always exists, does not fit into any concept of time you might hold. Always is a constant; there is no beginning or end. You think of things in time as having beginnings and endings, such as birth and death. You think of time in a continuum. If you consider reincarnation, you probably see your lifetimes unfolding in a sequenced order where you learn lessons and grow from incarnation to incarnation. From the human perspective of time, that seems to make sense. From the Divine perspective without time, there is no order.

When we talk about the "now", we are speaking of the eternal is-ness, that which is for all time, which is outside of time. When you begin to think of the ordering of events, with one thing coming before or after another, you are dealing with illusions and not Divine truth. This is a very difficult concept to grasp, let alone to accept, when you are in a body. It always appears that "now" is this moment, but there is a past and a future. There are things that came before and events that will follow. If your intention is to experience your Divinity, it is necessary to realize that this exists outside of time. The closest you can get to that understanding while you are in a body and your ego mind is running the show, is to try to be in the present moment, to attempt to remain in the "now" that you are experiencing - even though you remember a yesterday and anticipate a tomorrow. Simply hold the intention to let go of the focus on the past and the future. As fully and completely as possible you focus on this present moment. That is what "be here now" signifies.

Let's shift gears and talk about the immediate benefits that are there for you on your spiritual path as you focus on the "now". Time is one of the ego's greatest tools in convincing you of your separation from God. When you look at the past it is almost always with a focus on victimhood and fear. This usually takes one of two forms. In the first, you look at the past and see how you were the victim, whether of your parents, a lover, an accident, abuse, and on and on. You focus on this mistreatment to which you were a victim, to justify the bad place where you are now. You recreate in the present the pain and suffering you experienced in what seems to be the past. On a practical level...stop doing that to yourself. What possible benefit can be brought to your "now" by recreating old pain? Actually, there can be a benefit. If you take this old pain you are recreating and transform it using the *five-step process*, your past has now been of service. The intention is to simply be here now. If the past intrudes on your present, transform the energy so that you can be here now.

There is a second manner in which the ego uses the past. The ego will pull a pleasant memory from the past and say, "Look how wonderful that experience was. You can never get it back again." These pictures could be of your childhood, falling in love the first time, or the optimism of young adulthood. Those were the days my friend. Now, you can never relive them. The ego uses scarcity and fear to convince you that life will never be that good again, that the past is irretrievably lost. So, it's damned if you do and damned if you don't with the past. Joyful memories of the past leave you with sadness and grief for what has been lost, while painful memories leave you totally helpless. Above all, these memories take you out of the "now", and the "now" is where Divinity lives.

The ego also plays two kinds of games with the future. One is the fear based vision of what might happen to you. You will get older and your body will break down, your relationship will end, you won't have enough money, you won't ever realize your dreams, you will get sick or injured, you will die, a loved one will die, and on and on. The ego has no end of fears of possible futures to flash before your eyes. Even if one or more of these scenarios were to play out in the future, it is not happening now. Why would you wish to replace the ecstasy of the infinite "now" with fear of future possible events? Whatever the past or future may or may not be, they are not here now. What is here now? Let that be your focus. The other game that the ego plays with the future is to dangle dreams in front of you. You will find your perfect partner, your financial problems will be solved forever, you will be healed, and on and on. Behind these dreams is a shadow warning you that you are just fooling yourself and the future will only bring more frustration.

So we come back to the "now", and its truth is love. Fear belongs to time, to the past and the future. It is not part of the "now". In the "now" there is only love. If you are experiencing fear you are either in the past or the future. Just knowing that can be a motivation to let go. Your ego warns that if you don't remember the past it will repeat itself, but it is actually the memories themselves that bring about the repetition. The ego warns that if you don't prepare for the future, you will only be a helpless victim of what will happen. And so, you make your present a hostage to your fear of the future.

It always begins with intention. You choose to be in the "now". You choose to let go of the past and the future. When either of those illusions tries to invade your "now", give it to Spirit. Spirit will handle your future. Spirit will bring you the highest thing to support the realization of your Divinity. When the past comes creeping in, give that to Spirit also. If you are unable to let go of either the past or the future, it may be time to do the *five-step process*. Go into the fear and transform the energy now, into love, into the infinite "now". Guidance is always there for you. Be comfortable in your ignorance. Trust Spirit. Support is always there for you. There is nothing real but love. It is in the infinite "now" that you realize your ascension. It is not in your future, and it certainly is not in your past. It is not about doing a lot of work and spiritual practices to earn your right to heaven. It is about being absolutely present and timeless. You don't have to decide which door to choose. The "now" dissolves all doors. Nothing can take you where you want to go because you are already there. There is here. Be here now.

Good Now

Sanhia

What is the difference between a special and a holy relationship?

One of the goals of most people, including those on a consciously chosen spiritual path, is to find that special relationship, that special person, that soul mate that completes you. My job today is to throw cold water on that dream. This topic, like many we discuss, could be covered in book length form, but we will narrow the focus to making a few observations.

Let's start at a basic level. A pattern that tends to happen in relationships is that you are attracted to another person for certain qualities that they seem to have. Perhaps it is a physical attraction; you like the way they look. It might be their smile or there is an incredible sexual energy between the two of you. Maybe you are drawn to them intellectually; you like the way they think and you enjoy talking together. It may be common interests that draw you together - you share a love for music or the outdoors. Perhaps the connecting bond is of a more spiritual nature. In all likelihood, it is some combination of these different possibilities. What commonly happens is that the thing that initially attracted you eventually becomes an issue that you have difficulty dealing with. What you once loved now gets under your skin. Perhaps you then decide to leave and try another relationship. You go through the same cycle again and again. Or at some point you might decide to settle with the relationship you are in, rationalizing that overall, the pluses overrule the minuses. Maybe you have a lot of time invested in the relationship, and/or children, and/or shared property or a business. But these days, people are more likely to leave, choosing a relationship that fits them better.

Why does this pattern occur? Why don't we just fall in live and live together happily ever after? Let's focus on two reasons. First, as we mentioned, you are drawn to this other person because of certain qualities they possess. You want them to continue to be that way, to please you as they initially did. This is what we call conditional love - as opposed to loving them simply for whom they are, allowing their sense of identity and person-hood to evolve and change. Instead you love them for whom you perceive them to be, and if they perform in any other way you are upset and feel betrayed. Then you may begin to look around. The truth is that they never were who you thought they were. You projected upon the other person what you wanted to see. Conditional love is the first major roadblock to creating a successful relationship. The other person is not acting as you wish them to; this is not acceptable.

The second challenge is a little more subtle. You are looking for someone to make you whole. There may be thoughts such as "I can't live without you", or "You are my better half", or "We complete each other". You are thereby expressing the judgment that in order to be truly happy, you require someone else's loving approval. We call that codependency. You depend on somebody else to be satisfied. You have a need for the other, which brings on an anger directed at them for that dependency. It is a place where you can't win. Part of you wants to push the other away and the other part can't live without them and wants to hold on. It sounds pretty hopeless and sad. How can one ever have a successful relationship?

The relationships we have been talking about are special relationships. You hold the other as being more special than all other people. It's the flip side of you not being enough. You make them more than enough, so they must eventually let you down. You are not seeing yourself as Divine. You cannot experience your Divinity and, at the same time, have a need for a special relationship. Special relationships are built upon your fear of and separation from God. They stem from the belief that you have to be special in order for God to forgive you. Since God never judged you, no amount of specialness will do the trick. There is no need to earn forgiveness. God loves you unconditionally. However, the ego believes that if you can find somebody special who also believes that you are special, maybe God can find you special, too. If that specialness ceases to exist, what is God going to do to you?

The resolution of this quagmire is in seeking a holy relationship rather than a special one. A holy relationship is grounded in unconditional love. You have no expectations for the other person; you hold no judgments. No matter what your partner does, you love and accept them. This thought brings terror to the hearts of most people. It brings on fears of being a helpless victim. I want to remind you that your partner is your mirror. Whatever you judge in them, you judge in yourself. You can use your desire to control or change them to instead forgive and love yourself for whatever it is you perceive in them. Acknowledge that this is you. The ego wants to pretend it is not. The ego wants to point the finger so that you can stay special in God's eye. The ego wants the other to be the one punished. Take responsibility. Acknowledge that this is you and forgive yourself and your partner.

Accept that your record in choosing partners has been less than stellar. Give the job of attracting your next partner to Spirit. Your holy partner will have one function and one function only. That is to be aligned with you in realizing personal Divinity. It is possible for you to have a holy relationship where your partner does not share that intention, but it puts all the weight on your shoulder because your partner is expecting a special relationship. For you to act in the "right" way for them all of the time will be a major challenge for you. They will not be happy to find you choosing God over them.

I will tell you quite honestly that if your intention is to be absolutely true to yourself and to love yourself unconditionally in order to realize your Divinity, you have a real challenge to accomplish that within any relationship. There are few models out there in how to behave in a holy relationship. The mass consciousness only shows you special relationships as the ideal. In fact, you may find this work easier to do when you are not in a relationship. It is said that when the student is ready the teacher will appear. I will modify that to say that when the person on the ascension path is ready, the partner will appear. Many of you have this thinking reversed. You seek the partner first, who will magically bring you to heaven, rather than first becoming what you wish to attract. When you get to the point where you realize you don't need a partner to support your spiritual growth, you may attract one. Neediness will only attract a special relationship.

All that has been said up to this point is here to support you in being able to make the choice for a holy relationship. Once you have made that choice, you are really on your own. As mentioned, there are no models out there for how to proceed. You don't know how to behave in a holy relationship. The only thing certain is that the ego will struggle to salvage something special out of it. All that you can do is to notice moment by moment where you have attachment to anything about your partner or the relationship and give it to Spirit. The holy relationship is fully guided by Spirit, as the special relationship is guided by the ego. To give yourself a fighting chance in your holy relationship, it is helpful if your partner and you have this as a shared, expressed intention and agreement between you. In this way you travel through the darkness together. You did not create this illusion and physical body to be experienced alone. You created other people so that you could project your guilt and fear on them. By yourself you could live in the illusion that none of that exists, but when you are in the presence of others, your judgments are inescapable. This allows you to see them and to take ownership of them. Your partner is always going to fulfill this function for you above all others.

When you intentionally take on the holy relationship, you learn to take 100% responsibility for everything that happens. If you allow yourself to be a victim to or in blame of your partner about anything, you are in illusion and denial. This is the challenge. It is also a great gift and a great opportunity. When two people choose to have a holy relationship, the ascension process is accelerated for each of them. It supports both in looking at the truth and in doing the required work. The irony and ecstasy of it all is that when you release the expectations of conditional love, you open up the possibility of enjoying full and complete happiness in the relationship. There is no limit to the upside of a holy relationship. The downside is no different than that of a special relationship. But, you have the momentum with you that comes from having chosen a holy relationship. Spirit is always there to support you. The perfect thing is always happening in your holy relationship to support your realization of your Divinity. The only commitment that you can truly make in a holy relationship is to see Divinity in your partner and in yourself in every moment, and to forgive and let go of anything that does not live up to that. That is God's relationship with you always, except that there is no work involved for God. He always sees you as perfect.

Good Now

Sanhia

When should I share my spiritual perspective with others?

A question that comes up for many people on their spiritual path is how much of their experience and knowledge is it appropriate to share with others. On the one hand, you may be looking for support from others because your new beliefs are not reinforced by the mass consciousness. You may be seeking the assistance of cohorts to be able to be strong enough to hold on to your contrarian beliefs. On the other hand, you might feel that you have received some benefit from the ideas you are holding and wish to share them with friends because you love them and wish for them to avoid suffering.

As you are realizing the truth about your Divine nature, about the world being an illusion, about there being no such thing as wrong and right, about death not being real, and about your fear of God – as you are realizing that you wish to listen to Spirit instead of the ego, you will experience quite a struggle. The mass consciousness not only does not agree with you, but thinks you are both crazy and dangerous to think such things. If you share these ideas randomly with people you are likely to attract strong negative responses. We want to look at this, not because there is a right or wrong way to act, but because we wish to support you in being efficient in letting go of fear and in living in love and peace, experiencing the least amount of pain possible. When people attack you for your beliefs, you feel pain, perhaps anger and/or fear. Our suggestion is this: There is a saying, "discretion is the better part of valor". In other words, when in doubt don't say anything. It may be better to hold it within and to work it out yourself than to share it with others, unless you have strong guidance to speak.

If you do decide to share with another, ask yourself what your motive is. For the present, let us assume that your reason for communicating is your desire to receive support. We'll deal later with the issue of helping others. You have a desire to not feel alone in your process, to have comrades, fellow travelers, with whom you can honestly share your fears and the trials and tribulations of your spiritual path. Ask yourself why you wish to share with this specific individual who is before you. If the answer is that you want approval, you may be in for a rough time. This is connected to the expectations of conditional love. You may want to be loved for what you have to express. If you don't get that response you may feel vulnerable and then judgmental toward them. Of course you can learn through all of this, but it is more efficient to notice your need for approval and work through that on your own. Again, use discretion. One way to create more safety is by joining groups aligned with your spiritual understandings. You can also wade into the subject slowly and carefully, so that you sense the openness of the other. No matter what you choose, you can't do it wrong. You will learn from every choice and life will always offer you more opportunities. When you turn your guidance over to Spirit, the way becomes smoother.

Let's go to the second point. As you are working on your spiritual path and gaining understanding, it is natural to want to help, guide, and inspire others. This opens up another can of worms. You have an understanding on a mental level that all of this in the physical world is an illusion, it is not real, and that it is your creation. Because you have that mental understanding does not mean that you know it to be true. If you did, you would likely leave your body now. You would have no further use for it. You would realize your ascension. For now, all of these are ideas, rather than knowingness. You don't fully believe it. How do you get in touch with the part of you that does not believe? Notice where people around you don't seem to be acting in their own self-interest. They might act like victims with sickness, relationships, or finances. You look at them and wonder why they would choose that. Before you decide to communicate that question, I want to remind you that you are seeing your mirror. It is to yourself that you wish to direct that question. Your job is to forgive yourself, as well as the other person, for not choosing Divinity. If you were seeing the other person in truth, you would only see their Divinity, as God only sees your Divinity. Whatever else you think you are seeing is only your belief and fear that you are not Divine. Be grateful for this gift that the other person has brought you, give silent thanks, and do the work on yourself.

To simplify things, we'll say there are two different groups of people out there that you might be projecting these attacks upon. The first group is absolutely unaware of what they are doing, of their Divinity, of the fact that they are hiding from God in this imaginary world. They do not want to hear anything you might have to offer about this subject, and will likely grow irritated and angry with any attempts by you to educate them. Again, your job is to do the work on yourself. The second group is composed of those people who do have some spiritual understanding. They may be working with *A Course in Miracles*, or these messages, or some other form of teaching where they realize that they are not their bodies and this physical world is a mirage. Like you, they are students and they have fear and doubt. They want to believe, and it is a struggle. Do you choose to help those people when you observe them acting as victims? The answer again is, when in doubt – no. Discretion is still the better part of valor. First of all, the person does have awareness that their action or situation goes against the teaching. Is it your job to rub their face in that? Do you wish to add to their guilt? What happens when you point out what they are doing is that you may be projecting your own judgment, anger, and fear upon them. You are attacking them, and really, yourself. So be honest. Cut out the middleman. Let them alone and clean your own house. It is never about them. It is always about you. You are the creator of your life experiences. Again, give them silent thanks. Take responsibility. Forgive yourself and them; do the *five-step process*.

Does that mean to never try to support somebody else? There are two times when verbalizing spiritual advice might be appropriate. The first is when another person comes to you and asks support for what they are dealing with. Even then, it serves both of you to be very careful. Are you sharing in blame or anger or judgment? The truest way to support another is to give it to Spirit, asking what It would have you say. Listen and get out of the way. As you are talking, remain humble, remembering that this is your lesson as well. Spirit is talking to both of you, but first to you. When you are preparing to take off on an airline, you are given profound spiritual advice. The flight attendant informs you that in the unlikely case of a loss in cabin pressure, yellow oxygen masks will drop from above you. Those who have children or other dependent people with them are instructed to take care of their own mask first, before attempting to assist another. What a wonderful metaphor that is. You can't help anybody without first helping yourself. Whatever message is coming, it is for you first. Try it on and work with it.

If someone asks for help, take your time. Tell them you want to go inside first. Speak when you are ready and share with humility. It can be helpful to give the person at least three acknowledgements or appreciations before offering any advice. AND, it is always better to say nothing than to come from an energy of fear. If you are going through life and confronting each fear as you meet it, you are more likely to be prepared in each moment to support those who come asking for help, and others are more likely to be coming - drawn by your energy. You are living with your oxygen mask on, constantly drawing the breath of Spirit. If the other does not ask for help, love them and accept them exactly as they are. Silently thank them for whatever mirror gifts they are presenting and be compassionate. What help you offer in these cases is your energy and your love. If you hold another in judgment, they will feel that, rather than love. It is always appropriate to share appreciations. Give every situation to Spirit. You might be guided to say something. Take care of yourself first. Love yourself without conditions. Forgive yourself. That is what God does for you.

Good Now

Sanhia

What spiritual practices should I be doing? (Part 1)

What is important if you wish to realize your Divine self, if you want to ascend? What should you do to help let go of the illusion? I will start with the short answer. The short answer is, "Nothing is required". To elaborate on this response, if you think that something is required, that is the ego speaking. If you think that you cannot possibly ascend without practicing a specific physical discipline - such as yoga or meditation - that is from the ego. If you think a perfect diet must be followed - such as vegan, macrobiotic, fruitarian, or breatharian - that what you eat will determine what happens to your soul, again you are listening to the ego. Jesus was quoted fairly accurately in the New Testament when he said that man is not defiled by what goes into his mouth, but by what comes out of it. You create impurity in your life through your expressions, not through what you eat. If you fear that something you are about to consume is not good for you, give it to Spirit to purify. That is the true purpose of praying before you eat.

Does this mean that it makes no difference what you do? Can you live at McDonald's and never lift a finger? This is not what I wish for you to understand. Your body is an illusion. Ascension is about letting go of the illusion. If you think that taking care of your body is what is most important, then taking care of the illusion becomes your goal. You can succeed at taking care of your illusion so well that you could live forever or until you realize that the body has no meaning in and of itself. Its purpose is to help you understand that it has no purpose. It is merely a vehicle, so you take care of it like you would any vehicle. If you don't listen to it and provide for what it is asking, it may not get you to your destination. Any other function you might give to your body gives it a reality which substitutes the illusion of the temporary for the immortal truth of you. In the meantime while you are experiencing this body, take care of it. If you are hungry - eat. Listen to what it wants.

If it later communicates that it wishes you had not made that choice, perhaps you will choose differently the next time. But, ultimately it doesn't matter what you eat. If your choice brings you discomfort, accept it as a gift and do the *five-step process*. When you have chosen ascension, everything that comes into your life has the purpose of guiding you to that realization. It is not your diet that is to be a constant, but your listening to the Divine, your acceptance, and your trust. Have faith in the guidance you receive in each moment. If a book or a person suggests to you what you should eat, smile and let it go. Spirit never speaks in "shoulds", that is the domain of the ego. The same thing is true with physical activity. If you come away from this saying you are not going to exercise your body because Sanhia said you don't have to, you have missed my message. Basing what you do on what you think I have said is another way of placing your power outside of yourself. There is no particular physical activity that is required, but if your body is asking for movement - listen to it and move in a way that it desires.

We have been focusing on the body because it is the most obvious part of the illusion. That physicalness that you can see in the mirror and touch - and that others react to - seems to be you. But there are other aspects of you that may seem to demand correct spiritual practice. There is the mental focus where you may believe that you need to think the right thoughts, that you should only think positively, and that your choices must be aligned with the highest truth. It is good to be wary when the mind uses words like "should", "need to", or "must". That is the language of the ego. If your desire is to always manifest things in the world that please you, then choosing the highest thought is a "must". But choosing goals in the physical world, again, puts the focus upon the illusion, not on your Divine nature. If you are afraid to think wrongly, fear will run your life. There is a larger scope to this picture around spiritual correctness with your thinking. It assumes that you know. I want to be the first to let you know, in case nobody else already has done so, that you don't know. You haven't got a clue. If you knew, you would not be here in a body. If you think you know, you are being guided by illusion - also known as the ego. The only thing you can do is to give your mind to Spirit. Whatever response you then receive is your message for the moment, but not *the* truth for all time. It may not be your message a week from now, and is certainly not anybody else's message. Your mind may find this a tough assignment. How can you know the truth if it keeps shifting and we are not all sharing the same one? It is not the truth that changes, truth is the only thing that never changes, but the words used can never express the full truth. The question then becomes one of which "half-truth" serves you best in this moment. All you can receive is a piece of the truth, which always contains its own contradictions. The guidance for you in this moment may be total insanity for another to follow. Each person receives only the guidance that is appropriate for them at that moment. When you are ready for the full truth, you will be beyond words, and likely beyond any need for a body.

We wish to also deal with the emotional and spiritual/intuitive planes, but I think you have plenty to work with for now, so we will continue in the next message. The bottom line for now is that if you are feeling any fears or pressures around performing as you "should" with your spiritual practice, you can let all of that go. There is no right way. There is just your way, and nobody else can truly tell you what that is. So, follow your guidance and trust what comes back to you. It is all perfect. It is better than you could ever plan. It is Divine and so are you.

Good Now

Sanhia

What spiritual practices
should I be doing? (Part 2)

In the previous message we began discussing the question of what spiritual practices you should do, focusing primarily on those that touch on the physical and mental planes. It is highly recommended that you go back and read it, if you have not already done so or as a review before continuing today. Now we will talk about the emotional plane. One suggestion that is often proposed as a spiritual goal is to suppress any feelings other than those of unconditional love. The attempt to do this encourages some to choose celibacy and/or to live in a meditative retreat. This seems to make it easier to hold only the highest feelings, only love. If that is your goal, you may suppress or avoid every other kind of feeling, so you will carry anger, fear, judgment, jealousy, and other negative emotions around with you unconsciously. You won't want to see them and there may be no triggers present, no mirrors to reveal them to you. Other sources will encourage just the opposite. They will say that the best spiritual practice is to vomit all of your feelings on whoever is around you, to not hold anything back. This idea holds your raw emotions as something pure. Both of these approaches consider your fear and negative feelings to be real. The monkish approach is "out of sight out of mind" while the purging approach assumes that when you express the emotions, they are gone. Neither ends up working very well. In the former case, the emotions will eventually surface; in the latter they will surface over and over again. Expression does not release the fear because you still believe it is real.

There is nothing wrong with fear; it is simply an illusion. If you hide from it, you make it real for yourself. If you push it out on another, you also make it real. The only way to deal with an illusion is to go into the heart of it to see what is there. Face your fear. If you stay with your fear, you will eventually realize it is only illusion. It will disappear. It will transform. Only love will remain. This is why we recommend that you do the *five-step process.* Love is not something you find by running away from fear or by casting it off of yourself, it is what you realize when you go to the bottom of whatever is before you. It is absolute truth. It is all there is. Love is what is left when all illusion is gone. There are no words to describe it. Love is not a state you can try to attain. All you can do is face all your fears until only love remains. When you are in the illusion of fear, consciously or unconsciously, the fullness of love cannot be experienced. Do the process or simply ask Spirit to support you in facing your fears. There is nothing wrong about holding on to your fear, but it is no fun and leaves you feeling separate from God. The *five-step process* will not guarantee your ascension. It is not a spiritual practice. It is a tool, but it is not intended as a crutch. Facing your fears simply makes the period of time easier to bear, while you are in a body waiting to realize your Divinity. We are also not suggesting that you drop any or all of your spiritual practices. If you enjoy them, if you are guided to do them - do so. Try not to feel needy about them; let go of any attachment to your practice.

Last, but not least, is the spiritual plane. Here we have meditation and prayer. Many teachings suggest that if you meditate often enough and long enough, you will realize your Divinity. The Buddha did it, didn't he? If you are not being successful, you must not be doing it good enough or hard enough. Good luck with that. Of course there are wonderful benefits from meditation. You can have improved health, more calmness, more energy, more focus. Most of this, however, relates to making the illusion better. The true heart of meditation is in giving everything to Spirit. To meditate with a goal of improving your experience in a body will keep you anchored in the physical. The focus is on giving to Spirit rather than to the ego. Giving importance to this practice is an act of the ego. Give up any pride connected to the length and depth of your practice.

Do it from your heart; release the need for a schedule, for an enforced discipline.

The bottom line is that whatever plane your spiritual practice is connected to, if it has as a goal to improve your life, you are trying to create heaven on earth. Thus you will always be at cross purposes, because you created earth to hide from heaven, to hide from God. As you are deciding how to focus your time and energy, how to realize your spiritual goals, a constant question to hold is whether or not the practice is designed to enhance your physical existence. If that is the goal - be honest with yourself , there is nothing wrong with wanting to enjoy yourself - this is not the same as choosing to realize you ascension. Ascension is letting go of the physical. This does not come through reaching physical goals. It also does not come about through the denial of the physical. Fasting, celibacy, and physical discomfort make you more aware of your body, not less. This is why the Buddha spoke of the middle way. Both lack and excess leave a focus on the material. As you become aware of a particular importance you are giving to any spiritual practice, remind yourself that it doesn't matter. What you choose to do or not to do really makes no difference. As you realize that it doesn't matter, it becomes much easier to give it to Spirit. If you think it matters, the ego is attached to doing it right. If there is no "right" choice, then why not trust Spirit to choose for you. You have nothing to lose and everything to gain. You can trust that your ego choice will leave you rooted in your body, feeling separate from God.

You may doubt your ability to hear Spirit. Be willing to do nothing until you hear something. What if you fear you may not hear Spirit correctly? Trust and follow what you hear. Then keep listening. Following Spirit is not a one-time thing. It becomes the only constant in your spiritual life. The more you trust, the better you will hear. What evolves is a great simplicity. The ego's attempt to control all planes and make all the right choices is exhausting. You never get it figured out. There is always a new idea, a new direction, a new discipline. You will always be second guessing yourself. Giving it to Spirit makes it so easy. You simply accept that you don't know and trust whatever comes. If you have fear, face it. If you have confusion, give it to Spirit until you become mindless, only following the guidance of Spirit. Nothing else matters. Spirit might suggest that you follow some spiritual practice for a time. That is guidance for you now, not for anyone else or for always. Spirit is always in *the now*. All guidance is, at best, half-truths, designed to lead you out of your ego mind. Let it. Let it be simple. Let it be God.

Good Now

Sanhia

How can I see the Divinity in other people?

We had a message several years ago about seeing the Divinity in others (Book I: Message 57: *Is there Divinity in everyone?*). Some people have said that this is quite a challenge for them. They see someone acting in a certain way which makes it difficult for them to perceive that person as Divine. It is such a challenge for them to practice forgiveness, they say. They understand the value of all of this but find it so hard to put into practice. What can make it easier, they wonder? I will do my best to support you here, but I agree with you. This is not an easy process. True forgiveness and unconditional love are not simple states to attain. If they were, you would have realized your ascension long ago. This is where the pedal meets the metal. This is where the tires meet the road. This is the real work of ascension. It is easy to be in theory about what truth is, but it is the practice that makes reality real. Every day you create for yourself situations to do this work. What a blessing that is. There is never a rest. Every day. You can hide from the world, but your mind will still flash these "old stories" in front of you, and in addition, perhaps, project futures ones with endings not to your liking. The challenges that are before you can be called "seeing the Divinity in another" or "practicing forgiveness", which are actually "seeing the Divinity in you" and "practicing forgiving yourself". In a given moment the outer or the inner focus might prove easier to move through.

Think of those areas that are the most difficult for you to accept. You all have your own hot spots, but I will dangle a few in front of you. Some are general while others feel more personal. The general might include someone using their power in a way that seems to hurt many people. So you blame and are angry at politicians, businessmen, or criminals. On a personal level it may be an individual who seems to have insulted you, who doesn't return your love as you wish them to, or who judges you – which makes it hard to see them as Divine. We want to remind you that all of this is you. Nothing else you perceive to be out there is separate from you. It is all your creation. When someone is acting in a way that you don't approve of, that is you acting. It is you that you don't approve of. If you pretend that isn't the case and you assume that there really are others capable of hurting you without your permission, then you are truly stuck in an endless cycle of pain, negative emotion, and helplessness. This will continue lifetime after lifetime until you agree to take responsibility. You are the creator of your earthly experience. You are manufacturing these events in an attempt to externalize all the judgments you hold about yourself. You do this in a futile attempt to hide your failings from God. You hope that God will punish them instead of you. All of this is, as we have told you, a misunderstanding. God does not and could not judge you. You are innocent and have nothing to be judged for or to hide. However, as long as you perceive another person's actions as real and believe that there are victims, you aren't able to let go and forgive.

The first thing that we would suggest to you is to remember that the forgiveness you are asked to perform is always a forgiveness of self. Seeing the Divinity in another is always seeing your own Divinity. You cannot see the Divinity in another if you are not seeing it in you. On the other hand, if you judge another and cannot see them as Divine, then you cannot hold yourself as Divine. It doesn't matter where you start, whether you focus on the forgiveness and Divinity of yourself or the other person. It is all One. It is all your creation. So, now use your creation. You may have chosen another to be the scapegoat, but instead you can see them as your mirror. The reflection they provide can allow you to see the self-judgment you have been avoiding. Now that you can see clearly, you can forgive yourself and replace the judgment with love. You can feel gratitude for what your mirror has shown you.

You can thank them (silently) and feel love for them for providing such service. The easiest way to forgive another and to see the Divinity in them is to love them. As you observe them or think of them, send them love. Keep sending them love. If your ego mind wants to throw anything else in there that is less than Divine, you let that go and return to love. Love them not because they have earned it; love cannot be earned through actions. There is no logic in this love. If your mind demands a reason, the reason is that they are Divine. Wherever there is Divinity there is only love.

Much of this process is private. If the other individual is at a physical distance, your process has to be private. However, if the other person is right in front of you the situation is much different. Does this mean that you smile and lovingly accept whatever the other is doing? Not necessarily. *A Course in Miracles* speaks of something called "level confusion". This recognizes that while you are in a body you are always acting in part from the ego. The choices you are making to forgive, to see Divinity, and to act from love - to choose Spirit over ego - can only be made from the ego mind. If you fully accepted your Divinity, there would be no choice to be made. This choosing of Spirit, of love, has to be made over and over. When you are confronted with a challenging situation with another, it can only be because you projected your "old story" upon them. This is difficult to deal with in that moment. It will be hard to speak to them without projecting. Deep inside you may believe that you deserve to be punished. I am not suggesting that you stand there and receive your punishment. That is not the teaching. Listen to Spirit as best as you can and do what comes to you to do in that moment. It might be to say no to whatever is coming at you. Later, when you work with the residual energy of what happened, is the time to see how everything was your creation. You do this not by blaming yourself instead of the other, but in acknowledgment that it could be no other way, that everything happens to help you see your Divinity - as well as the other person's Divinity. No matter what happened or how you or they reacted, as you look back on the situation focus on loving them and yourself. When we talk of this loving, we mean without qualification. The love is never earned; it is an automatic deserved response to everyone in every situation. Nothing can disqualify them or you from this love. If something seems to be unlovable, that is your own self-judgment – take responsibility and replace it with love. In the end, forgiveness is the realization that there is nothing to forgive.

There is a stereotype of a parent who loves their child so much that, even as an adult, nothing their child could do could cause that parent to drop their loving defense. No matter what the world's judgments may be, they stand fully behind their child. The child may lie, steal, murder, or rape, but the parent says, "Oh if you knew the heart of my child, you would love and forgive them, too." This is what you are aiming for. Those of you who have children likely make exceptions for them you wouldn't make for others. Make everyone your child. See them all as innocent babies. That is what you are surrounded by - millions of innocent babies. That's all that you are - an innocent baby.

If you want to see others as Divine, the first thing is to do everything you can to think of them with love. Let go of any judgments you notice yourself holding, and see them lovingly. If you are in their presence, act however you act. Away from the moment, let go of all of that. Hold that person and yourself to the highest love you can find. This is what opens the Divinity in them to you. Now, full forgiveness becomes possible, knowing that in truth there is nothing to forgive, there is only Divinity – knowing that none of this has anything to do with them, that it is all about you. The answer to today's question is unconditional love, feeling it for others and for yourself. Your ego mind always tells you that you should have handled things differently. Of course, you are in a body. You act from the ego.

But, that is not the truth of you. You are Divine. What would it be like to feel God's unconditional love all of the time? Feel that now. Give that to yourself. Give that to everyone else. That's all we ask of you now. It is a very simple thing, just open up to that love. It is the only reality. God loves you.

Good Now

Sanhia

How do you define yourself?

Today's question, rather than being one that is asked of me, is one I wish to ask of you. The question is "How do you define yourself?" If your only answer is that you are a Divine, eternal, unconditionally loved and loving, infinitely creative child of God – and that is all that ever comes into your mind when you think about who you are, that is fantastic.....and you can stop reading now and enjoy your Oneness with God. There may be other ways that you see yourself that seem to stand in the way of realizing personal Divinity, even if you have been making efforts to see the truth. For example, you might define yourself by some traumatic event that has come into your life, which was painful when it happened and you cannot forget about it or let go. Perhaps you tell this story to others, maybe often, and/or it regularly comes up in your thoughts (Book I: Message 64: *What do you mean by my old story?*). These are places where you allow yourself to believe in your separation from God. Rather than one traumatic event, there may be a painful pattern you have noticed in your life, perhaps dealing with money, relationships, deservedness, loneliness, or lovableness.

There are two things I wish to say concerning these things you hold about yourself. The first I have already mentioned. You define yourself by these issues. This is part of who you believe yourself to be. That's why you relate these stories to others. It gives your fearful ego self a boost to have others understand what you have been through, and to receive some compassionate thoughts from them. Some of these identities you have carried for so long that it is difficult to imagine yourself without them. Not only is letting them go difficult, it is fear provoking. Who would you be without this story? An example of this is a parent who has lost a child, who thinks they can never recover from this and will never be the same again. Another example could be the belief that you were shaped by how your parents raised you. A third could be that money is always a struggle for you. Whatever your story is, it defines you.

I mentioned there were two things I wished to say. The second is to remind you that your story is not true; it is a fiction. It is a movie that you are acting out a role in. You are pretending to be a victim of some event or series of events. It simply is not true. What is actually there for you is an enormous gift. Whatever you see as an anchor weighing you down in your life is a blessing from Spirit. Whatever limiting, fear provoking message this event is telling you is something you came in with in this body. Out of the fear you brought with you, you created the event. You didn't do this to punish yourself. It was part of your pre-planning for this lifetime. You created this to overcome the false beliefs and separation from God that you have carried through all your incarnations. You are presented with these enormous gifts so that you can choose to overcome. There is no real consequence to holding on to the story, other than your continued pain and suffering in this body and the next and the next, until you decide to let this illusion go. God doesn't care how long you hold onto it. He doesn't see your story. He sees only your perfection. God can only see what is real, which is the loving, Divine you.

If you want to take the bull by the horns, if you want to be proactive – make a pact with yourself. First, become aware of these limiting definitions that are less than Divine. Notice the stories you tell yourself and others. Agree to stop telling them. If one comes into your awareness, do the *five-step process*. Now, look at the fear connected with this story until it transforms. Let go of the hopelessness of feeling that you will have the story with you forever, and look it right in the face. The reason that you cannot seem to get away from it is because it is your creation. It will follow you wherever you go until you confront it and let it dissolve. It is not real, but until you look at it and feel it fully and completely without backing down, it will feel real. This is not a work that anybody else can do for you. In fact you will likely react angrily toward anybody who would try to help. That would probably be too frightening.

You need to be in control here. The action is to come from you. You are to admit that you have chosen to be a victim. Nothing has happened to you. It is 100% voluntary. Because you have chosen the "old story", you can unchoose it. The truth is that only things that are real can stay forever.

Something that can assist you in being proactive with this "old story" is to change it in your mind. Ask your guidance to show you how this "old story" has already been a blessing for you or how it could be seen in that light. For example, if you have had a severe financial crisis in your life, you might now recognize that you have survived the "worst possible thing" and no longer have the same fears about money. If you have a parent who you felt treated you in an abusive way, you could thank them for doing such a loving thing because it forced you to find your strength within you, to love yourself instead of looking for approval from others. There is always a true story in the gift presented by each piece of this identity you have given yourself. Ask for support in finding the truth of the benefit from each situation. Now you can burn your candle at both ends. At one end you face and transform your fear. At the other end you see the event as a blessing. Develop the habit of doing both of these things until you notice your fear evaporating and everything being a blessing for you. There is no reason or need for you to continue to suffer or be a victim any longer, absolutely none. Nor is there any judgment if you continue to do so, absolutely none. You are free. Choose as you will. Go in peace.

Good Now

Sanhia

How can we deal with the world immigration problem?

I have been asked to say some words about the issues of racism, immigration, and the reactive rise of conservative political parties around the world. There are important questions about how to deal with the people who have been dislocated by wars and abusive governments. There is also the ongoing story of racism, both in the United States and in Europe. We always wish to begin by having an awareness of the illusion. If there is any part of the illusion that is triggering fear in you – whether it be expressed in anger, judgment, or confusion – take that and work with it, seeing it as a gift. The truth is that there are no victims or victimizers. Everything comes out of the creation of the individual.

When one believes one's self to be separate from God, whether or not the awareness is conscious, there is fear and projection. The projection may be upon the victim and how in some way they deserve what they got. There could be projection upon the heartlessness of the victimizer. People may be seen as power driven, ignorant of what is going on, or stupid. So, forgiveness is called for on both sides. Keep in mind that all of this is about you. If these events and people did not touch on something deep within you, we would not be having this conversation. As long as you believe that this is all outside of yourself and a part of the world, a part of others, it will continue to trigger fear and helplessness in your life. It is not about the events themselves or about the unfairness, the pain, and the suffering. It is about the fear that is triggered in you by these events, by these stories. One way of dealing with these fears, of course, is to use the *five-step process* to transform the fear that is generated.

The route to spiritual awareness often passes through territory of intense fear and suffering. If your world appears to be okay, there may not be anything to drive you to go past your self-imposed limitations. If the world is absolutely insufferable, you feel a need to find a way to deal with it. The only way to truly make sense of what is going on in the world is to realize that nothing real is happening. If you take it seriously, you will never find a solution. If these racial/immigration situations can help you to face your fear or to realize that love or fear can be chosen as a response to any situation, a great gift has been realized.

If you are choosing to help others because you see them as victims who cannot help themselves, that is fear based. You cannot see another as a helpless victim unless you hold yourself in the same light. You can choose to project your sense of victimhood on others – and the world will be so generous in providing you an endless list of sufferers – or you can deal with your own fear of vulnerability. I am not picking out any group of people and labeling them as victims. To be human is to believe that you are a martyr. Every human does that. You believe in your separation from God. The history of humanity is the history of victimhood. Your job as a human is to realize that you are Divine. As a human, all you can do is pick your poison. Which side do you wish to view as the victims, those who have been driven from their homes or those whose homeland is being changed? Either way there are good guys and bad guys, winners and losers. Either way there is separation. Either way there is fear. The only way out of the morass is to no longer see yourself as a victim. You begin by forgiving both the victims and the victimizers, however you may have those roles distributed. You can't have one without the other. Both are your creations and both represent your belief about your identity.

Let's look at the Swedish immigration situation. The question is one of how to experience things from a position of unconditional love. If you hear someone state that the immigrants are destroying "our" way of life, how can that be looked upon with love? The bottom line is that fear begets, or gives birth to, fear. When you act out of fear, you create the very thing you are afraid of. Reacting out of fear is always self-defeating. It can never bring a solution; it can only make things appear to be worse. The approach to take with those who act from fear is not to throw fuel on the fire by accusing them of racism, hatred, or selfishness. It is of greater service to acknowledge their fear and to help them to do the same, without judgment. Realize that you could not feel fear in them without holding it yourself. The question then becomes one of asking how this fear can be transformed.

The same question is there for those who see all of the immigrants as victims and those who oppose them as victimizers. What is the fear? What are they terrified of? What are you terrified of? Your job is always to see the Divinity of everyone involved. The truth is that everybody just wants to find their way back home and they don't have a clue how to get there. Back home might look like pre-immigrant Sweden. Perhaps, if we could get back there, there would just be peace, love, and safety. Or getting back home might be possible if everyone just opened their doors to all the world's victims. Then, everything would be fine. If we all just found a place in our hearts to take care of them, we could live in peace, love, and safety.

In truth, there is no idealistic past to return to, except the Garden and the reality before your imagined separation from God. There was no perfect time in Sweden or in the United States. Every "present" was a time of fear and of longing for an earlier "perfect time". On the other hand, if you try to be the white knight for all the victims of the world and bring perfection to *the now*, you will quickly realize that there are more victims than you could ever be able to handle. If you tried to bring all those in need of help to Sweden, the number would be many times greater than the current Swedish population.

Are you prepared to invite anywhere from 10 to 100 people into your home? Are you ready to care for all their financial, emotional and psychological problems? On a logical level, this is obviously an insane solution, but far beyond that, it cannot deal with the problem because it does not recognize the true cause.

The solution does not come through changing the outside. It is your inside that creates the outside. If you are placing the blame on the outside and think you can do something about it, you are in denial of your own victimhood and helplessness. How can you save the world if you cannot save yourself? Ultimately there is no difference between feeling sorry for the immigrants and blaming the victimizers than in judging the immigrants and saying that it is their problem and not yours. It is just a different choice of how to deal with your projection. You can blame yourself and believe that you can't do enough to make the situation right, or you can blame the victim and therefore can't do enough to eliminate that problem.

The only solution begins with owning and facing your own fear. This requires taking responsibility for creating the world, rather than acting as a victim to your creation. It is not that solutions cannot be found, it is that the answer begins within you. First you find your own Divinity and then see it reflected in every other human. You see all as creators and none as victims. From that place you can invite others in love to look within for solutions. Since you know that every apparent outer problem is a gift from Spirit to help you open to your Divine self, you can support others to do the same. This is not to say that you ignore the outer because it is only illusion. You support each person in the way that you are guided without taking their problems seriously. You know it isn't real, but sharing that with another who is not ready to hear it may not be the greatest support you can offer. On the other hand, buying into their story only helps to cement it in place.

If this dance is a difficult one for you, you probably have more work to do with yourself. Silently thank your victim "mirrors" and go back to transforming your fears. Be kind to yourself about this. If you are in a body you have fear and you believe in the reality of the illusion. If you have made the intention to release the illusion and to let Spirit guide you, there is still work to do. It may be part of Spirit's plan for you to be here to support others. You are not here to help them solve their problems (a Sisyphean task if there ever was one) but to help them take responsibility, to take their power, to find their Divinity. Whenever it all feels like too much, remember that it doesn't really matter. It is truly all illusion. You cannot take a wrong step. Nothing outside needs to change. Within is love and Divinity. Ask Spirit to help you find it.

Good Now

Sanhia

Why is it so hard for me to forgive?

It may seem that forgiveness is a common topic in these messages. That is true. It is true because there is probably no single concept that is of greater importance than that of forgiveness. If you wish to realize your ascension, it is absolutely central that you learn to forgive fully and completely. Without forgiveness, it is difficult to experience unconditional love. To try to love without forgiving first, is putting the cart before the horse. Forgiveness is what drives your realization of your ascension. The most efficient use of your energies is to figure out how to truly forgive. That's where we are going today.

One of the reasons that forgiveness is difficult for you is that you may understand it to be something that is bestowed upon another because they have done something that requires forgiving. Whatever act that they have committed, you recognize it as a crime. You decide that it needs to be forgiven because otherwise you are stuck in this ego cycle. If you are a "good" person you will learn how to forgive them. What actually happens is that in this process you ever so subtly (or perhaps not so subtly) suggest that you are better than the offender. You will be the bigger person and forgive them for being such an idiot. I exaggerate to provide a little humor, but this is precisely how the attempt at forgiveness often takes place. You are still holding on to the judgment when you try to forgive in this manner. If you look deeply within, you will find that the forgiveness has never really taken place. Your belief is that the person has done wrong and needs forgiveness. No matter how much forgiving you do, that person still has done wrong. This misunderstanding is why forgiveness is so difficult.

The first step in true forgiveness is to acknowledge that nothing wrong has been done. To repeat, nothing wrong has been done. The judgment that a wrong has been committed needs to be released. The truth is that the other person didn't do anything. If they had done something real, something that could truly hurt another, the victim would be hurt forever and ever, for eternity. Nobody has the power to do such a thing. The truth of all human souls is that they are Divine children of God and exist forever. Nothing Divine can be hurt. Only something that is not real can be damaged. Whatever it is that you are judging in this other person did not really happen. To repeat, it did not happen. Nothing real can be hurt. When you judge someone for the action you perceive them doing, it is no different than judging them for their previous night's dream. There you can recognize that nothing really happened. It is the same in your "waking" world. The action that you have judged didn't really happen, nobody was really injured. Nothing real, nothing Divine, can be hurt. You will wake up from this physical illusion too, some day. So, this is your job. You don't forgive another for what they have done because you are a good person, above them and better – so that you are able to forgive. Rather, you realize that there is absolutely nothing to forgive.

Let's look at it from another perspective. We talked several messages ago about how you define yourself. How many of you define yourself, in part, by what other people say to you or about you? Nothing that can change is real. Nobody can hurt anyone else. How could spoken words have any effect upon you? You are Divine. How can the illusion affect reality? It is time to turn this around. Nobody does anything to you. No one. There is nothing to forgive because no one does anything to you. This illusion is all your creation. You have created other people in your physical life. In this illusion of being human, you "hire" others to say and do things to you. Imagine that you have written a script. You hand it your friend and ask them to read it to you. It says horrible things about you. They ask if you are serious about having them read it out loud. You tell them to go ahead. They tell you how horrible you are. Then you get upset. You feel bad about yourself and are not happy with them. Pretty silly, huh? That's exactly how it happens.

You are getting a two for one today. First, you are realizing that there is never really anything to forgive in anyone else. The second is to realize that whatever anybody does to you has come from your instruction. It is the only way it can be. They are telling you the judgment you have about yourself. They are telling you what you have not forgiven yourself for, the illusion that you believe to be true. As long as you pretend that it is them and not you that is the source of this information, you are stuck in a pattern of having to be superior to them for the harm they have done. As you accept that you are the source of everything that is not Divine, you realize that you have made up this whole fairy tale, this whole story. The forgiveness called for is of self. If you think that you have been wrong to think or act as you have, does this mean you now have to be better than yourself and forgive? How can you do that? You might believe that you can be better than another, but how can you be a better person than yourself? That gets pretty tricky. Now is the time to realize that this is all absolutely crazy, that there is nothing to forgive.

You have been projecting your beliefs upon God. You have created an unforgiving God. Now it gets even trickier. If God is really the one judging you, and you want to forgive, you have to be better than God. Then you can forgive yourself, which God obviously can't do. This is the insanity of the ego. When you look at it in black and white (as you are doing now), it's a pretty funny story. It's really humorous. Close your eyes and feel the enormous freedom that comes from absolute forgiveness. This is not the forgiveness of your sins, but the forgiveness that says there is no sin. There never has been sin. You have always been loved unconditionally. There is nothing you ever could have done or ever could do to change that. Nobody is defining you as in need of forgiveness but you. You do not have to grovel before God begging forgiveness. Only you are holding the judgmental picture of yourself. Let it go. No amount of pleading will ever buy you forgiveness. No amount of atonement, no penance, will ever be enough. You cannot perform community service for God. You cannot make up for what never was and never will be. Such actions can only keep you in the cycle of judgment and fear. Forgiveness is only made easy when you know there is no need for it. Anyone can do it. No special skill is needed. You don't have to be better than anybody else. There is nothing to do. Be like God.

Good Now

Sanhia

What do you mean when you call the world an illusion?

We have talked many times about the illusion, but there has never been a single message fully describing what is meant by this term. Now the time has come. I am going to start with the ending and then go back and fill in the spaces. This is the ending: Everything, without exception, that you experience in this physical world is an illusion. Everything. None of it is real. No exceptions.

Now we will take a giant step backward. In the illusion, you can do that. In reality, there is no place to take a step and no time in which it can be accomplished. What is reality? Let me tell this as a story. In the first part of the story there is God. God is unconditional love, unlimited creativity, unlimited power, and unlimited joy. There is no duality, only the is-ness of these qualities. These descriptors are human terms and unable to do justice to what Jesus called "the Kingdom of God". The only thing that is absolutely true and real is this kingdom. In the second part of the story, God chose to create beings or entities in the image of Himself. Remember, as always, that the language is limited. There are no serviceable gender free terms, but be clear that Divinity, that God, does not have gender. There is no duality in Divinity. As a default, we will refer to God as "Him". To continue, these entities were created in the image of God, beings of unconditional love, creativity and so on, and, of course, gender free. These could be called the Children of God.

In the third part of the story, a group or a portion of the Children of God, who *A Course in Miracles* calls the Son of God, in their infinite creativity, decided it would be fun to construct something that would be secret and separate from God. To begin with, this was an impossible task. There can be nothing separate from God. I will now use the term "We", because you and I are a part of this group. We are One with God and God cannot be separate from Himself. We allowed ourselves the thought that we could create separately from

God and then went into that creation. We then experienced the illusion of separation. This experience was not real because we could not actually create something separate from God. We could say that this creation was like a dream. We went into this collective dream. God could not see this dream any more than a mother can see her child's dream. In the dream we felt separate from God and had our first experience with fear. We were afraid that we could never find our way back to God and that He would be angry with us for creating behind His back. These fears were false. It is not possible for God to be angry or judgmental. However, in this nightmare we had created, all of this seemed possible. The ego is what we call that part of us that feared God and believed in the illusion.

In this way we created the physical universe. It is a part of this dream, of this illusion. We have been hiding here in the physical from God. The truth of us is still One with God. This is just a bad dream. As soon as God recognized what we had done, he created the solution. He imagined the means by which the part of our Divine selves stuck in the nightmare could reconnect with the Oneness. Because there is no time in Divinity, the solution was instantaneous. The problem was immediately solved. You could say that it was over before it began. Boom, boom. However in the illusion there is time. There is duality. So, it seems that we have been trapped in this dream for thousands upon thousands of years, for lifetime after seemingly endless lifetime. Trapped. The idea we have of hell is right here. This earth is it, but it is not real. The idea of heaven is our true home, the Kingdom of God, the place of unconditional love and unlimited joy. The challenge for us through these eons of time in the illusion has been to simply wake up to our Divinity, realizing that we are and always have been the Children of God. I have called this waking up our Ascension. These physical bodies are not who we are.

This entire physical world, every aspect of it, is an illusion. We created it, not God. This is our nightmare. As long as we hold onto it and defend its reality, it will seem real. The ego's job is to convince us in whatever ways possible that the illusion is real and that we have no choice but to stay here. The solution that God created is called Spirit, or Holy Spirit. Spirit is the intermediary between God and the illusion. God doesn't directly experience our dream because it isn't real. If He were able to observe it, it would make it real. That's the last road we would want to go down. Then our illusion would be true and we might really be stuck here. Fortunately, this isn't the case, and God cannot get directly involved with things that don't exist. Spirit, however, is the link between God and our ego illusion. We can listen to the voice of Spirit and be led home, or we can listen to the voice of the ego and continue spinning through lifetimes of pain, fear, and suffering. Sounds like a slam dunk choice here. However, the ego is whispering in your other ear telling you not to trust Spirit, asking you how these things that you can feel can be less real than some ideas that probably aren't even true. Ego tells you that your Divine nature is the illusion and that God is out to get you. You will have to pay for what you have done. You are guilty, guilty, guilty. Why would you want to go home to a God who is just going to punish you? Instead, you play all kinds of games trying to win God's favor and His forgiveness. You project blame onto others, hoping God, and yourself, will be fooled and will go after them instead. All of this is impossible because there is no judgment or favor to be won. How can God love you more than unconditionally? It can't be done. The only thing standing between you and realizing your Divinity is you. It is your choice to listen to the ego and to believe its claims that this illusion that keeps you trapped here is real.

Your job is to remind yourself every day that everything except your Divinity is illusion. _NOTHING_ that you see in this world is real. No exceptions. Scream it from the rooftops. The bodies are not real. The objects are not real. The stories are not real. The weather is not real. Your problems are not real. Money is not real; well, you probably knew that. None of it is real. The only thing that is real is your Divinity and unconditional love. Whenever you make something else more important than your Divinity, you stay trapped in the cycle of pain, suffering, and illusion. That's all there is to it. It is very simple. When you feel trapped, give it to Spirit. Spirit is the link between the illusion and Divinity, so that you can ask for support and guidance as you deal with your fears and difficulties in the illusion. Spirit is, always has been, and always will be involved in every moment of your life. Spirit directs your story, presenting you with exactly what you need in this moment to find your way back home. Meanwhile, the ego is telling you to fear the gift of Spirit, so you push away in terror what Spirit brings to you. Maybe Spirit brings a death into your life. When you resist what Spirit brings, you are saying that you want to stay here in illusion rather than go home. Spirit is bringing death into your life to show that death is not real. It is bringing a material loss into your life to show you that things don't matter. Spirit brings failure into your life to show you that your earthly goals are not important.

The question again is a very simple one. Do you want to listen to the ego, which will have goals for you in the physical, or do you want to listen to Spirit, realize your Divinity, and go home? The more successful you are in reaching goals in the illusion, the more attached you will be to staying there. This is why Jesus said that it is easier for a camel to go through the eye of a needle than for a rich man to enter the Kingdom of Heaven. You can't take it with you, not one part is real. It is all part of your dream. That is what I mean by illusion. I am not using a metaphor. I am trying to express as clearly, directly, and honestly as I can. There is nothing in this physical world that is real. You are to give up all attachment to everything physical and to trust that Spirit is always there bringing you exactly what you need to find your way home. Trust everything that comes into your life. Give up the fight and the struggle. If that is hard, give it to Spirit. If it is still hard, do the *five-step process* in addition. That is also a gift from Spirit to you.

Everything that happens in your life is guidance and a gift from Spirit to lead you home. Nothing here can ever be lost because nothing here is real. It is all illusion. Spirit will play with your attachments until you come into that full realization. The illusion and duality dissolve as you listen to and trust only Spirit, letting the ego go. Then you have no need for the illusion. You have no reason to create heaven on earth because your true heaven is right before you and infinitely more fantastic than anything you could dream up here. Welcome home.

Good Now

Sanhia

Are other people a part of the illusion?

In the previous message we talked about the illusion, and I meant every word I said. Now, it is time for some balancing words. It is true that your physical body is an illusion, but it is not true that you are an illusion. You are very real. It is true that the physical bodies of others are illusions. But it is not true that other people are illusions. As you are working with this truth of the illusion, I wish to suggest that it is fine to look at everything in the physical world going on about you as illusion, including things and events. Remind yourself that they are not real. However, it is not recommended that you look at other people and tell yourself that they are illusions, that they are not real. There is a practical reason for this. Whatever you see in others, you see in yourself. I have called this the mirror effect. If you identify others as illusions, you will view yourself in the same light – or lack of light. When you see yourself as an illusion, nothing is left that is real. That can be a depressing way to exist. That will pass. No permanent damage can be done. Denying your reality, your Divinity, can never change it. You are real and so are others. In the meantime, holding yourself as an illusion may not feel so comforting.

To avoid this, simply don't think of others as illusions or as part of the illusion. This doesn't mean that you look at them and say, "Ah! This physicalness is real." All physicalness is illusion. But, when you look at someone, the truth of you sees the truth of them, recognizing their Divinity. If you say that they are illusions, you are saying that the Divine is an illusion. Here is what I suggest instead. As you are observing other people around you, practice seeing them as Divine. Forget about whatever you notice them doing or about how they physically act or appear. See them with your Divine eyes, as Jesus saw everyone. Behold their Divinity. If that is a challenge for you, and some individuals will present you with enormous challenges in perceiving their Divinity, ask Spirit for support.

As you master seeing others as Divine, so will you identify yourself.

Remember that when it is hard for you to recognize the Divinity in another, you are looking in a mirror. You are projecting upon the other whatever is most difficult for you to love and forgive in yourself. You are not truly seeing the other. If you were, you would recognize Divinity. If you are identifying anything less, you are seeing your mirror. Of course, when you perceive the Divinity in another, you are also seeing your mirror. When you look with judgment you are watching through the eyes of your ego. Your Divine eyes can only see with true vision, can only perceive the Divinity in another.

Knowing that the action, rather than the actor, is illusion allows you to see the Divinity. This helps you to let go of the false picture of the other person. Your projection, your judgment of the action, is what is not real. The person is real. The truth of everyone involved is unaffected by the action. No harm can be done to Divinity. This is where the illusion is significant to realize. The players are real and are Divine. Only the action is not real. So don't throw the baby out with the bathwater. Discard the illusion of the action without rejecting the Divinity of the actor. This is true forgiveness. Whatever you see that is not Divine is your projection. It is what you don't want to notice in yourself, because it is too painful, too frightening. Hold everything in the physical as illusion except for other people (and of course yourself).

That is it for now. Short and sweet. See the Divinity in others so that you can see the Divinity in yourself. That is what is real. All the rest is illusion. You are real.

Good Now

Sanhia

Is there any place for fun on the ascension path?

The last several messages have been somewhat intense, so I thought we would have a little more fun this time. In this message we will talk about fun, joy, and play. Perhaps you are taking things too seriously. If what you are experiencing is an illusion, why not have more fun with it? I have an assignment for you. Each time you find yourself being weighed down by the seriousness of your now moment, think up a joke about your situation. Make it so funny that you can't wait to find an audience to share it with.

You are aware that your Divine nature is the truth of you. You understand that you don't have a lot of control over how long it will take until you fully realize your Divinity and leave this physical illusion. In the meantime, since you have nothing really important to do – except, of course, whatever Spirit has in mind for you – you might as well have fun. If there is to be a choice between joy and misery, between fun and boredom..... is this a hard decision to make?

It is not so easy to have fun when you are feeling like a victim, so those thoughts and feelings will have to be jettisoned. It is also quite a challenge to enjoy yourself when you feel weighed down by lots of responsibilities. It is time to let go of them as well. Perhaps you feel that you have to earn your fun time, so you will work now and play later. Try turning that one around. If you are truly doing God's work you will be feeling ecstatic. The teaching from the mass consciousness is that this world is a very serious place and that you have to apply yourself, work hard, and make the right choices or life will just run you over. Such a responsibility you have! When you look at that it is overwhelming. Sometimes it just makes you want to lie down and die. That couldn't be any worse than living with that much pressure. But, unfortunately, it is not okay to die. That is not one of the choices. You have to let God kill you. Am I the only one seeing the humor in all of this? Instead, be counter-intuitive. Decide that nothing here matters, that there is nothing important to do. None of it means anything. You might as well dance and sing and play and do whatever is fun. This leads to the hilarious irony of the human condition. When you want to leave because you can't take it any longer, you can't. You are stuck. Even if you break the biggest taboo and off yourself, you will eventually come back and pick up where you left off. But, when you are having so much fun that you couldn't imagine wanting to be anywhere else, that's when you might leave.

The world has it pictured that if you want to go to heaven, ascend, or get off the wheel you will have to work really hard. To achieve such a goal you have to pray, be good, and deny yourself. There is so much that is required every day, every moment. It's impossibly hard. Then you die and you come back and do it all again. The counter-intuitive thing is not to try to do any of those things. You don't try to be good. You don't try to be right. You don't try to do any of the things that the ego says you should do. Instead you ask yourself what would be fun today. What is your play in this moment? Even if there are dishes piled up in the sink, have fun. Maybe you put on earphones and listen to music while you are cleaning. Maybe you play with bubbles. Allow it to be fun. Tell yourself that if it isn't fun, it isn't worth doing. Joy becomes your value. This becomes your training. When that voice comes in and says "Yes, but you should....", you jump up and say, "I know who you are! I don't listen to you anymore." You can recognize the voice when you hear the devil. The devil's middle name is "Should".

The funny thing is that this is true about everything. Whatever you think it is that you want – let it go. Just have fun. You think you want a relationship. Let it go. Look around at your friend's relationship. Does that look like fun? Let it go. Have fun. Maybe one day part of your fun will include playing with someone else, someone who wants to have as much fun as you do. But, what is important is having fun, not having the relationship. If you have to give up fun to have a relationship, well that's no fun at all. Replace the word relationship with anything else...money, dependable car, children who listen – it doesn't matter what it is. If you really think you want whatever it is, then give it to Spirit. Spirit runs a highly efficient lost and found department. Everything gets to where it is needed. If it will truly increase your joy, it will come to you. If it is something that will end up taking away your joy, that will be a struggle – do you really want that? It's a strange thing. You say to God or Spirit that you want something. You ask for it because you think it will make you happy. Cut out the middle man. Don't ask for what you think will make you happy. Just ask for happiness. Ask to be eternally joyous. If you knew how to do that, you would have done it long ago. But admit that you don't know anything, especially about how to be happy. So who are you to be demanding certain things, thinking they will bring you happiness. Be a happy idiot. Turn it all over to Spirit.

This includes ascension. Look at the fuel you have given to the ego when you ask for that. "You think that *you* can ascend? You think *you* are good enough for that. Oh, you've got a lot of work to do." And you are off to the races. What you want is total ecstasy. When you experience that in a body, there is an opening to realize ascension. Ascension is not getting out of jail; it is the knowing that there is no jail. When in doubt, laugh. When unable to laugh, cry. Then let it all go. You probably didn't hear it here first, but "don't worry, be happy". Remember always....

Good Blesses You

Sanhia

Do we have free will?

The question of whether or not humans have free will has always been a hot topic. The answer is yes.....and no. In the duality there is always duality. There is no simple answer. The truth of you, the Divine you, has absolute free will to create anything it desires. Absolute. There is no limit. In the illusion, your ego thinks it has absolute free will. And it does. It has absolute free will to keep you stuck here. That is the job of your ego, to keep you in the illusion. Otherwise it disappears. Your ego has a vested interest in your free will, both in your believing that you have a choice and that there is a right choice. In truth, in the illusion you have no choice. You have no free will whatsoever. It has already been decided that the illusion will end. The script has been written, in fact, the play is already over. The illusion ends; it disappears. You realize the truth of who you are and always have been. This is the truth of who you are at this very moment – even though you think you are this body and that the physical world is real.

Because the physical is not real, it cannot be sustained indefinitely. Things that are real last forever; things that are not real begin and end. Knowing this makes understanding easier. Just look around and see what lasts forever. Probably there is nothing like that that you can see. Your human eyes and senses are unable to detect anything that will not change and ultimately end. So, we come back to the question of free will. Your only "true" free will is whether you listen to Spirit or to your ego. As you choose to listen to Spirit, the voice of your ego grows weaker and weaker. Eventually you won't hear it at all. Then the physical begins to drop away and you will fully realize your Divinity. You realize your ascension.

What you are referring to when you say you have free will is really the voice of your ego. It says, "I want to choose what I want". Even choosing ascension is a choice of your ego. Your Divinity cannot choose to ascend because it is already in that state. You are not trying to achieve something here, only to wake up. To choose something is to believe yourself to be separate from it. Every choice you can make is an affirmation of separation. Whatever your ego tells you is the way to realize Divinity, comes from fear and separation.

The goals you have in this world come from fear and separation. If you say that you want to get your finances in line so you don't worry about money anymore, if you are seeking a nurturing supportive relationship, if you are seeking to find your right livelihood – the work you came here to do – none of that will lead you to realize your Divinity. I am not suggesting that you never have earthly desires, but, even should they be fulfilled, you will be left with the need to replace them with other earthly goals. Behind it all will lurk a feeling of lack, a desire for what you don't have. Your ego's eyes are infinitely large, always wanting more, never fulfilled. There seems to be a gap where you feel separated from God. No matter how hard you try to fill it, the task is impossible. How can you fill an imaginary hole with imaginary achievements? Eventually, whether in this body or another, you will decide to give your life to Spirit. There is no free will about this. It will be the only choice remaining for you. You will ask Spirit to tell you what to do. You will tell Spirit you are here to serve and that your wills are One. Everyone will make this surrender eventually. You will give your free will to Spirit. Until that time you will continue to have pain, fear, and suffering on the physical plane. No matter what goals you may set for yourself, there will be no heaven on earth.

Ego does not run the show here. Everything is directed by Spirit. Ego has absolutely no power; it all belongs to Spirit. Whether or not you pay it any attention, Spirit runs your life. The only thing you truly want is to wake up to your Divinity. Everything else is just your ego pulling your leg. Spirit brings to you in each moment exactly what you require to realize your ascension. Your only job is to accept what is presented. Welcome it. When you resist and think that what has happened is not what you want, you are trying to give control to your ego. Change your mind about that. Surrender your earthly will to the Divine will. You are simply agreeing to a done deal. Like it or not, Spirit is running your life. Let go of thinking that you know where your happiness and, eventually, your salvation lie. If you knew how to get yourself out of this illusion and into your Divinity, you would have done it long ago. Your life has already been scripted by Spirit. The end of the story is that you are back home. Your choices cannot affect this plan, though your cooperation may speed it along.

Your Divine self played with the idea that it could create something separate from God. A "part" of you went off into that idea, into that dream. It was a dream because nothing real could be separate from God. We could identify the part of you that thought this separation could happen as your ego. It is the part that is in guilt and terror. The moment you created that dream, or that nightmare, God recognized it and created Holy Spirit to follow you into the illusion in order to wake you up and show that it wasn't real. So, within this insanity of the physical world there is a voice of sanity. The truth of Spirit, of Divinity, never waivers. The duality jumps back and forth. On the one hand your ego says you can create anything you want here. You are God; you can create heaven on earth. On the other hand your ego says you are a worthless piece of shit who has failed at everything you have tried, deserving of punishment for your sins and ineptitude. Your ego is always in duality. There is constant conflict. In the truth of Spirit, you simply are. You are Divine. There is no good or bad, no judgment, only Oneness.

If you think of the most joy you have had in this body, it is a small taste of the infinite joy that is a part of your true nature. Some of you have had moments where you felt yourself stepping out of the duality into a place of peace and love. This, also, was but a taste of your true nature. Unlike this temporary appearance, your true self is eternally experiencing this joy.

There is no other possibility.

In conclusion, you have the free will to surrender your free will. There is no choice to make. Choices only exist in duality. While you are experiencing this duality, it is the only place you can operate from. So, exercise your apparent free will by choosing Spirit over your ego. Establish a dialogue with Spirit. Your will and Spirit's will are the same. Spirit will tell you what to do. Surrender to that guidance. Absolutely. All of your fear will come up because you are afraid of God. Ego tells you that only your free will can save you. Spirit reminds you that nothing can save you because you already are saved. So listen, surrender, wake up, and go home. Spirit tells you exactly what to let go of to give up the belief in separation. Your only job is to say "Thank you" and "What is your instruction today?" If you don't hear a clear message, open your eyes and look around. Whatever you see is what Spirit has brought you today. You can do this. You will do this. Ultimately, you have no choice. That is your terror and your salvation. Don't forget the *five-step process*. It can help you move through the terror more quickly. Your free will is a prison. Give it up, and let the gates be opened. There is nowhere to go, nothing to do. There is only God, only Spirit, only love.

Good Now

Sanhia

What if this was the last day of your life?

A question that sometimes is asked of a person, often in connection with their spiritual path, is "What would you do if you had but one day left to live?" This, of course, is not a question of what heroic efforts might save your life, but rather one that forces you to choose what is truly important. This necessitates a great personal investigation. What do you place such a high value on that you would be sure to make it a part of your last day on earth? Conversely, what things would you definitely not do, not waste your precious moments with. As you are working with this process, you are not limited to pretending that you have only one day to live, you can give yourself a week, a month, or even a year. Perhaps what remains undone seems large and would require more time. Whatever the time span, the purpose is to become aware of the deep passions and desires that you are not exercising in your day to day life, to look at how much of your existence is spent with things that are not truly meaningful for you. It is about using your time productively. On that level it is a wonderful process, but that's not where we are going today. We are moving to another level. That is always what these messages are about...taking things to another level, or looking at things from an ascension perspective. So, let's be a little counter-intuitive again today.

You have likely done some of this kind of work already, looking at what your passion or your purpose is. You are aware of what gives you joy. Perhaps you don't fill your days with these things to the level you would wish, but you have awareness. You are not choosing to live your life in absolute denial of where your heart or Spirit leads you. So what is this different perspective I am suggesting that you take? If you are on a serious ascension path, rather than holding spirituality as an interesting hobby that you enjoy exploring, there is another way to play this game. If your intention is to realize your Divine self, to experience that this is all an illusion, and to let it go – and that this takes precedence over everything else – you may wish to look at what you would do with the last day of your life from a different perspective. Whatever your answer to this month's question might be, that is what stands between you and the realization of your ascension. Whatever you feel is undone or has not been completed yet, is what keeps you tied to this body. You will stay until you either complete it or let it go. The purpose of the "last day" process is not one of learning to stop wasting time. Time is an illusion that cannot be wasted. It is not about doing what you came here to do. There is nothing that is really important to do here. This is not real. If there is anything important for you to do (I am just throwing this contradiction in here because the ego mind goes absolutely crazy with inconsistency, while absolute truth can never be communicated in words), you have no clue in your conscious thinking mind what it is. But, there is a plan that Spirit has for you.

The best you might do with today's process would be to say to yourself that if you have only one day (week, month, year...) you are going to listen to Spirit and do whatever you are directed to do. Anything else is coming from your ego. It amounts to your ego placing an importance upon you in this body in this illusion. Take some deep breaths and let this be assimilated into your being. What does this mean? It means that while you are in this process of waiting for the grace of God to lead to a full awakening to your Divine nature, you could be compressing time by looking at what you think you still have to do or want to do – perhaps what some people refer to as their "bucket list". One choice would be to achieve all of those things so that they no longer stand in your way. The more efficient path would be to release the desires, to give up all your plans. Give them all to Spirit. If Spirit so guides you, take an action, but as for your ego self, there are no directions to be taken. You simply do the things that allow you to remain in your body in the moment...breathe, drink, eat, exercise, play with your mirrors...and then let them go. We are not just speaking of actions, of achievements, and of concrete goals. There may also be emotional, relationship desires you want fulfilled. Perhaps you want to feel loved or to have others express love to you in certain ways. Maybe there are spiritual gifts you want to demonstrate, such as translocation, channeling, time travel, or direct manifestation of objects. There is no limit to the number of things that your ego may want to experience. I wish to remind you that each one of these desires, including those that you may not even be conscious about now, keeps you rooted in the physical. They are all things you need to do in a body.

There is no judgment here. To be human is to have ego desires. There is no punishment for holding on to them. We are only suggesting that you become fully conscious of what your desires are. If you wish to release some desires, judging yourself for having them is perhaps the most inefficient technique you could come up with. Let them go when you are ready. A motivation for choosing to let go of these goals is to realize that whatever joy or satisfaction this experience or achievement might bring you, it will not relieve you of the pain of believing yourself to be separate from God. It will not bring you nearly the joy, pleasure, and ecstasy that are the truth of who you are when you let go of the illusion of being this physical body. You will get but a taste of Divine love.

It is a very simple process for today. Ask yourself what you would do if your time remaining in this body was limited; then let go of all need or desire to do those things. If that isn't easy, give it to Spirit. If you don't have the will to let go of something...go do it. Have that experience. Manifest it. Create it. One day you will simply say to yourself:

"Enough! I give up all my desire for earthly experiences. I surrender it to Spirit and let myself be guided by Spirit to whatever actions are part of His plan for me while still in a body. Let me become One with the Divine plan, which is truly my plan."

Good Now

Sanhia

Can we create heaven on earth?

Can we create heaven on earth? This is an exceedingly popular question, one that many spiritual practices and teachers give much energy to. Most people have little hope that there could be heaven on earth. They tend to possess a helpless victim-like approach to their existence here, though there is usually some hopefulness that something might improve. On the whole though, they expect there will always be problems. Governments will misuse their power. Businesses will always care more for their profits than for the environment or the well being of their customers. Health will be a concern; we are victims to disease and accidents. We will never have enough money and our bosses don't really care about us. Relationships and friendships are not fully satisfying. Those that start out ecstatically devolve into, at best, a ho-hum day-to-day survival. However, many of those who are on a spiritual path as well as a lot of spiritual teachers have decided that all of this can be overcome, that we can have heaven on earth. Working with an understanding that we are the power in our lives and that what we focus on and believe in will happen gives us the power to determine our futures on the planet. There is an underlying truth in this belief, but when we look at the wholeness of what is suggested here, the insanity of trying to create heaven on earth may become clear to you. This idea has its birth in the ego; it does not come from Spirit.

When we look at creating heaven on earth, there are several things to be aware of. First of all, this physical illusion of the earth and the universe is based on duality; it is based on opposites. In Divinity there is no polarity: no good and bad, no male and female, no hot and cold, no opposites. There is simply *is-ness*. The whole appearance of physicalness is based on the illusion of duality that does not exist in Divinity. One thing this means is that when you try to create "good" in the universe, an equal amount of "bad" must also be created. Opposites always balance out each other. "Good" cannot exist without "bad". There simply cannot be heaven on earth without hell on earth. In duality, you cannot create one thing without creating its opposite. So, if you succeed in creating a "good" in this illusion, somebody has to create a balancing "bad". To further confuse the issue, your "good" may be another's "bad" and vice-versa. Everyone is trying to create heaven on earth according to their own personal model of what that is, and how to achieve it. If this sounds insane, please understand that insanity is the basis of duality. If you wish to follow this reasoning as far as you can, then if you wish to create "good" coming out of others, you should create as much "bad" as possible yourself, so that the balancing energy could be released. If this is an absolutely insane proposition, welcome to planet earth. It is just a dance where every action brings an equal and opposite reaction.

Creating heaven on earth is an impossibility. Heaven is your true home. It is where you are right now, though you are having a dream/nightmare that you are in a physical body on earth. There is no real earth. Your true self is in heaven as you are reading this. So, here you are trying to reinvent the wheel, trying to create something that already is. In this case, rather than having God's absolute perfection, we have humans who don't believe in their Divinity and are therefore capable of using only a small fraction of their infinite creative power trying to compete with God in creating heaven in the midst of duality. It is not too hard to see the futility in this. But, it could be no other way, because this earthly physical illusion only came about as the result of a crazy idea. You thought that maybe you could create something better than God was capable of doing. That was an insane idea. Then you compounded this by going into terror and fear and disappearing into your creation to hide. All humans hold guilt about this choice to separate from God. Fortunately, you didn't succeed. It was not possible to separate from God, any more than it is possible for God to judge you, withdraw His love, or punish you. It is possible to be in a dream, to be in an illusion where you forget who you are. You cannot change who you are, but you can experience amnesia in your dream. Your job is not the impossible; it is not to attempt to compete with God, by trying – and failing – to create heaven on earth. Your job is much easier than that. Forgive yourself. Be aware that God has no anger or judgment about what you have done. In fact, nothing has really happened. Realize that the easy thing to do is to allow yourself to be in heaven, not to try to create the impossible on earth. It is not only easier, it is also inevitable.

You will all wake up from this dream and realize your true home. You have no choice about this. All you can do is drag your feet and slow your progress down on your trip back home. You can extend time, but time is just one of the illusions of duality. Only what is real can last forever. These bodies, this earth are finite. You are real; your body and the hell around in the dream are not. Even now, as you dream of being here on earth in a body, the truth of you is in heaven. Rather than focus energy on bringing heaven here, wake up! The heaven you will find yourself in will far surpass anything you could even dream of in this illusion. Instead of doing the impossible, do the inevitable. Rather than dragging your feet, lift them up. Let Spirit carry you home. By choosing to hear that voice each day you can shrink time. You can cut off years or lifetimes. In the long run, it makes no difference. Once you awaken, this will all seem as if it never happened. In the meantime, you experience some amount of pain and suffering. Why prolong it?

If you try to create heaven on earth, you will fail. This will bring about some amount of pain and suffering. The part of you that feels helpless at not being able to create heaven on earth, but feels equally helpless in figuring out how to wake up, can feel doomed to suffer until ascension finally happens. There is a fear of seeing the earth being slowly destroyed, of wars, of corruption, and of friends, loved ones and eventually yourself succumbing to disease and then death. Does one just have to put up with all of this, to stand helplessly by? That is one choice, but it is not the only one. You can focus your energy and intention on seeing that none of this is real, just like the show you watched on television the other day. Not real. Made up. Imaginary. As you get that, you can find that watching it becomes less and less painful. In fact, it may become quite entertaining. When you know it is not real, it is not so hard to experience anything. The closest you can get to creating heaven on earth is by realizing that everything that is happening is being scripted by Spirit for one purpose only, and that is to guide you to your awakening...to your ascension. It is there to help you become aware that none of it is real and that you are and always have been in heaven. This means that whatever is happening is perfect. Realizing that it is perfect, accepting rather than judging and trying to change the gift of Spirit, allows you to begin to experience heaven. Perfection is not something that you create; it is what already exists. Your job is not to make the world perfect; it is to recognize the perfection that is already in place. When you think that something has to change, you are not accepting the perfection.

This bears repeating. You do not need to change anything to bring heaven on earth. Spirit is taking care of that. All that you need to do is to relax and accept the perfection of Spirit's gifts, to feel gratitude. Your only response is to Spirit, as you learn to ignore the insane ranting of your ego. You don't ask for any part of the world to be fixed. The only thing you pray for help with is your willingness and ability to hear and receive Spirit.

Help me to trust the perfection that surrounds me. Help me to know that this is not real, that no child of God can ever be truly hurt, that death is an illusion. Help me to choose your voice instead of the voice of ego, to choose love over fear. Help me to choose to believe in my innocence rather than in my guilt. Help me to reclaim my true home in heaven.

Good Now

Sanhia

Do you confuse cause and effect?

One of the biggest confusions that the ego throws into every situation is its determination of what the "cause" is and what the "effect" is. We are all familiar with the terms, "cause" is what makes something happen and "effect" is what happens. There seems to be no control over the effect. It appears to automatically follow the cause. According to the ego's picture of the world, you also have no control over the cause. Therefore, you have no control whatsoever. To the ego mind, the cause is always out there in the world. Perhaps because some person did something, it causes you to have something happen in your life. Maybe it is because the government infringes on your rights, because the doctor messes up, because the weather ruins your plans, and on and on, that negative effects come into your life. In that view of reality the cause is always out there in the world and you are a helpless victim with no control whatsoever over what happens. Shit happens. The universe is random or there is a spiteful god. Anything could happen to you at any time. You feel nothing but terror when you consider the future, not to speak of the immediate present. There seems to be no rhyme or reason to it all. It is simply a chaotic universe. If that is the case you truly better live for today, for there is no guarantee for anything but the moment, and it may not last long. Anything might just fall out of the sky, ending life as you know it.

We are just having fun with you here. I want to remind you that the cause is never out there. It is always in here, in your mind. Please don't take this scrap of information and rush off and blame yourself for everything in the world. That is another trick of the ego. It wants to know why, if you are the creator of all of this, you are doing such a lousy job. It does you no good whatsoever if you replace responsibility with blame. Responsibility is the acknowledgement that it could be no other way. The world is your creation, not God's. You did this by making the choice to separate from God, create this universe, and disappear into it. However, you are unconscious of the part of you that made these choices – as you are unconscious of your Divinity. You are absolutely unaware that you are in heaven with God right now and this world is just a dream. If you were conscious of all of this you would wake up and leave the dream. This taking of responsibility is the third step of the *five-step process.*

Perhaps it is best now to turn to the *five-step process*, because it clearly shows the relationship of cause and effect. An event (or multiple events) is going on in your world. You react to it with fear and helplessness, believing it is something outside of yourself and that you are victim to it. Perhaps your brain-mind, your conscious thinking mind, assigns blame. Maybe you are not aware of what is causing your fear, but you clearly feel the discomfort in your body. It might register as a pain, a discomfort or an illness. This is the first step of the process, identifying the problem (effect). In the second step, you face the fear or the discomfort. You go right into it. Eventually the fear will transform. Because it is not real, your steady focus upon the fear allows it to transform to love. Then you are ready and able to move to the third step, as previously mentioned, and claim your Divinity by taking responsibility. You acknowledge that you, not the world, are the cause, and that it could be no other way because of your Divine nature. You could never be the victim. Remember there is no blame here. What transpires in the world is not real. None of it ever happened. There can be no fault, only confusion in your perception. The third step is to help clarify your perception. As *A Course in Miracles* (*ACIM*) teaches, "There is no order of difficulty in miracles". No step in this process is any more important than any other. They all need to take place. In the fourth step, in the state of peace that you have found, you go inside and listen to the guidance. You go to true cause.

While you are in the illusion, while seeming to be in a physical body, you are always in duality. Even when you have moved into the third and fourth steps of the process and are experiencing peace, you are still in duality. If the experience remains of being in the world, of being in a body, you are in duality. Even though you may have the awareness that none of it is real, you are still fully in the experience of the illusion. If I were to say to you at that juncture to let go of the body and the world, you might ask, "But how?" You feel yourself stuck in duality. What the fourth step is really about is turning your life over to the only force that can lead you home, and that is Spirit. Listen to and follow what Spirit has to say. No matter how supportive anything in the world may be for you - whether it be *ACIM*, these messages from me, other pure non-dualistic texts, guidance from any spiritual teachers or leaders, support from spiritual practices such as meditation or yoga – it has the sole purpose to train you to listen to and follow Spirit instead of the ego. The only thing that will take you home is a total surrender to the voice of Spirit within you. Everything else is still a part of the illusion because it recognizes the duality of Spirit and the ego. The ego will continue to throw its tantrums, but your job is to return over and over to the voice of Spirit until that is all that remains.

Once you have realized that everything is created in your mind, there is always a choice of what you instruct your mind to listen to. Ever since you have been in a body – lifetime after lifetime – you have chosen to listen to ego. Otherwise, you wouldn't be here. You would be aware only of your Divine home. There would be no choice of voices to listen to. There would be only One, only Spirit, only God, only Divinity. In duality this will always appear as a choice, do you choose Spirit or do you choose ego? There are steps that you can take toward realizing your Divinity. The first step is to realize that you do have a choice. You can choose between listening to Spirit and listening to ego. The second step is to be aware of which voice you are listening to. Ego will always tell you that the cause is in the world. There are no limits to where the ego will assert itself. It will tell you that you are hungry because you haven't eaten for four hours, that you are tired because you didn't sleep well last night. The cause will always be out there in the world according to the ego. It never is. This is not to say you should pretend that the world doesn't exist. While you are in a body you will have to have food and sleep. Otherwise you will die and come back to try it in another way. What is not true is that your discomfort comes from not eating or sleeping. The cause of discomfort comes from your mind, from your fear and separation from God, from your guilt. So, you create pain in your life. If you are hungry, eat. If you are tired, sleep. Don't pretend that that has solved the situation. It won't be long before hunger and sleepiness return. So it is with every other "problem" in your life. The situation is never healed. Eat and sleep, but remember that the truth lies within you. Remind yourself that the only end to hunger and tiredness comes through listening to Spirit. Eat and sleep, but give your discomfort to Spirit.

We have been down this road together several times. I wish to remind you that Spirit is always bringing to you exactly the perfect thing in each moment to guide you home. I want to remind you that, as ego is your creation and as the world is your creation, so is the existence of Spirit being there to guide you home also your creation. In your Oneness with God, you have co-created your way to wake up. However, you are the sole creator of the dream. This is not God's dream. Nobody else can wake you up, but yourself. Nobody else is dreaming this but you. Spirit can grab you by the shoulder and gently shake you and whisper to wake up, but you can pull the cover over your face and continue to sleep for as long as you want. Or...you can choose to wake up. For most people, if it comfortable enough to stay in the dream, they will stay. It is familiar; it is known; it feels relatively safe. Waking up is an absolute unknown to the unconscious mind. Letting go of the world is terrifying. As we mentioned in the last message, trying to create heaven on earth seems like a safer bet. You, however, have made the choice to try to listen to Spirit rather than the ego. Spirit is going to bring situations to you that feel uncomfortable in order to help you wake up. If you see these events as the cause of your suffering, you will stay asleep. As you accept them as the gifts that they are from your own true mind, you begin to awaken.

Spirit will never give you more than you have asked for. Spirit will help you see where you have given power to the illusion, where you have become a victim to fear. This requires that you face these fears head on. It is not easy, but it is doable. Eventually, you will do it. The world is never the cause. When you fully realize this, the world can cause you no pain or suffering. There will be nothing to fear. You will know that the cause is in you and you will choose to go home. That is what Spirit is teaching you. When things come into your lives that feel painful, this is not a failing on your part. It is not a weakness. If anything, it is a strength. It is a sign of spiritual maturity, a sign that you are now ready for this test. You are ready to give this to Spirit, to take responsibility, to let go of having the earth be your cause. If the earth were at cause there would be only despair. Knowing you are at cause, that it is all from Spirit, from Divinity – there is nothing to despair of. Everything is perfect; all is aligned.

The thought for today is that the cause is always within you. Everything in the world is the effect from your mind's cause, and you have caused it for only one reason. You have done this to help yourself wake up. If it is your deep desire to awaken, feel nothing but gratitude for whatever the world seems to bring to you. So simple. So pure. So beautiful. Just accept it with thankfulness.

Good Now

Sanhia

Am I really supposed to accept everything that happens to me?

In any situation when something happens, you have the choice to listen to the voice of ego or the voice of Spirit. If you listen to the voice of ego, you stay on the merry-go-round. You keep going round and round, or up and down, and stay stuck in the belief that this illusion is real. Or, you can listen to the voice of Spirit, which will eventually guide you back home. We have talked about this before, but I want to describe it today using different terminology. It is not always easy in the moment to recognize what is coming from Spirit and what is of the ego. Here is a method for making this discernment, to become more aware with whom you are playing and giving energy. The two significant terms here are *acceptance* and *analysis*. It isn't hard to guess which aligns with Spirit and which with the ego, but I'll tell you anyway. When you simply accept what is happening or has happened, whatever it might be, you are opening up to the voice of Spirit. When you attempt to understand, to analyze, and to deal with the situation, you are listening to the voice of ego. Spirit accepts; ego analyzes.

Let's talk in more depth about what each of these choices is like. I the last message we talked about cause and effect. When you analyze, you are acting as if the effect is the cause. You are turning things around. You are looking at how to change the world. You are accepting the world as real, and as the cause of your problem. You are trying to make your world better. That is always the voice of ego trying to make heaven on earth. Remember that the cause is always within your mind, not out in the world. When you analyze, you are pretending that the world is cause. So, you may be thinking, "Sanhia, should I accept everything that happens to me without resistance?" And I respond, "Yes". This is what Jesus was referring to when he said to turn the other cheek. Don't fight what is happening, surrender to it. Accept it. Know not only that you are the cause, which means that anything and everything that happens in your life that does not feel Divine is experienced because you believe that you are separated from God. You fear that you are going to be punished, deserve punishment, and need forgiveness from God. This is why you have created everything that is uncomfortable in your life. Acceptance is merely the acknowledgment that it could be no other way. The cause must be in you and so it is useless to try to change the world. Rather than trying to change the effect, you go to the cause. You change what it is in you that feels you are guilty, that judges yourself. What you want to heal is your belief in your separation from God, this thought that you are not worthy, this idea that you have sinned against God and been found guilty. These false beliefs are what you want to change.

Another side of the story is this. Spirit always, with no exceptions ever, anywhere in time, has a plan. Everything that is happening to you is exactly perfect and as it should be. Spirit's plan for you is that you wake up and come home. Every event in your life is part of this wake up call. When you fight what is happening or try to change it after careful or not so careful analysis, you are questioning the judgment and ability of Spirit. Only the voice of ego would have the temerity to try and pull that off. Ego is trying to protect its own turf by claiming to have a better plan than the Divine plan. You have bought this promise lifetime after lifetime. The reason for acceptance is to have faith in the voice of Spirit, trusting that Spirit is bringing you the perfect thing in each moment. Acceptance is the shortest way home. No need to question, to analyze, to understand...you simply accept that this is the best way. If it is hard to accept, you can do the *five-step process* to ease your experience. Rather than asking Spirit for understanding, ask for support in letting go of your illusions and the belief that they are real. Ask for support in giving up your self-hatred and your fear of God, letting go of your self-condemnation. If Spirit in Its plan provides you with understanding, then of course you will accept that insight, but it is not your job to figure things out. That is Spirit's job. Your only responsibility is to accept what comes and to trust, knowing that Spirit will provide you with everything that you need. So, cover your ears. Shut out the voice of ego. Starve it. Do this through acceptance.

As you have the conscious intention to choose acceptance over analysis, you will become more proficient at it. You will find that the more often you choose acceptance the easier it becomes. All things begin to look more Divine, especially in places you would have previously had difficulty in finding perfection. Eventually, everything will look Divine. That is the state of mastery that precedes the full realization of ascension. Jesus was able to look at those who were putting him to death and see them as Divine. He could see every moment as holy, including the one where a spear was jabbed into his side. He accepted. He saw the Divinity. He saw that nothing else was real. In full acceptance there is unconditional love. There is no pain, no fear. You will all get there. That is already in Spirit's plan. You get there by taking one step at a time, by noticing where you are analyzing rather than accepting.

Let's take a few more moments to look at the analyzing process so that you may more easily recognize it. You are so skilled at this ability of looking at another and seeing how they are making choices that are not in their best interests. You want to help them. You want to point out to them what they are doing. That is the voice of ego. What you see out here, what you see them doing, is you. It is not them. It is always you. Your self-analysis is projected upon another. You are trying to heal it out there, instead of taking responsibility for your own thoughts. You are trying to change the effect instead of the cause. The other person is always showing you the effect of your mind. When you recognize how that process works, you begin to accept the behavior of everyone else and stop analyzing them or trying to change or assist them. You simply acknowledge that you are seeing places where you do not accept yourself and you take that inside and forgive. You accept everything as yours and give it all to Spirit. Think about how much time and energy you spend thinking about and worrying about others. You may hold it as your holy responsibility to do that. But, that is all from the ego. It is all analysis. It is all projection. It is not your job to help anyone else. Your job is to save yourself and you do that by accepting everything around you.

So, with all of this time and energy not being spent in your habitual manner, what do you now talk or think about? What is left if there is no more problem solving or "loving" spiritual gossip to share? This is a big space; it can feel like an enormous void. You give that space to Spirit. You accept that everything you see is your projection of your separation from God. You work on forgiving yourself and God; forgiving the other.... reminding yourself constantly that none of this out there is real. In truth there is nothing to forgive. Everyone is innocent and Divine. I am aware that you are surrounded by spiritual teachings that contradict this. You are to be the Good Samaritan. You are to help others. You are to be a "good" person. There is nothing wrong about helping another, but that is done by simply loving them unconditionally, by accepting them as they are. If you think it is your job to fix them, you see them as broken, not as Divine. That is the service you will provide them. And as you see them, so do you see yourself. So we have the blind leading the blind. This does not mean that you don't help somebody who asks for help. Be kind. But don't confuse the issue by thinking you are healing somebody by giving them assistance. For more on this subject you can reread Message 9: *When should I share my spiritual perspective with others?* You have no obligation here. It is not your job to heal. That is Spirit's job. Spirit may use you in the healing process, but not through your conscious deliberation of what is needed, not through your analysis of the situation. You give yourself to Spirit and wait for Spirit to direct you. If you truly want to help others, then realize your own ascension. That is the greatest gift you have to offer to the whole. If Spirit has a role for you to play, that will unfold. It's not up to you. There is nothing to figure out. Let go of that weight. Free yourself. Your job is to simply accept everything. You don't have to do the right thing. Whatever you do is perfect. It doesn't matter. What everyone else does is perfect. It doesn't matter. If it looks like somebody out there needs correction, the truth is you think you need correction. You are all Divine, but asleep. You have to awaken yourself before you can awaken another.

Let's close with this image. You are watching a movie on a screen. You don't like what is happening so you get up and try to change the screen. But you can't do anything. The movie continues. That is because the movie is not created on the screen. It is created by cameras and then projected on the screen. The screen is the world and the projector is your mind. The only way to change what is happening on the screen is to change your mind. This means that what is on the screen or in the world is not real. Only your thoughts are real. So change your mind. The catch is that you don't really know how to do that. So it all comes back to the thought for today. Accept the movie as it is. Take responsibility for it. Forgive yourself. Give it to Spirit in the realization that Spirit is the true creator of the movie. All you can do is accept what you are seeing. Stop analyzing the show and give it all to Spirit. It is so simple. Analyze, listen to ego, and continue to suffer. Accept, listen to Spirit, reclaim your Divine heritage, and go home. No matter which choice you make in this moment....

God Blesses You

Sanhia

What is meant by pure non-duality?

I have been talking about the illusion. The last message dealt with acceptance and analysis while the preceding one considered cause and effect. All of this is connected to what we call pure non-duality. I am going to take a moment to define this term. Duality has to do with opposites. The physical experience is a creation of duality. Without it, there can be no physicality. Whether the split is male/female, hot/cold, light/dark, right/wrong, heaven/hell or ego/Spirit – everything in this world is based in duality. Non-duality implies Oneness. Non-duality is God, is Divinity, and is your true nature. When you think you are human and in a body in the physical world, you are in duality. Ascension requires the release of duality. If you want to get off the wheel, to stop experiencing heaven and hell, reincarnation, suffering, and pain – so that you can go home and experience only Divinity with God – the route to follow is pure non-dualism, absolute and complete. Anything, any belief system or teaching that finds an ultimate value or purpose in the physical, such as those who wish to create heaven on earth (*Message 21*), is not teaching pure non-duality. This is fine. It is not our job to criticize or to tell you what to believe, but we want to let you know that there are consequences to every choice that you make. The truth of you will never be hurt or damaged no matter how long you chase after illusions. One day you will wake up. It makes no difference how attached you are to the duality. Eventually you will choose to let it go. The focus here is not to try to talk you into non-dualism. If you have an attachment to the physical and want to stay, then this message will probably not have much attraction for you. For those of you who wish to go home now, who are ready to release the physical and let go of duality, you will wish to read on. That being said, it is one thing to intend to focus on pure non-dualism, but another to fully realize it. The mass consciousness does not support such thinking in any way whatsoever. Even religions that began out of the seed of pure non-dualism have been altered, so you are unlikely to find support in any church or temple. Even many of those who purport to teach from non-dualistic sources, such as *A Course in Miracles*, often misinterpret and dilute the message.

Here comes a primer in pure non-dualism. Everything in your physical experience is an illusion: nothing physical is real. It is not the truth. All that you perceive in the physical world comes from your mind. You are the creator of this physical "dream", not God. It is in this dream of physicality that you think you can hide from God. As long as you "live" in this dream you experience duality. There is a balance in the physical where every "positive" is "counter-balanced" by a "negative". Duality is based upon judgment, upon what is thought to be good or bad. The ultimate judgment is that you are guilty, that you have sinned against God and He will punish you. So, you have to be good, or at least punish yourself first, to get back in God's good graces. That is the insanity of duality. You are welcome to try and improve the duality; you have been attempting this for eons. Beat your head against the wall as long as you want, but the only way out of the quagmire is to give up duality and practice pure non-dualism. This recognizes that God does not and could not judge you, that you are innocent and loved unconditionally. You cannot earn God's forgiveness because it is always freely granted. Pure non-dualism means letting go of your belief in your separation from God's love and choosing to wake up from this dream and be home with God. When you make this choice, we are here at your service. The practice of pure non-dualism is not complicated; it is very simple. It does require a great deal of effort and trust because you will be asked to go against everything that the ego is screaming into your ear, ideas that seem to be logical. Ego's voice will come from within your own mind, from others, from the mass media, and from other spiritual paths. You will find yourself surrounded by this cacophony. No matter how daunting the odds may seem, you have no choice but to eventually succeed. We are here to expedite your journey.

There are just three steps in moving from dualism to pure non-dualism. The first one is perhaps the most challenging. This step is for you to simply accept that there are two voices you can hear in any situation. You can hear the voice of the ego, which confuses you through duality, or you hear the voice of Spirit, which reinforces pure non-dualism. This step asks you to train yourself into an awareness at each moment of your life – with each thought, with each action, with each feeling, with everything that is transpiring – that you are being presented with a choice of listening to ego or to Spirit. This may sound like a small step, but how easy it is to unconsciously accept ego as the only voice, as, for the most part, you have always done. Examples of listening to the ego include entertaining thoughts of victimhood, of judgment of self and others, of comparing yourself favorably or not to another. You may contemplate why things are happening, may feel fear, may feel unloved. There are many levels and ways that the ego carries on this onslaught. Training yourself in each moment to be aware that you are listening to either ego or Spirit is an enormous accomplishment. We are not even yet talking about the discernment of which voice you are hearing – though it is likely that of the ego at this stage – only the awareness that you have a choice of two voices in this very moment, that nothing is set in stone. In step one it is just for you to be aware that you are listening to a voice. Until you become aware that you are listening to a voice, you will unconsciously be listening to ego and will stay rooted in duality. Remember that there is no judgment about this choice. God loves you no matter who you listen to. The only punishment will be self-imposed under the direction of the ego. The ego plays "good cop, bad cop". Ego will tell you how wonderful you are in comparison to another, which may feel good. Then it will tell you how bad you are in comparison to another individual, which may not feel so good. Ego constantly plays these games with you. Be aware of that. Until you develop the awareness that you are listening to a voice, you can go no further. Ego will run your life. If you notice once a month that you are listening to a voice, you will experience slow progress. As the awareness becomes weekly, or daily, or multiple times a day – you will truly begin to move your consciousness. Ultimately, your awareness will be constant. That is the state of the master. As long as you are still in a body, ego will do its best to keep you listening, to keep you rooted in the physical. Your goal can be to have constant vigilance about noticing that you are listening to a voice.

The second step is a small but significant one. The question is, "What voice are you listening to?" Is this ego or Spirit? As you are starting down this road it won't always be easy to discern. In general the voice of fear comes from ego and Spirit is the voice of love. But, sometimes fear can feel like love – and vice versa. When ego whispers in your ear how you are better than others, it can feel like love, though it is truly separation. We want to give you some more tips on how to recognize the voice of Spirit. Spirit never compares or judges. As we pointed out last time, Spirit accepts, ego analyzes. Thinking about things opens the door to ego. Accepting whatever appears opens you to Spirit. Spirit always reminds you of your innocence, of your pureness, of your Divinity. There is never blame or judgment of yourself or anybody else. You can know that it is ego if blame or judgment is heard. Spirit never compares, that also is the realm of ego. When Spirit speaks, it is always a win-win situation. There are no losers. With ego there is always some sort of competition. With Spirit there are no "shoulds". That word implies a rightness or wrongness in a choice. It suggests that to be "good" you will make a certain choice. If you follow a voice out of the fear of what will happen if you don't, you are following ego. If you don't follow that voice there may be fear of repercussions. Attachment to a certain result is also from ego. Acceptance of any outcome is the voice of Spirit. Whatever happens is perfect. If there is any guilt involved, that is the voice of ego. Spirit always communicates unconditional love and acceptance. As you practice identifying the source of the voice you are hearing, you will get better. It doesn't matter how many times you are fooled. Your only jobs are to be vigilant (step one) and to make a decision (step two). Your accuracy will improve. Just keep getting back on that horse. You are still in duality. Otherwise there would not be the illusion of having two voices to listen to. Only the truth of Spirit could be heard. Ego lies. It is trying to maintain its existence by deceiving you. Spirit is patient. Time is on Its side. Ultimately the truth will out and will stand alone.

Step three is perhaps the easiest, or maybe the hardest. This step is for you to take action. It does little good to identify the speaker as Spirit if you don't follow what He says to do. This is where you put your money where your mouth is. You act in alliance with the voice of Spirit that you have identified. There is integrity, because when you are true with Spirit you are true with yourself. Here are some suggestions to ease the creation of this alignment. Begin each day by talking with Spirit. Ask Spirit to be with you all day and to help you notice when you have a choice of voices, to identify His voice, and finally to follow it. Ask Spirit for His guidance for the day. If you wake up with something from your sleep or dreams, or from the previous day that causes you confusion, ask Spirit for direction and support. You can complete your day by having a similar communication with Spirit before going to sleep. Let go of everything that feels incomplete, unsuccessful, unfulfilling, or simply stressful. Give it all to Spirit to handle while you enjoy revitalizing sleep. Wake up freed of this heavy load and filled with love. That is the whole purpose of that *third* of your life; it is a time to plug into Spirit and recharge. Ask to be told what to do. There is a subtle but powerful difference here between this guidance and the voice of ego. Ego tells you what you *should* do; Spirit tells you what *to* do. There is no right or wrong about it. It is now time to trust, to fully let go of ego and only listen to Spirit. You do this in order to let go of the world and fully realize your Divinity. You trust Spirit as the only voice to get you there. You realize that you have no separate voice of your own. That separate voice was always the ego. It kept you apart from God. Spirit is now telling you the most direct way home. Spirit is not the best voice to listen to, it is the only voice. It comes from within you and from nowhere else. Nobody else can tell you what you should do. Spirit speaks only to you and loves you beyond measure. This is the only way for you. That is a terrifying thought to the ego. It is probably screaming in your ear right now telling you not to give up your autonomy. Of course the joke is that you have been doing just that for lifetimes – giving your autonomy to ego. Now, you are giving it to the Divine truth within you. If you are tired of living in the duality, your job is to do your best in every moment to turn your life over to Spirit, to truly practice pure non-dualism. This is a tall order, but you will do it. You will all do this eventually. In reality it is already done and you are home with God in Divine love. The play has already been written and acted out. Within the dream it feels like the illusion is still going on; it may feel like it is taking endless time. To reduce the time, follow step three in every moment possible. This, of course, requires first following step one and step two, but the goal is for those steps to become such habits that all of your focus can be on listening to and following Spirit.

Another support for step three is to be proactive by filling your mind through readings that support pure non-dualism. The world is filled with dualistic energy. You are bombarded by it daily from all sides. Taking some time to read and meditate on pure information can be a great support, not only in resisting the world but also in noticing where you still tend to make it real. Here is a short list of places to start:

1. *A Course in Miracles*
2. Gary Renard's books (starting with *The Disappearance of the Universe*)
3. The *One With God* series (by Marjorie Tyler, Jo Sjolander, Margaret Bollonoff)

4. Anything by Ken Wapnick
5. Channeling from Sanhia (either from
    channelswithout borders.com or the book *God Blesses You*)

Start reading where you are guided. Find time wherever you can. Love yourself whether you read or not, but have the intention. You can also have the intention of finding allies, that is, others who have made the choice to experience pure non-dualism. Having even one friend with which to share mutual support can make your voyage faster. Perhaps there is a group out there for you. You do not need to be in a state of feeling alone with your path. As you progress, you will find yourself drawing like-minded energy. Give that to Spirit, asking to be supported in the highest way. If you find yourself alone though, know that that is the perfect way for you now.

While following these steps provides an enormous challenge, you also have an enormous resource to support you. The loving energy of Spirit (or Jesus, or Buddha, or Sanhia, or whatever expression of Divine Oneness you feel most connected with) is so far above and beyond the ego's obstacle of fear that I hesitate to mention them in the same breath. As you choose and act from Spirit's guidance, you fill yourself with more and more love. The accumulation of this love makes it increasingly easy to follow these three steps. This love builds on itself, spiraling higher and higher. It all starts with step one. Ask Spirit for support. Remember that all is perfect and is proceeding as it should. Accept Spirit's gifts each day. Don't fight, don't resist. Trust. Listen. Then your load truly lightens. No matter what happens.......

God Blesses You

Sanhia

Do I have to be perfect to ascend?

I have been covering a lot of territory in the past few messages, talking about pure non-duality, confusing cause and effect, accepting everything that comes to you, and the impossibility of creating heaven on earth. Sometimes, and it is perfectly understandable, you might have the reaction that this is all too much. On a conceptual level you might believe in what I have shared; that you are creating it all, that none of it is real, to forgive yourself for everything that has happened and to not judge anyone, and, and, and...... You might be thinking "But Sanhia, it feels enormous. It feels so big. I don't think I'm up to it. I don't think I can do all of this. How could anyone accomplish such a feat? You would have to be perfect." Wow! That was quite a rant. Is there anything more? Don't hold back. Excuse me while I chuckle just a bit, not at you but with you. You are absolutely right. It is too much. It is too big. Fortunately, you are not expected to be perfect. In the illusion in duality, it is an absolute impossibility. You cannot go through your day and not have a negative emotional response, not get angry, not blame someone, or feel like a victim. It's going to happen. It is the human condition. If it did not happen, you would not be here in a body; you would be finished with all of this.

Maybe, you notice that these reactions are not happening as often as they once did. Think about how it was before you begin working with non-dualistic thinking. Over time, this change in how you react to the world will increase in its occurrence. But, you will never realize a time where the ego's thoughts don't grab a hold of you. If you have it in your mind that your ascension can only come about through perfection, that day is never going to come. There will never be a time where your ego is absolutely unable to get a foot in the door, or even a toe. Hearing this may bring on a wave of sadness or hopelessness for you. You may feel that you can never make it. That is not the case; it is but an opening for the ego's voice. In fact, the opposite is true. You are going to make it; you have no choice. We are in charge of that, not you. You can slow the process down by digging in your heals and refusing to listen to Spirit, by insisting on being a victim and projecting your guilt on others. You can do that and slow things down, but you can't stop it. So, if you can do your worst and are still guaranteed your place in heaven with God, where in fact you truly are right now though lacking the awareness of being there, how much more quickly are you going to realize your Oneness with God if you are trying to work with the process instead of against it?

The secret is not in being perfect in every moment. The secret is in becoming aware after you have let the ego run rampant, that you have done so. With this awareness there are two steps to take. First, give whatever it is to Spirit. Don't tell Spirit what to do; this is not yours to handle. Just let it go and let Spirit handle it. The second step is equally important. *Be kind to yourself.* Let it be okay that you did what you did, or that you didn't do what you didn't do. Let that be okay. It is not the expectation that you will never stumble. There is no thought about that. There is no judgment. Remember that nothing here is real. Nothing you do is wrong. Nobody is hurt, not even yourself. It is all an illusion. That is the forgiveness process, so be kind to yourself and forgive yourself. It is perfectly okay that you listened to the ego. The important thing is that you noticed and have chosen to try not to do that next time. You might still do it again. No biggie. What is important is that you notice, even if it takes days to do so. It makes no difference how long it takes you to notice. Time doesn't matter, except when you are in pain. Holding on to your blame and victimhood is always painful...well, after the initial rush that comes from feeling yourself to be a righteous martyr. As soon as you realize that you have projected, that you have confused the cause and the effect, the pain eases. This is an enormous accomplishment, the noticing that you have been listening to ego and now want to give it to Spirit. Nobody is counting how many times you trip, except yourself. So stop counting; be kind to yourself.

Let go of seeking perfection. You are already perfect. You are perfection pretending to not be perfect. As long as you are in a body, that dance will go on.....it will for all humanity. You cannot be perfect in duality, because in duality there are always opposites. You cannot help listening to ego in some moments, and you are not judged for that or for anything else. So give it to Spirit and be kind to yourself. I want to remind you that as you are looking for perfection, you can be looking in all the wrong places. Perfection is not found in the world, which will never mirror heaven, which will never replicate the infinite love of God. You created the world, thinking you could do better than God. That was a mad idea. The world is not the place to look for perfection. However, there is a perfect plan for you and the Sonship to awaken. When something occurs in your life and you react in such a way as to be a victim, this is a perfect part of Spirit's plan. If you were to spend your life in the belief that you are doing everything perfectly, you would be in denial. Your head would be deeply buried in the sand as you repeat to yourself "Everything is fine". You would ignore your pain until it kills you. Then you would come back and try it again. It is through feeling the pain that you experience when you listen to the ego that you realize you need to choose differently. Without this suffering you would not choose to listen to Spirit. Each time you go through the cycle of listening to ego, feeling pain, giving it to Spirit, forgiving, and being kind to yourself – you are one step closer to letting go of the illusion. This is only possible if all of the steps are followed. You cannot learn without first making a mistake. So, the more mistakes you make the faster you learn, as long as you realize your missteps. There is perfection in your errors. You each have your vulnerable spots – your hot buttons – the places where you are most likely to go into victimhood, projection, and blame. Those hotspots are a gift that Spirit will use to help you learn to let go of the ego. Choosing wrongly is the necessary first step.

If you are in a body, you believe that you are separate from God and you fear God and his wrath. That is painful. It is not your job to hide from the pain. Spirit makes that easy for you. Spirit presents choices that make it likely that you came into contact with your pain. Spirit does not cause the pain. It is your belief in your separation and your need for punishment that cause the pain. If you are not conscious that you carry this guilt energy with you, how can you let it go? There is perfection in everything that is presented to you. There is not perfection in your ability to choose Spirit in each moment. That you will never have. You will simply, eventually reach the point that you give your pain so quickly, so automatically to Spirit that Spirit will say, "Come with me now", and it will be the end of your earthly experience. This happens not from your per-fection of action, but from your surrender of your little self to the Oneness of God. You cannot choose this moment. You can only remember that choosing to listen to the ego for an instant does not further separate you from God. It is a window of opportunity that is there to lead you home. You may have many rungs to climb up out of the hell of physicality. You will not likely be taking the express elevator out, though the ego will whisper in your ear that if you were really so Divine you would take that express ride right out of here, so you must really be a fuck up. Smile, and give all of that to Spirit. Let go of the need for perfection. Each rung will bring a lightening of the load you carry. You don't need to demonstrate perfection; you are perfection...no matter what the ego might be saying to you. You are innocent. You are perfection.

Good Now

Sanhia

Is it part of my purpose to help heal others?

As you are working with your spiritual process, with real-izing your Divinity, with noticing you are listening to a voice, with learning to discern whether it is Spirit or the ego you are listening to, and with learning to hear, trust, and follow Spirit – as you are doing all of these things and you look around at your friends, relatives, co-workers, and perhaps even strangers – you notice that they are making what seems to you to be wrong choices. They may seem to be acting in ways that bring them pain and confusion as they listen to the ego and make the illusion real. A very natural reaction you may likely have is to say to yourself, "Oh, if they only knew what they were doing!" You think that perhaps you can be of help to them. You could point out how they are listening to the ego, how what they are seeing isn't real, how their choices cannot work out for them. You may wonder if that is part of your path. As you are gain-ing wisdom, should you be sharing it with those around you? My answer to this is a very simple and clear "No". That is not your job. That is my job. That is Spirit's job. It is not your job. Perhaps that is not what you wanted to hear. Or maybe you are letting go a sigh of relief.

Let me explain why healing others is not your job. There are myriad reasons, so I will wander about and touch on this and that. I will begin by reminding that when you want to intercede when observing another in pain – what you are seeing *is* you. This is where the voice of the ego in you likely goes crazy and says, "No! That is them." No, this *is* your creation. Do not con-fuse the cause and the effect. Whatever you see in the world is your creation. Everything is created by your mind. You are not a disconnected observer. What you see is born in your mind, not in the world. So, everything in the world is your mirror. When you see another choosing ego, it is you choosing ego. The work, then, is not to fix them, but to heal yourself. Your only job, your only purpose for being here, is to heal yourself.

You have no responsibility for dealing with what you perceive as others' challenges or problems.

Now, your mind may be asking, "But, what if they ask me for help?" That is a different question. Any requests you receive for support are to be given to Spirit. Allow Spirit to speak through you. Trust what comes and share it with the one who has requested support. Then, let it go. Have no attachment to it being heard, received, or acted on in the "right" way. That is none of your business. Your only job is to share what Spirit gives to you and let it go.

When you perceive that another has a challenge or might not be choosing in the highest way, what is truly going on is that you are judging them. This can feel like a thin line, discerning what is noticing and what is judging. If any kind of emotional reaction is present, know that judgment is involved. This can include positive as well as negative emotions. Let's take it a step further. The truth of the other is that they are Divine, as are you. Any lack you perceive in them is an expression of denial of their Divinity. Thus, you are saying that you, also, are not really Divine. A good rule of thumb to use when looking at others is that if you cannot make your perception true for all others, it is not true. To judge one person for something you do not judge another for is to create separation. When you separate any son of God from another, you separate yourself from God. You could, instead, think in the following fashion. When you observe someone acting from the ego, you can say that they are not fully awake yet. That is true of all who are in the human condition, including yourself. To single out one individual as separate from God, while holding another as special or connected to God, creates the illusion of separation and cannot be a true observation. God is unity and Oneness. Any differences come from separation and the ego. As soon as you label any one person as out of balance, you have separated yourself from them and from God. In truth, of course, you are never separate from God, but this is your human experience.

If you wish to realize the truth of your Oneness with God and to let go of this physical illusion, don't ever take on the cloak of the wise teacher, of being the healer. That is not your job. That, again, does not mean that Spirit may not use you, but it is for Spirit to decide. In truth, you cannot help but to teach what you have learned, but you will do this through your surrender to Spirit. Your job is not to teach, but to learn. If you are in doubt whether the words you receive are coming from Spirit, say nothing. The same words can come from the voice of ego or Spirit. What matters is if pure love is behind them. If you are unsure whether it is your ego or the voice of Spirit wishing to express, err on the side of discernment and caution. Give your doubt and confusion to Spirit. Continue to give to Spirit all of your perceptions of pain or fear or doubt or victimization or victimizing that you see expressed through others. Your task is to love them unconditionally and see yourself as One with them. If that is too great a challenge in the moment, it is no biggie. Give it to Spirit. You are the one crying out for help. When you turn the situation over to Spirit, you don't tell Him how you want things handled. If you have any expectations about results, you have not let go, have not truly given it to Spirit. Remember that thinking you knew better than God is what got you here in the first place. Maybe Spirit has a message for you to share, maybe not. It is not your business. It does not matter what is going on in the world. That is effect not cause.

Your business is to heal your separation. You do this through forgiveness and reminding yourself of your innocence, not by noticing the log in your neighbor's eye. Your healing will never be realized through projection. Own everything you see as yours; ask Spirit to help you forgive yourself and open to God's love. You become frantic to heal the other, because you are frantic to heal yourself. When you try to heal the shadow rather than changing the projector you cannot succeed. At best, you end up with good slapstick comedy. Remember that it is never about the form. It is never about what appears to you to be going on in the world. It is always about the content of your mind. Is your focus on the truth of your Divinity, your innocence, on you being unconditionally loved by God – or – is it on your fear and guilt, on the belief that you have been kicked out of heaven, on trying to please God? It is never about fixing the world. It is not about saying the right words at the right time to the right person. None of that matters. Yes, Spirit will use humans in the process of ending the illusion, but it never matters when or how. The end is already certain. It was decided before any present perception, words, or actions transpire. When you speak with the influence of the ego there will be a shadow of judgment in your voice or an attachment to the end result. You may feel the listener must follow your advice to a successful conclusion or you have both failed. When influenced by Spirit you may never know why He has used you, what the purpose is. Let go of any need to know.

Your job is not to do "good". Good is one half of the duality and we all know what the other half is. One cannot exist without the other. Love does not recognize good or evil. It shines on all until everything is dissolved but truth. The reason you want to heal another is your desire to be rewarded by God. God may then single you out for redemption because you are better than another. How fortunate that you noticed their failure so that you can help them because you are better than them. Look God! No hands! Your imagined redemption comes only after you see your absolute equality with every Son of God. God doesn't need your help. Let go of thinking you have a better way. Be humble. Give up your need to be an individual, to stand out, to be better. Just be. Instead of healing another, simply be kind to them; be loving. That's what God does. No matter how many times you fall on your face, you are loved beyond measure. No matter what you do or feel or say...

God Blesses You

Sanhia

How do I give it to Spirit?

We have been talking for years about giving it to Spirit. People have been asking me lately just what that means and how to actually go about giving something to Spirit. To begin with, I wish to remind you – and I can never say this too many times – whatever it is that you want to give to Spirit, doesn't really exist. The problem isn't really there. It is a figment of your imagination. That does not mean that it doesn't feel absolutely real to you. It doesn't mean that strong emotions are not triggered; appearing to cause you discomfort and pain. I am well aware of all of that. I have walked in your moccasins. I bring the illusion up as a starting point because you will find it easier to give something to Spirit if you can remind yourself beforehand that it is not a big deal, that it ultimately doesn't really matter. If you believe that something is crucially important, it is harder to trust it to Spirit. When you give it to Spirit, you *do* let go of it. If you don't fully let go, you haven't given it to Spirit and you are left holding the bag. That is the acid test. If you find yourself still holding on, try again. Give it again, as many times as necessary, until you have fully let go.

I am going to share some ideas to ease your process of letting go. For some of you it may be hard to visualize what Spirit is. What is this entity you are trusting? It might be easier to substitute Jesus for Spirit. For others it might be easier to give it to Buddha, or to the Divine or the Divine Presence. You can give it to Sanhia. It makes no difference as long as you are giving it to an energy of pure non-dualism. I don't recommend that you give it to a spiritual leader who is in a body, because they, like you, are still in dualism. No matter how learned and advanced a human teacher may be, he or she is still in the illusion of duality. They are a projection for you rather than Divinity or Spirit.

When you give whatever it is to Spirit, you absolutely release it. There are no strings attached. That is why you never ask Spirit to solve a problem for you. Have no attachment to what Spirit does with your request. You don't ask Spirit to fix your financial problems. Don't ask Spirit to bring you your perfect relationship. Don't ask for a specific outcome or a solution. When you direct Spirit to a specific action you are making the illusion real. You are saying that if this problem can be solved, you can have a little bit of heaven on earth. This keeps you stuck in the cycle of duality. Asking for a solution is confusing cause and effect. You are not unhappy because of what is going on in your life. You are not a victim of that; you are the creator of that. In your mind you hold a belief that you are separate from God and deserve punishment. The challenge you are experiencing comes from that wrong-thinking mind. This is not an easy concept to wrap your head around when you are in a body. Your ego has done a very effective job of convincing you that the world is doing you in. Then, you want Spirit to come in and save you. I want to impress upon you that you don't want us to do that because as long as you remain the victim you will stay in hell indefinitely. If we were to solve this problem, you would just create a new one, because your belief in victimhood and helplessness would continue unabated.

So, your request to Spirit is never one of asking for a solution to a problem. There is only one prayer for you to make to Spirit. Ask Spirit to wake you up, to help you realize that this is your creation. Ask for help in realizing that all of this comes from your belief in separation, from your fear of God, from your belief that you deserve punishment, from your belief that this world is real and that you are a victim of it. You want Spirit to take all of that from you and wake you up. You want to be reminded that you are, always have been, and always will be the unconditionally loved Son of God, that you are welcome to come home. That is the only thing to ask Spirit to do. When you call on Spirit, you give Him this burden, this tangled muddy mess of victimhood and confusion. You ask Spirit just to take it from you, that you no longer want to be immersed in fear and limitation. You ask not for solutions, only for freedom from the worry and the weight. You are free now, say, of your financial worries because they are not real so there is nothing to worry about, not because Spirit is going to pay your bills. Your belief that your problems were real is gone because you have given it to Spirit. Your beliefs will be cleansed by Spirit. Spirit is your cosmic laundry service. Your only job is to let go.

If you should notice that you are still holding the fear, it only means that you didn't fully let go. Perhaps you let go of one level of your fear. No big deal. Give it to Spirit again. This is like the last step of the *five-step process*. It may come back. That is fine. When you successfully give it to Spirit and let go, you are living in the holy moment. This is that time where there is no time. You have let go of the past and your guilt. You have let go of the future and your fear. All of that has been given to Spirit. All that is left is the holy moment.

Another issue that may come up for some of you, perhaps for everyone, is the issue of trust. You wonder if you are just fooling yourself. Is there really a Spirit out there that you can give this too? Is it really true that you are the Divine Son of God, that this is just a dream that you can let go of? Is all of this really true and the entire world around you an illusion? Of course, I can assure you that Spirit is the only thing you can trust in, but that won't necessarily alleviate your doubt. For most of you your choice really comes down to a combination of two things. First, you have tried it every other way and nothing has worked for you, so what do you have left to lose? You have tried and tried to create heaven on earth, to solve all of these problems and you have failed, so why not leave it to Spirit? The second thing is that you have been working with what I am talking about. This is not new. There have been times when you were able to let something go. You experienced a healing around a fear, even if it didn't last. The more you practice giving it to Spirit, the more you will notice these kinds of results. This is not the outcome of seeing your problems solved, but the fruition of seeing your fear dissolve, of feeling at peace.

Maybe your finances don't look any different, but you don't worry about them much now.

This is why you, not God but the Divine You, created Spirit being here. You wanted a constant and clear voice reminding you of the truth, because you also created the ego, a constant and clear voice reminding you of what is not true. Both of those voices are always there for you. You have been learning how to discern which voice you are hearing and to choose the voice of Spirit. As you continue to work in this way, your trust and faith will strengthen. It is a matter of persistence, of self-discipline. Your fear will decrease, but while you are in a body it never fully disappears. This is perfect. Whatever stands in your way from leaving the physical and returning home is there for you to see and to give to Spirit. It is so simple. You have only one job. Give everything to Spirit. There is nothing you have to decide or to solve. Everything is off of your shoulders. Spirit is your absolute guide in each moment. Returning for a moment to the *five-step process*, the second step is truly giving it to Spirit. You can choose to incorporate this into your internal directions to yourself. Surrender fully to the energy you are feeling in your body and at the same time hand it over to Spirit. You are already doing that when you stare into the face of your fear. It disappears because it is not real. When the discomfort of the fear transforms to that warm feeling of love, you have made your surrender to Spirit. As you look into the face of your fear, Spirit is there with you. The ego mind tells you to look away, warning you that it is not safe to face your fear. As you are facing the fear you can verbally add that you are giving this fear to Spirit. Again, you are not pushing the fear away, only offering it to Spirit. Perhaps in your practice of giving things to Spirit that we talked about earlier, failure comes about because you are pushing your fear away rather than simply surrendering it. So, if you are having trouble giving something to Spirit, we recommend doing the *five-step process.*

Finally, giving it to Spirit is a lightening of your load. It is not a foisting off onto Spirit to handle your problem. You give to Spirit in a spirit of love and gratitude, in the awareness that your fear is not real. It is a request for support in fully awakening. This request is always heard and always answered.

Good Now

Sanhia

How can we not see children as innocent victims?

It's a funny thing, but I have never talked to a human who didn't have parents. Sometimes, one might not know who his birth mother was; there was an adoption and the mother's identity is hidden. In this case there are two mothers that you have stories with, one that abandoned you and one that you can have the everyday issues with. Even if there are no identifiable mothers, you will have numerous tales with foster parents, relatives, or orphanages, along with the actual birth mother relationship. There is always a father, also, even if the mother doesn't know who it is. Present or absent, which is of course its own drama, you have a history with him along with any other men who have played that role for you. Within the illusion, everyone has two parents, and many stories come with those relationships. An interesting thing about the parent-child relationship is that it is a lifelong one. Most relationships are for a short period – perhaps only a one time meeting, or for a length of time – but only a few traverse your whole life. The relationship with a parent is carried deep within you, particularly if you haven't taken full responsibility for it. This is true even if there has been a separation, whether through death or from personal choice. The relationship is a constant presence. If there were an order of importance of relationships in the illusion, these might be the biggest ones. Many of you, if you are honest with yourselves, blame your parents for one thing or another. You believe you are the way you are because your father was so cruel or because your mother was so judgmental. So, you are a victim all of your life because of whom your parents were. This is not true. That is the ego's story. It is another way of confusing cause and effect.

The mass consciousness presents the illusion that a pure, innocent, helpless baby is born. The child is a blank screen onto which the parents will begin to write. Such a responsibility! If they do things right, the child will thrive; if they do things wrong, the child will suffer. What a burden! Fortunately it is an illusion. Children hardly come in as blank slates; they arrive fully formed. Of course we are not speaking physically, but as we know the physical you is not the true you. Physically, infants are helpless, but mentally they carry with them all of the ego beliefs of guilt, fear, and victimhood they have burdened themselves with through countless incarnations since their imagined separation from God. What happens is that children create experiences in the world just as you do as an adult. From the first day onward, and even before that in their prenatal experiences, children create in accordance with these beliefs. Like you, they project their guilt onto others and receive punishments they believe they deserve, which will hopefully square them in God's eye. Now they have others, particularly their parents, who they can blame and point a finger at. You all did this, and you are *still* doing it.

I want to talk about this from a few different perspectives – firstly from your specific relationship with your parents. As you were growing up it certainly seemed that you had no choice. You couldn't pick up and leave or select different parents. You couldn't avoid abusive situations at school, in your neighborhood, or with relatives. You felt yourself to be a victim. You simply had to endure these experiences. But then, as now, you always had the ability to say that the outer world did not affect you. In some places you made this choice and your parents' words and deeds did not touch you. You knew they were not the truth. You created your own truth in these situations. If you are not an only child, you see how your siblings developed differently – none of you are alike. If you were blank slates written on by the same parents, you should have turned out the same. Yet, you and your siblings are quite different. Why? Because you each created your own experiences and made your own choices in dealing with them. It was not so much a question of what happened to you as how you dealt with it internally. Did you practice forgiveness and seeing the

Divinity in your parent, or were those skills yet to be developed? The potential was there to access those truths. This is not to point a finger or to say that it was your fault that you were not more aware, but simply to shine light on the reality of the situation. You came to wake up and Spirit provided you from birth on with the opportunities to do just that. You came in believing in your victimhood and you proved yourself right.

At some point you left home. Now you are on your own. Your parents are no longer in your day-to-day life. Yet, in how many ways are they still running it? What judgments did they make about you that you took on as your own? What fears did they instill in you that follow you around even when your parents' physical presence doesn't? Unless you do a forgiveness process, your parents will continue forever to run your life, even though you have been an independent adult for years. If you tell yourself that you are over all of that, that you are an adult and your own person now –wonderful! But take a good look at each of your parents and notice where you have any judgment remaining about them, or about the way they raised you – or about things they are still doing today. Where you find judgments you are discovering the places where they still run your life. This is projection, a confusion of cause and effect. You are always the cause of everything that happens to you. The world is always the effect. This is true now; it was true when you were a child. Your judgments of your parents are a refusal to admit the truth. It is time to grow up. Stop being a helpless child. If you were not really a victim then, you are even less so now. Be an adult and take responsibility. It is yourself you are judging. Handle it. You know how to do that – kindly, gently, lovingly, but firmly. There is no kindness to your parents or to yourself in projection and blame. They are attacks. Blame is a statement that you are a helpless victim. You pretend that you didn't choose these parents, but you did. You may scream that you didn't ask to be born, but you did. You created the perfect parents for you, the best classroom for you to learn the lessons you came to master so that you could awaken – leaving the pain, the guilt, the suffering, and the belief in separation from God that are a part of the world of duality – and come home. You chose the perfect parents to support you in doing that. Their job ended years ago. It's over, complete. Now the only work left to be done is yours.

Until you do this work, you will recreate your parents in all of the authority figures you meet in your life. It might be your boss and it certainly will be your partner. If you have not forgiven your opposite sex parent, you will find yourself married to that parent. It will make no difference what your spouse does; you will perceive them acting as your parent did. Remember that it is all you. There is no other. You are the creator of everyone in your life. You will create your mother and father everywhere you go. Make it simple for yourself. Rather than dealing with challenges with every person you meet every day of your life, just heal with your parents. Give gratitude to Spirit and to them for playing this game with you, for being your teachers. Look where you have judgment. Let Spirit lift that and help you to forgive. Ask for gratitude for having these perfect parents who came into your life to teach you exactly the lessons you came to learn. If you are not certain what the lessons were, request to understand what you came to learn from your parents.

In conclusion, you are all children. When you were a physical child it seemed that your parents were on another level. They certainly had the physical power. In truth, you were all children, asleep and hoping to awaken to your true selves. You and your parents are siblings, as is your brother Jesus. Your only job is to love them and to love yourself, to forgive them and to forgive yourself. To enter the kingdom of God you become like a child: innocent, pure, forgiven – the very idea that the mass consciousness holds of the newborn. Become the child you never got to be in this body. You are the Child of God.

Good Now

Sanhia

How can I be a better parent?

In the last message we talked about the relationship you had with your parents, about taking responsibility for all that happened and forgiving them and yourself. If you have not taken these steps, you will likely find yourself repeating your childhood with your own children. For those of you who do not have children, this projection will take place with others for whom you act as an authority figure, though the impact is usually stronger and more focused with your own children.

Many people have very idealistic thoughts about their children and how they will raise them. You tell yourself you are not going to be like your mother or your father; you will bring them up in a different way. You may consider the best techniques to use with your offspring so that they don't have to go through what you had to endure. The truth is that if you haven't healed with your parents, you will find yourself becoming your parents as you are in the midst of bringing up your children. They will constantly frustrate you. It hardly seems fair – first your parents controlled and hindered you, and now your children are doing the same thing. What kind of world is this? The illusion is that you have the responsibility as a parent to turn out the perfect child, when in actuality it doesn't matter what you do as a parent. It truly doesn't. This does not mean that I am encouraging you to beat or sexually abuse your children, but it doesn't make a difference for them. It does make a difference for you. Whatever you send out to another is what you believe that you deserve, and will therefore receive. However, the truth of them is not harmed. If that is what they seem to receive from you, it is their creation. They will deal with it however they deal with it, as you did with your parents.

Your children came in with their egos fully formed and are creating what they need to have in their classroom to help them wake up to their Divinity. They chose you as their parent. Your basic job is to see that they survive childhood – to see that they are fed, clothed, housed, physically protected, and adequately educated. It is not your job to make sure they excel as students or have perfect behavior, whatever that might be. If they survive childhood, you have done a wonderful job. Even if they don't, you have done the best you could. If you manage not to project your fears upon them, that is just gravy. Again, your children are the creators of their experience, not you. You are just a tool. If you want to do more than the basics and provide some of that gravy, the best way of doing that is to heal with your parents. Remember, if you still hold yourself as being a victim to your parents, you will create being a victim to your children. You will perceive your children as victims, too. You will worry about them, about what the world is doing to them. You will judge them for their weaknesses and fear for their future. In short, you will treat them as you treat yourself.

What you teach your children does not come from your words, but from your example. If you are coming from unconditional love, they will receive that no matter what your words or actions might be. They always have the choice to reject or misinterpret you, but loving them anyway gives them more space to choose love themselves. If through your living example your children are shown that you are never a victim to anything, you could not do more as a parent. Of course, this includes not being a victim to being a parent. If your children get the message of the parental role being one of martyrdom – that you have had to make so many sacrifices in order to be a good parent – you have put an enormous guilt load on your their shoulders. That's okay; it was a lesson they apparently needed to deal with, but it leaves you feeling a failure, feeling defeated.

But this message is not about your children, it is about you. Where you have judgment about your children and want to change them – that is the place you are not accepting yourself. Thank your children for being your teachers. Herein lies the crux of this message. There is no true hierarchy among you and your children. You, they, and everyone else are just human. You are all Divinity pretending not to be Divine, trying to wake up. Just because your child is in a smaller, more physically vulnerable body – as you were once upon a time – does not mean they are not your peer. Yes, it is your role to help them survive to adulthood, not because you are more evolved, but simply because you are physically mature. So thank your children for being your teachers, and learn from them. Seek the place where you have no judgment.

One of the biggest confusions that a parent can act on is to demand some kind of love from their children. When you demand love from anybody else, silently or overtly, it comes from a place of not loving yourself. You have denied yourself God's love, even though it is always there. You have separated yourself from it, pretending it is not there. You seek human love to replace Divine love, but that can never work. When you don't believe that God loves you unconditionally, you create the world from that mindset. You are unlovable. It is not possible for anyone to fill that void, least of all your children. How can they love you when they are dependent on you? It is hard to truly love your boss or the policeman who just pulled you over?

Another thing that happens in the relationship between children and parents is brought about by your desire to create heaven on earth. The dream is that you will create this heavenly family where you can finally find love and feel needed. In addition you will release these wonderful, perfect children into the world who will make such a difference, or at least have the level of success that you never reached. You are a wonderful parent and they are wonderful children. If you now have adult children or – god forbid – teenagers (just kidding), you know what has happened to that dream. How much fear do you have for your child or your adult child? What concerns do you have about their choices? Where do you see them as helpless victims of other people or the world? When you worry about your children, you aren't seeing their Divinity. You are not seeing the perfection of the lessons they are drawing into their classroom as they attempt to awaken from the dream. This has nothing to do with your children. They are simply your projection of your inner fears and separation from God. Own all of that. It does not matter what you or your children accomplish on the earth plane. Heal yourself. Set your children free to find their own Divinity. Again, the best support you can provide them with is your own self-healing.

Your role as parent ends when your children leave home. It was probably over long before that, but now it is impossible to ignore. You succeeded. They survived childhood. If you ignored your own needs in order to be a parent, you can stop that now. Take care of yourself. This is much easier to do if you have also given up the role of being a child to your parents. If you haven't, if they still run your life through the power you give them in your mind, it is never too late to reverse that. Free yourself from your parents as you set your children free. Your primary relationship is now with Spirit. Your children and your parents are all peers, siblings, as you heal the rift with your true parent, with God. Your job is to see all your family members through the eyes of Jesus, to see them as perfect, innocent, unconditionally loved Children of God. This is the true relationship between parent and child.

When the relationship with your parents is not healed and there is frustration with your children, you will probably experience your marriage as less than ideal, also. All these relationships are being created by the same unhealed mind. You might make the decision to stay together for the children, fearing that they would be badly damaged by a divorce. It is not my job to tell you whether you should stay or leave; you must trust your own guidance to make that call. However, if you blame your partner for the problems in the marriage and leave, you will likely go out and create the same problems in another relationship. Don't confuse cause and effect. Your mind is the creator of all your experiences, so that is what needs changing. However, if you put on a front for the children and stay together for their sake, it will be another example of telling them one thing and then doing another. They will know, at least on an unconscious level. This will not give them support in navigating relationships on their own as adults. Yes, this will be their creation, but don't fool yourself into believing that you help your children by living a lie. Be honest with your children that you are having difficulties in the marriage and that they have nothing to do with them. Tell them that you are doing your best to sort things out. In that awareness, you still may realize that you and your partner's goals are so different that a change to a relationship with greater alignment is desired. If you are unable to solve the marital problems, let your children know, without putting them in the center of the situation, and separate. If you find that you are not able to create an amicable split with your partner, you are not a victim. Whatever you do, try not to ever put the children in the center of your marriage/divorce. Don't try to get them on your side or set them against your partner. This is not appropriate. It can never serve the child. A child is not ready to be your adult friend. Your relationship with your spouse is about you, don't project it anywhere else. Take responsibility.

As you can see, this subject of parents and children is enormous. Humans learn through relationships more than anywhere else because of the nature of projection and the fear and difficulty connected with looking at the self honestly. No relationship is more fraught with confusing entanglements than that of parent and child. Therefore, no relationship provides more fertile soil for spiritual growth. Fortunately, as with all relationships, you don't need their presence or their cooperation to heal. What is your creation can be totally balanced by you alone, of course with the support of Spirit. Don't be shy about asking for that help. You are a Divine child and a Divine parent.

Good Now

Sanhia

Why is it so difficult to let go of the illusion of the world?

Most people have this experience – we could call it schizophrenia – where on the one hand they understand the spiritual truth of pure non-dualism on a mental level; they read these messages and have read and studied *A Course in Miracles*, perhaps multiple times. That side of them believes in the truth of Oneness with Spirit and with God and correspondingly disbelieves in the ego and the reality of the physical world. Yet when it comes to the push and shove of daily life, they seem to live in another world. There appears to be such a split. They ask, "Why, Sanhia, is it so hard for me to live the truth? Why do I know that it is all a dream, and yet take the dream so seriously and get upset and angry, am filled with judgment, pain, hurt, fear, and feelings of victimhood. I know it's not real, but I am still overwhelmed by all of these feelings! Why Sanhia? Why? Can you help me?" I can't help you because there is no problem here. I hope you are laughing with me now. You are just being human and cannot be expected to be behaving any differently.

There is a term that psychologists use that goes back to Freud called dissociation. Freud also talked about projection, where people assign their own self judgments to others so that they can live with themselves (though probably not so happily). Jesus also told us all about this phenomenon. Dissociation can be described or explained in the following way: you want to change your life, to change your experience of things, to give up all of the pain and suffering and to implement a new plan; but a part of you disconnects from that new plan and does the same old thing. You sabotage your own strongly desired program. The old story simply continues to run your life with all of the old pain and suffering included. Even though you consciously say that you don't want this, you keep doing it. That is dissociation; that is schizophrenia. In therapy, you have decided on a course of treatment, but you don't seem to be able to carry it out. In spiritual healing, you decide to listen to Spirit instead of the ego, but the ego keeps running things.

Why would anybody do that? Why would they act against their own self interest? The short answer is, "because the ego made me do it". A slightly longer version is that it is more comfortable to keep choosing the ego. It could be said that the known devil is preferable to the unknown devil. So far you have all survived while listening to the ego. It may have been painful, but it is familiar. It is comfortable like your old clothes. A big part of you doesn't want to let go of that. And…what is this unknown? What would you be letting go of the ego for?

Before answering that question, let's take a giant step backwards. As a child you often felt pretty helpless in a hostile world. Your protection was to build a wall and hide behind it. You didn't let anybody penetrate that wall. In your private world you were an innocent victim of your parents, teachers, siblings, neighborhood bullies, and whoever else seemed to be more powerful than you. You blamed them for your troubles, and forgiveness was out of the question. The truth behind your wall and behind everybody's walls was that you were terrified of God. This fear felt too dangerous to face, so you hid it, even from yourself. In this way you could pretend that God would take pity on you and punish those who were so harsh to you. The only problem was that none of that was true. You now have the spiritual awareness of why it wasn't true and why it ultimately wouldn't work for you then, or now. But, you also have this habit, and it seems to have kept you alive.

So, you are not just letting go of the ego; you have to tear down this entire wall that has seemed to protect you, though at an increasingly high cost. And what are you getting in exchange? You are willing to give up the pain, the fear, the suffering, the anger, the judgment, and the victimhood. You will also be giving up your personal identity, which is absolutely tied up in all of this. For you to fully release the illusion, you will have to fully release your attachment to your separate identity. This is fertile ground for the ego to grab hold of. Are you sure you are ready to do that? To become One with God and Spirit it is necessary to lose your uniqueness, to lose your sense of self, this sense of you. That is what letting go of the ego entails. What you do then, unconsciously of course, is to keep a foot in each camp. On the one hand you keep your spiritual disciple going through reading, studying, affirming, and asking Spirit for support. On the other hand you keep the other foot firmly planted in the ego's camp, holding on to your specialness and that of others. So you have your support group of people you judge as *specially* good and the opposition group which is *specially* bad. You have special love and special hate. You hold that for yourself as well. You tell yourself all of the things that make you a special person: you are on a spiritual path, you recycle and care for the environment, you are against war, and you try to help the disadvantaged, and so on. You pat yourself on the back for being good. Then your special hate for yourself surfaces and you judge yourself for failing to be perfect with your spiritual practice, for not eating well enough, for losing your temper, for catching yourself judging, and so on. So you bounce back and forth between being so enlightened and being such an asshole who will never get it.

Boy does ego like all of this back and forth crap. If you choose Spirit you have to let go of it all, the special hate *and* the special love. This is enormous. It is bigger than your separated mind can even hold on to. That's how big it is. The fear is gargantuan. There is no way that you can survive it. *Sanhia! What are you saying?* I mean that you as a separated, individual self cannot survive. If you let go of the ego comfort zone and pull that foot out of the game you will leave your personal identity and fall back into the Oneness of God. Sooner or later you will have to do this, but right now you are driving with a heavy foot on the brakes. The only choice you have is for how long and how slowly you want to rip that bandage off. The fear is usually way too big to rip it all off at once. For one thing you have no idea how long the bandage is, nor how many hairs will have to be ripped out. Beyond that, you have no idea what replaces the bandage and the accompanying pain. You know what a separate self feels like, but Oneness can feel like it might be an endless void. You have no conception of what the experience of "no you" is like.

Spirit demands nothing. You will never be forced to come home. Spirit knows that of course you dissociate. Of course you try to maintain your separate self. That's what humans do. No problem. There is nothing you have to do about it. You are not wrong to continue, nor are you right to stop. But since you do want to listen, Spirit whispers to you to notice that you dissociate. Then Spirit suggests that you have a willingness to look right at the areas where you have a special hate toward yourself or others. If you say to me that you don't have any hate for anybody, I suggest you are dissociating. It is fear provoking to admit your hate and judgment. Everybody in a body carries hate. It goes with the territory. You hate yourself for separating from God or you project that hate onto God for abandoning you. The fear is that if the hate is exposed, God will punish you. That is an insane thought, expecting something God is not capable of. But, if you pretend it is not there, you can't deal with it. It remains hidden behind your wall and you stay in the hell of separation. Part of dissociation is pretending you are healed when you are not, pretending that you don't have a problem. The ego here might suggest to you that since the problem isn't real, there is no reason to look at it. *But*, you believe it is real. So, look right at it.

You look at it, not because you have a work that you have to do to transform this fear, but simply in recognition that you have a judgment. Notice that you have this judgment, this anger, this hate; become aware that you feel you are a victim, that you blame this person, that you blame yourself, and on and on. Just be conscious that you are doing that. Bring that to me. Bring that to Spirit. We'll look at it together. That's all you have to do. When you look at what is not real side-by-side with what is real, only the truth will eventually remain. The fear will disappear, will evaporate, will be burned away. This is like the second step in the *five-step process*. Love and fear cannot long occupy the same space. Do this throughout the day. Whenever you notice yourself experiencing any of the aforementioned manifestations of fear and separation, don't try to hide or ignore what you are feeling or believing. On the other hand, don't accept it in helpless self hatred. Look right at it and invite me, invite Spirit in at that moment. Ask us to look at it with you. Let go of the judgment and just look with us. This can be called "looking down upon the battlefield". We will see you acting from this dispassionate viewpoint. We will remind you of your innocence and that you are unconditionally loved. As we watch together, you will become aware that you are the only one judging, and will realize there is no benefit to you from continuing, but plenty to gain from loving yourself. The fear is too great to face alone. Fortunately, you are never alone. You are always welcome to come join with us. Welcome us in. Invite us to gently shake you and to point out when you are dissociating. Allow us to remind you that it is safe to bring those judgments out into the open with us.

Good Now

Sanhia

How can I become One with God?

A common statement or intention expressed through many spiritual disciplines is that of becoming One with God. People ask me, "What in the hell does that mean, Sanhia? And even if I think I have some idea of what it means, how could I possibly achieve that?" There are so many fun ways we could answer this question, so let's see how many roads we can go down (How many roads can a man go down before they call him One with God?). "How do I become One with God?" is one of those nonsense questions. To be horribly trite, it is like asking a fish how to become one with water. You are now One with God. You have always been One with God. There is no time, no past, no present. You simply *are* One with God. You could not be anything else. That's just how it is. Well, that was a short message! ….. Okay, we'll go on to the next part. Being One with God without being aware of being One with God is not so desirable. When you have a fight with your partner it may not feel like you are One with God. When you are stuck in traffic it may not feel like being One with God. When you listen to or read the news it certainly doesn't feel like you are One with God. So, I'm guessing you want to know a little more about the realizing side of this reality.

We have told this old story before, so I'm not going to go into great detail about it, but let me give you just the outline. The story goes like this: God created you in His own image….. which makes you an angry old man. Wait, that's not the right story…..that is the one about you creating God in your own image. This means you have no physicalness; the truth of you is absolutely One and in unity with God. At the same time you are not God, but are the Son. You did not create yourself. Like God you have no beginning or end, because there is no time. You simply are. In your infinite creativity you had a thought, a crazy, mad thought, "What if I could create something separate from God, something apart from God, something God didn't know about?" That thought took off like a runaway train. Part of you disappeared into that idea. That part decided to create an identity, uniqueness, specialness. That all seemed like a great deal of fun; it seemed absolutely fantastic. The truth, however, was that no, you couldn't do that. You are One with God, You are absolutely connected. There is no part of you that isn't a part of God. God is everything; nothing could be created separate from that. So that mad idea couldn't create anything real. It remained an idea. The universe it spawned was not real, only an idea. As you birthed this idea, you, the One Son, splintered into millions, billions of pieces – each one with an identity separate from the others. This allowed you to create this imaginary universe of specialness. Well, we all know how that worked out. It's so funny; you have to join me in laughing at all of this. You created your specialness, your individuality, your separation from God and you discovered it was a terrifying place to be. Alone! In pain! Having to defend yourself constantly! That's how it feels for the human believing he is separate from God. So the question is not one of how you become One with God, it is one of how to remember who you really are – that you *are* One with God. You cannot create what already is; you can only deny it. You have spent eons in that denial out of the fear of God's anger. You project that He wants to get revenge for your abandonment of Him. Some of you take this denial into a place where you convince yourself there is no God, therefore nobody to punish you. This only frees you to stay here perpetually in the hell of your creation with no way out. This is the planet of free suffering. I hope you are still laughing with me here.

Now we come to the really meaty part of this message. You know about this work. You have an understanding about the importance of forgiveness, stopping the blind adherence to ego, listening to that soft, gentle, humorous, loving voice of Spirit, and letting *that* voice guide you home. To some degree or other, with whatever amount of dissociation (remember the previous message) that is involved in your process, you are slowly waking up to the awareness of this truth of yourself as One with God. I want to tell you about the biggest crevice you have to leap over, the largest challenge you face. Some of you have felt this already. For some it is so scary I almost hate to tell you about it. You might not sleep well tonight. But, then you probably aren't sleeping well anyway. If you look this fear straight in the face, you might begin to sleep better. Well, here it goes. You came into this illusion, into this dream or this nightmare, with your own personal identity. The only way out of this dream or nightmare is to leave your personal identity at the door as you exit. You can't take it with you. Your personal identity is your separation from God, not to speak of the rest of the Son-ship. To realize your Oneness with God you have to abandon this illusion of having a separate identity. Otherwise you keep cycling around in this place that feels so distant from heaven, so far away from home. You remain with the pain, the suffering, and the guilt that we have talked about so many times, that you are so familiar with. But! And here is the crux of the matter. Giving up your personal identity feels like a permanent death, not death as in death and rebirth, or reincarnation. This is the black hole death, the void. This is the nothingness, the terror that the ego feeds in you. Actually it is the ego that will die, because it exists only in separation. This fear tells you that you have no existence outside of your personal identity. The truth is just the opposite; you have no real existence in your personal identity. You want to feel nothing but love, but that is not possible here. You want to feel unconditional acceptance, to experience that you are absolutely guilt free. That cannot be accomplished without releasing the separation of your personal identity. Each one of you will do that eventually.

You have had other lifetimes where you had different names and different bodies, perhaps a different gender, race, or religion. None of those things are you. You are not this name that calls you to dinner. It has nothing to do with you. It is like you have come to a strange planet knowing nothing about it and you pick up a foreign object wondering what it is and you make up a name for it. Let's say you call it *glook*. So, to you it is a *glook*, but it is not. That is simply a name you have given to something that doesn't really exist. You are not your name. You are not your body. You can keep trading these bodies in. There is only one thing you truly carry with you from lifetime to lifetime; that is your guilt. You can be certain that as long as you hold on to your identity, your guilt will be waiting for you in the next infant version of your separation that comes flying down the tube, or more likely is reluctantly pulled from the womb, from not your true mother into not your true home. The guilt and the fear will be right there with you. That's all that you carry with you. This identity that you hold as so valuable is your pain and suffering.

Sooner or later the weight will become so strong that you will be exhausted by it and ready to let it go. If that day is approaching for you, I can give you a few hints to make it easier. Whenever you see another and see them as different from you, remind yourself that they are not. Remind yourself that there are only two things that all humans ever express. They either say "I love you" or "Help me". That's all they do. That's all you do. You are all exactly the same. If you meet somebody today and you do not feel "I love you" coming from them, they are crying out for help. If you have a hard time receiving that plea it is because they are your mirror. You are projecting your cry for help onto them. Thank them for being a fellow traveler in pain. It's not your job to remove their pain; your job is to remove yours. Thank them for the reminder and stop the separation. Give up pointing at them, making them to be the one in pain. Don't blame them. Don't make them the asshole. Don't make them the cause of their problems, or yours. Don't feed the separation. Don't allow yourself to feel superior..."well at least I'm not as bad off as they are". Every time you choose separation, you choose to remain in hell. Every time! Pretty silly isn't it. As we look at it together, isn't that a really funny thing? You think it is somebody else when it is really yourself. You could choose to forgive and love, but you have chosen to project and blame. And then it hurts you! And all the time you pretend not to be doing it. You have to see the humor in that, so laugh with me and let it go. Forgive yourself and the other.

You are all in this together. That's why we suggest that you be as kind as you can with each other. When you are kind to another you are kind to yourself. When you are kind to yourself you may actually reach the point of realizing your innocence, that you don't deserve punishment. If you look out at one other, just one person, and think he is guilty and should be punished – you can be looking at the other six billion and see them all as innocent – that one is you. That is you that you want to send to hell. It just takes one, but let's be honest – there is more than one such person for you. Each one of them you wish to see punished is you. So funny! Laugh again with me. So simple! The ego wants you to stay in separation, in guilt, in pain; Spirit wants to wake you up, bring you home to the love of God. It's not a hard call to make. Come here with us. We will look at everything with you and help you to laugh. And always, as always......remember.....

God Blesses You

Sanhia

What is the meaning of the Coronavirus?

With the Coronavirus everybody is on the same page. You can search through your memory banks and be unable to find another time when the whole world was on the same page. Americans of a certain age remember the time when all of that country was on the same page following the Kennedy assassination or 9-11. Swedes had a similar unity around the assassination of Olof Palme. However, outside of your respective countries the effect was not so big and it became still smaller when extended to other continents. But here, now, everyone in the world is touched by the Coronavirus, no matter what continent, race, religion, or age. This is, indeed, a very interesting time. Look at what has been manifested here. Everyone has, seemingly, no choice but to focus on this phenomenon. It is affecting every aspect of your life.

As always, there are two voices that you can listen to, the voice of love or the voice of fear – the voice of Spirit or the voice of ego. You are surrounded by the voices of fear. There is no need for me to repeat the fear scenarios that are present. You can turn on the television, go online, or pick up a newspaper and be inundated with fearful stories and fingers pointed at those who can be blamed for causing, spreading, or failing to slow or halt the virus. My job today is to speak to you from Spirit, to remind you that there are no accidents and that everything is in perfection. You have a heightened opportunity now to choose love over fear. We have spoken often of the advice, and you have heard it many other places (thank you Ram Dass[1]), to be here now, to be present, and to be in *the now*. When you are absolutely present, you are with Spirit. When you are not present, you are with ego. All that truly exists is this moment. It exists forever. In this moment you are One with God; you are One with Spirit; you are One with me; you are One with each other. All there is *is* love.

---

1) Ram Dass (1971). *Be Here Now.* San Cristobal, New Mexico: Lama Foundation

The Coronavirus has been given to you by Spirit as an enormous gift to help you let go of the ego and be here now. Many of the normal distractions of your earthly experience are denied to you in this moment. You don't feel the freedom to go where you want; you can't watch the game on television or even read about it. You are likely at home most of the time, some of you not able to go to work. Your opportunities to socialize are minimized. What you do have is this enormous gift to help you let go. You can choose to be with ego, to be lamenting and sorrowful about what you are asked to give up, fearful or terrified about what the future might bring – or – you can receive this gift. You can revel in the stillness. You can take this as an opportunity to communicate with Spirit, to give all your fears, all of your judgments, all of your anger, everything that takes away from the peace that is your birthright – and give all of that to Spirit.

Now is the time to let death die. In the eternal now there is no death. Death is of the ego. It is not real. Yes of course, bodies die. You are not your body. You do not die. You cannot die. Jesus demonstrated that for us. This is a time given to you by Spirit to release and let go of all your fear of death. Give your death to Spirit. Know that if Spirit has use for you in your body to help all to awaken, you will stay in your body. If Spirit says that you have done what you came here to do and now it is time to come home into the Oneness, then you will let go of your body in love and joy, not in fear. That is not a death, but a full awakening. Invite Spirit into your heart today. Use your quarantine to be with Spirit. It is just the two of you; your challenge is to make it the One of you by surrendering your fearful, ego-based will. Ask, "What is it that you wish me to do with this space you have provided for me through the gift of the Coronavirus?" You now have this opportunity that you would not normally have. You would be so busy with your daily life and with what the ego says is important to do. Now this intervention precludes business as usual. Not only is there the space to listen to Spirit, but also the motivation to deal with those fears the Coronavirus has triggered in you. Besides the fear of death, you may be experiencing financial worries, loss of opportunities, fears about losing loved ones, uncertainties about the future, anger, or blame. This just might be the perfect storm that gives you the gentle shove that encourages you to let go of your attachment to the drama and finally surrender to Spirit. What an opportunity for healing! Now is the time to give all that fear, judgment, and projection to Spirit and listen to the messages and guidance that are there for you.

While everything that has been said here goes to the core of what this event is truly about, we don't suggest that you ignore the recommendations of health officials. Unless you are personally guided in a different direction, quarantine yourself, use proper cleaning techniques, pay attention to your own health signs, and strengthen your immune system. If you fear you have drawn something your way, be conscious in protecting yourself. On the other hand, whatever happens is perfect and is in Spirit's hand. Trust in God and tether your camel.

I want to encourage you to feel an enormous gratitude for this gift of the Coronavirus and for Spirit bringing this potentiality for awakening into your now. Take this opportunity to hold each of your mirrors, every other human, in a place of loving acceptance and kindness. Part of the magic of this gift is that you are all in it together. When you find yourself talking with another about this situation, ask Spirit why He has brought this person to you. Are you to receive something from them or is there something that you are asked to give. Allow whatever it is to happen. If you meet your neighbor and they are in pain or fear, remember he is your mirror. He is reflecting that part of you which may be hard for you to see. Give silent thanks for that gift and take your pain and fear to Spirit. Perhaps you have a gift to share with your neighbor about the perfection of what is unfolding, about his Divinity, about his safety – but first take your concerns to Spirit and see what you are guided to say to the other. It is not your job to heal them. That is Spirit's work. If you are to be a tool for Spirit, He will let you know. It is your job to bring all the fears that are triggered by the Coronavirus and others' responses to it to Spirit to be lifted to love. Always thank Spirit for this opportunity to awaken.

Good Now

Sanhia

How long will the Coronavirus last?

Interestingly, in the past five years there were two messages that drew the greatest attention. First was the perspective on the election of Donald Trump (Book I: Message 74: *What can I do with the fear I feel over Trump's election?*) and in a close runner up position (and the polls are still open) was the previous message on the Coronavirus. It seems that what draws our attention is the biggest fear, which is not in the least surprising. Fear is mother's milk for the awakening process. I now hear the question voiced as to how long the Coronavirus will continue to be appearing to run the show on the planet. Is it ever going to fully go away? Will it fade away only to return? Is it just the first in a wave of epidemics still to come? Is this to become a permanent part of life on earth now, like airport security and terrorism? I love these questions. First of all, it is not my job to make predictions about the future. I only predict certainties such as that you, the reader, will wake up. When that will happen is a prediction and that is none of my business. My only job is to tell what there is for you to hear in this moment about the truth of yourself and the events going on around you. The choices that you make with that information are your business and not mine. I know that you are coming home, the timing is not important – unless you are experiencing severe pain or fear. Then it may be time to take a bigger step. Thank you, Coronavirus.

We have recently talked about the psychological subjects of projection and dissociation. Projection, again, is where you pretend that what is actually going on with you is being expressed by another. Dissociation is where you have spiritual intention but conveniently live your life as if it weren't there. You have awareness of the truth, but continue to make the old, comfortable choices that fly in the face of what you want to achieve. Everyone does both of these things; it is human nature. Fortunately, you are not human, but Divine, and are thus fully capable of overcoming both of these habits. There is an aphorism which states that there are no atheists in a foxhole. A foxhole is a trench a soldier digs to hide in and shoot out from at the enemy. We don't wish to argue for the veracity of that statement, but rather to notice its suggestion that when the bullets are flying and death feels near, people tend to look at the subject of God and prayer in a different light, often making profound changes in their lives. So let's replace foxhole with pandemic. The greatest gift that is coming now is that this virus is forcing each and every one of you to face your fears. Ultimately behind all fear is the fear of God, but that is not necessarily the one you are directly confronting. More likely you may be facing the fear of death, but it also might be felt as fears about financial support, scarcity of food, bad health, or separation from loved ones and on. The greatest gift that you can ever receive is the one that triggers the most fear. Maybe you don't want to hear that. The part of you that dissociates wants to believe that this world is real and that it can be made livable if not heavenly. You want to believe that what happens here really does matter. The Coronavirus and the election of four years ago are here to remind you that things here don't matter. If they did, it would all be too hopeless. So, maybe if the scariest thing happens and all of your buttons are pushed, you will wake up and realize that none of this matters, except as stimuli for awakening.

If you are asking the question, "How long is this virus going to last?" you are asking the wrong question. What then is the question? Perhaps the question is, "Why do I fear it lasting?" This is the gift. This is why Corona went viral! Come on, laugh with me here. What most scares you? You can choose to dis-associate and listen to the ego. You can try to fight and hide and resist the fear or to pray that God/Spirit will come in and rescue you. Or, you can look at your fear with Spirit, asking for help in staring right at it. Ask Spirit to help you welcome the fear in. Look at all the extra time you are being given to do this. Thank you, thank you Coronavirus for all this time. You just never stop giving gifts. All the things that you thought had to happen every day turn out to not be essential, whether it is your work, entertainment, sports, or whatever else has been disrupted. Yet here you are – alive and still breathing – dealing with your fear. And the illusion of the world goes on. And you go on. Eventually the world will no longer go on, but you will always go on. Even that is a little misleading because going on suggests the passage of time, so it is more accurate to say that you always are. You will always be. Your fear will disappear, but it will persist as long as you resist. It will not leave by pretending it is not there. Face your fear. Go right into the heart of it. Do the *five-step process*. Embrace your fear. It will dissolve. There is nothing there; there is only love. You won't know that until you are courageous, until you stand up to it and look it right in the eye. The Coronavirus is here to encourage you to do just that.

Though you share many of the Corona gifts with others, some are special for just some of you. Perhaps you have been working too hard at your job. You have been too busy, too stressed. You haven't allowed yourself to have the space to be alone, to be silent, and to listen to your heart. There has been no peace and little time to be at home. Now you have this gift. Perhaps this space is terrifying. If so, face it. This is an enormous gift for you. On the other side of the fear are countless treasures. Nobody will go back to business as usual if and when the virus winds down. All has changed. Those of you who have reveled in this free extra time will not relinquish it easily. You may choose to hold on to the more relaxed and free pace, to the peace. Some of you have found value in places where you did not hold it before. All of you have experienced some changes in your values. You may have found that you can live without and even thrive without things you thought were necessary. Spirit is here to remind you that there isn't anything you can't live without. You are dependent on nothing. I encourage you to take some moments today to think about the gifts the Coronavirus has brought to you, and to feel and express gratitude for those things. Take some time also to acknowledge the fears that remain. Give thanks for being made aware of those fears – they have nothing to do with the virus, you have simply projected your own fears there – and face them. What an invaluable gift the Coronavirus will have been if you wake up on the other side fearless; if you wake up trusting Spirit and willing to listen and follow. What a gift if it helps you give up your addiction to the ego.

Countries have had varied responses to the pandemic. You may have found yourself upset with the way that your country has responded. Perhaps you have judgment with the hoarders, whether it is of toilet paper or other products, or with those who are trying to cash in on the virus. I encourage you to let go of that victim thinking. See the perfection of what Spirit is bringing. These actions you judge are expressions of fear. Your judgment makes them real. Have compassion. On one hand trust Spirit to provide you with what you need when you need it. More importantly, remember those whom you judge are your mirrors, your projections. You have taken the last bit for yourself in the past, even if it was just the last piece of pie. You have done something that went against your heart to make money. That is you. Do you want to keep yourself in hell? Ask Spirit to help you forgive yourself, to realize your innocence, and to feel the absolute love in which God holds you. The love is real; the toilet paper is not. Which do you want more? Is it really more important to win a tug of war over toilet paper than to release your guilt, pain, and separation? Wake up. Forgive. Bring everything to Spirit. Give thanks to the virus for encouraging all of this movement.

Some of you are bored with being home, feeling confined and restless like a prisoner. Remember that there are no accidents and there is no such thing as punishment. You can look at this experience from the perspective of Spirit. What does Spirit want to communicate to you? Deep down inside, what do you want to be doing? Now you have the space to find this and to act upon it. What is it that you have denied yourself that wants to emerge? For some this awareness is clouded over by the guilt over not being productive as the ego dictates that you should be. But now you have this gift of time and space. Nothing is expected of you. You are free. You don't have to prove your worth. You don't have to earn your way. Be a child again. Before you can unwrap this gift of time you may first need to face this fear, this guilt over being "inactive". This is also a wonderful place to use the *five-step process*. Let your fear and guilt dissolve so that you can hear Spirit's loving, guiding voice. Imagine the joy in feeling free of the burden of guilt, of feeling your true innocence, of the ecstasy of following your inner voice. That is where you are headed. The Coronavirus is giving you this glorious opportunity to choose Spirit, love, joy, and freedom over the ego, fear, guilt, and imprisonment. The ego is not evil; it is not something to fight. It is simply something to not give energy to because it does not lead you to love, joy, and freedom. There is no better time to fully commit to this choice in each moment of your quarantine. Stay home forever in the heart of God.

Good Now

Sanhia

Is the ego part of me or is it separate?

We talk about the ego a lot. People are sometimes a little confused about what the ego actually is. Is it a real entity? Is it like the Christian devil? Is it something outside of us or inside of us? These are all very good questions. We will start by saying that the ego is neither inside you nor outside you because, in truth, it does not exist. Neither do you, not the part you think of as an individual and separate from others. The ego has existence only in the sense that the world has existence, and your physical body exists. It is part of the dream. We could say that the birth of the ego was that single crazy, mad thought that came into the mind of the Son of God that said "Maybe we could create something separate from God". For an instant that idea flashed through and the mind of the Son of God entertained it. The thought was absolutely insane, impossible. Nothing can exist outside of God. Part of the Son's mind found the idea to be fun and wanted to run with it. A second part of the mind of the Son recognized the insanity and dismissed the thought immediately. Since the idea was not possible, it could only manifest as a dream. What instigated the idea for that dream? We call that insane voice the ego. Still, there was yet a third part of the mind of the Son of God that found itself in the middle. It realized that the idea was crazy and couldn't happen, but felt a need to rescue the first part of the mind. This validated the dream for both of these parts of the Son. Meanwhile, the second part simply held that the dream didn't exist. This part warned the third part not to go after something that wasn't real. You, the reader, are this third part of the mind of the Son. You came in to rescue, when there is nothing that needs rescuing. So it appeared that there was a split in the Son of God, in the Oneness, but nothing really happened.

You came attacking an enemy that doesn't exist. You came to protect God who needs no protection. You came to take God's place. This enemy is what we call the ego. The ego is the voice that tells you there is some meaning to this dream. It is the part of you that believes you can be separate from God. The ego is the voice of insanity. It only has the reality you have given it. If you were to ignore that voice and listen only to those who never entertained the illusion – which we call the voice of Spirit – it would disappear because it is not real. In truth, neither the ego nor Spirit is real. They exist only in the dream. In truth there is only Oneness. It doesn't matter whether you consider the ego or Spirit to be a part of you or outside of you. None of the players here are real. What part of your dream last night was you and what part was separate from you? That seems like a crazy question. It was just a dream. Today it doesn't exist. What difference does it make if that was part of you or not? It wasn't real. Welcome to your life, to your dream. It is no more real. We could say that it is all part of you, because you are creating the dream, but that doesn't make it any more real. No part of what you consider to be your separate self has any true existence.

Meanwhile, as you are experiencing yourself being in this dream, in this world – which I like to call hell, for lack of a better term – there seems to be both an ego and Spirit along for the ride. The important question is not whether an imaginary ego is inside or outside of an imaginary you, but whether you are *listening* to its imaginary voice or the imaginary voice of Spirit. Even though neither exists, ego keeps you in hell and Spirit guides you home, that is, toward the place of peace, love, and joy. This is a choice that I call a no-brainer. You may think that it is not that easy. Yes, that is the voice of the ego. The ego says that you are stuck with the world. It is real. The best you can do is to make it better. Is that voice within you or coming from the outside? If you are crazy, is that craziness from within you or from the outside? If the answer to a question you are asking yourself seems impossible to determine, you may be asking the wrong question. The right question is easy to answer. For example would you choose love or fear? Do you choose peace and joy or pain and suffering? If you tell me that you want love and peace, but choose to listen to a voice that can only lead you to more pain and suffering – isn't that crazy? We call that dissociation. The important question is not this "how many angels can dance on the head of a pin?"[2] query about where the ego is located, but whether the decider part of you, the part that is your mind, is going to listen to that ego – or not. As a human you have this illusion that you are separated from God and from each other, but that is not true. The truth of you is *One*. How can you be two places at once when you are not anywhere at all? There is no inside and outside. This question is an ego question. The truth of you is not even separate from the ego. The ego simply does not exist. The only question is "Are you going to listen to this insane voice?"

You all will wake up. You all will come home. It is a matter of time and time is also not real. It is only the way in which you measure your pain. It is certain that you will go home, because you never left. You are there now, if there was such a designation as "there". This is only a dream from which you will awaken. Spirit and the ego are there with you in your dream. One softly invites you to awaken; the other encourages you to dream better. Where you are, even in the dream, is in *the now*. If your now encompasses listening to the ego, now feels like forever, is painful, and is hell. How painful does it have to be before you choose Spirit? Is it hot enough for you yet? Should we turn the heat up a little more? This is not a question of good or bad – Spirit good, ego bad. Ego is not the enemy. The world is not evil. It is just a question of truth. Spirit speaks truth, knows only truth. Ego lies, know only untruth. Your mind

---

2) "**How many angels can dance on the head of a pin?**" (alternatively "How many angels can stand on the point of a pin?") is a *reductio ad absurdum* challenge to medieval scholasticism in general, and its *angelology* in particular, as represented by figures such as Duns Scotus and Thomas Aquinas. It is first recorded in the 17th century, in the context of Protestant apologetics.

recognizes truth and will eventually choose it, resulting in the disappearance of the lie.

Let's look at the elephant in the room. Your fear of God is so enormous concerning your alleged separation from Him, the ensuing guilt, and your hiding from his imagined retribution. Not only does this feel bigger than you can handle but also as something you can't deal with by yourself. It amounts to a gigantic feeling of stuckness, magnified by the fact that you have a difficult time even facing the fullness of your guilt. Ego, like a good politician, promises all kinds of ways to avoid the wrath of God. Its promises are equally empty, providing at best a temporary reprieve from your guilt, pain, and suffering. Spirit makes no promises. Spirit only asks you to listen and to trust. Spirit holds your hand while you face your fear, rather than distracting you from it. Spirit faces your fear with you, whispering the truth of your innocence in your ear as you stand together. Spirit doesn't ask you to confront more of your fear than you are able to handle. Will it be scary? Yes. Will you get through it? Yes. Eventually, all of it disappears: the ego, Spirit, fear, a separate you, and the world. Only your Divine Self is left. The truth of you remains as it has always been: One with God, One with the Son, in Eternal Love. The trip begins as you commit to listening to Spirit rather than the ego. Bon voyage!

Good Now

Sanhia

What is the nature of power?

One of the greatest concerns or questions of humans is about the nature of power. Most of you, probably all of you, have some issues with power. As you look out at the world it seems that power is being used inappropriately, selfishly, and destructively and that there are victims and victimizers. Such a story! I want to talk about power and about how to be absolutely powerful. You can begin by letting go of every belief you have about what power is in the world. If you define power as the ability to affect your will upon your experience of the world, you may have an above average chance of succeeding at bringing some of your dreams into fruition. At the same time, it is unlikely that these achievements will bring you any lasting sense of peace or joy. If realizing those creations *is* your intention, you may as well stop reading now and find another source that will support you in being successful – there are many of them out there. You may have to go out and prove this for yourself, but I will tell you why succeeding won't bring you peace. Quite simply, reaching your goals will not bring you peace because you haven't a clue what will bring you peace. You are shooting in the dark. If you did know, you would manifest peace right now, because you are that powerful. If you think that finding the right partner, following the right career, reaching financial success, developing your art or talent, making the world a better place, or being in service to others will bring you peace, I encourage you to go for it. If you find you are still not at peace, come back and we'll pick up the conversation right here.

The reason that none of these endeavors will work for you is simply that if you knew how to find absolute and lasting peace, you would have already done it. You wouldn't be here in a body. The truth is that you don't have a clue as to what to do to bring yourself a permanent sense of love, joy, and peace. If you want to act powerfully upon the world in such a way that it will bring you, and perhaps others, permanent love, peace, and joy – you don't know what changes to make. The ones you have tried so far have been less than effective. You cannot change the world because the world is the effect and not the cause. The cause comes from your mind. You cannot change the world except through changing your mind. Your mind is real; the world is not. If you want to be absolutely powerful in the world, the first step is to give up your power, absolutely surrender it. Give it to Spirit. When you are trying to change the world you are also giving away your power, but in that case you are surrendering it to the ego. The ego promises that if you achieve a certain something you will be happy. Ego is a good salesman, but not so good at leaving the customer satisfied. Whatever is delivered is not enough. It cannot be because the ego is not capable of delivering pure love; it is rooted in fear. Now, you may wonder how you can possibly feel powerful if you give up all of your power, especially if you stop trying to make the world a better place. This may just sound like everything is hopeless and you are helpless and have to accept whatever shit comes your way. It sounds like you have to give up your free will. Actually, you don't because you never had free will to begin with. You have nothing, so you have nothing to lose.

Now I am going to reverse myself. You do have free will to choose which voice you are going to listen to. Any attempt to change the world comes from listening to the voice of the ego. You *can* choose to listen to the voice of Spirit. Spirit has a plan. Spirit knows exactly what you should do. Each moment of each day Spirit brings to you absolutely the perfect opportunity for you to realize love, joy, and peace. That is all Spirit does, constantly – 24/7. At the same time ego says that this isn't what you want; that isn't what you had planned; that doesn't seem to be the dream – 24/7. Only waking up from the dream will bring you love, peace, and joy. Ego cannot tell you how to do that. When you stop giving power to the world, the ego begins to die. It is so simple. Your only job is to say yes to whatever Spirit brings you in each moment. Yes, thank you! If you have any other reaction, bring that to Spirit for support. If nothing looks like what you thought it would, ask to have your doubt released. Request help in healing your judgment and guilt. Spirit is bringing the perfect event to support you in those healings. It is not the world or your body or your emotions that you want to heal, it is your mind – your mind that still wants to choose ego over Spirit, wants to hear the voice of fear instead of the voice of love. The only thing that stands in your way is your free will to choose the ego. The only thing that can help you is your free will to choose to give it all to Spirit. This is what free will truly is, your ability to accept or reject what comes to you.

You are not here to accomplish things in the physical world. Your only reason for being here is to wake up. Everything that happens in the world occurs to support you in that quest. Nothing has any other meaning. What happens has no other importance in the context of the world to you or to anybody else. It is all a dream. Again, the only thing is waking up. When you say yes to Spirit in response to everything, even if you don't understand how it serves you, when you ask for acceptance, ego slowly loses its grip over you. Allow yourself to be reminded of your innocence and of how you are loved unconditionally. Forgive yourself and everyone else for these things that have never really happened. This is the true nature of power. It is unconditional love; it is forgiveness. Power is Oneness with Spirit, with God. When you say yes to Spirit, when you accept whatever is happening, you align yourself with Power. When you resist what is happening and want things to change, not only do you feel the pain of fear and resistance, but you choose to go to battle with the Power of the universe. If there were such a possibility as victory in this imaginary battle, on which side would you place your bet? How can you possibly believe that you can confront the Oneness, the Power of God and come out on the other side with love, peace, and joy? How can you find love by flying in the face of the Isness that accepts you unconditionally? How can you feel joy by choosing the voice that says that you and the world are not enough, that demands that you prove your worth? Choosing the ego is insanity, but it was listening to a single mad idea from the ego that brought about this dream.

True power is acceptance without exception. As you move through your resistance, your projection, and your disassociation and bring true acceptance to everything or, at least, bring it to Spirit for support, peace begins. Out the window go the prayers to change what is happening or might happen in the future. This is the end of "I don't like this, fix this, make me healthy, settle my financial problems, or bring me my soul mate". Instead you have but one response to life: "Everything is perfect. This is exactly what will support me in waking up. Thank you. Help me to accept." This is absolute power. This is absolute simplicity. This is a no-brainer. You don't have to figure anything out. You don't have to be smart. You don't have to be talented. You don't have to be beautiful or handsome. All you have to do is to accept. Just say yes. This is an absolute leveling of the playing field. Everyone has the ability to choose Spirit over ego, to accept rather than resist, to trust in Divine guidance rather than thinking you know better than God.

You may be thinking that this seems like an enormous mountain to climb. How can you develop this trust? How can you be certain that this is true? And even if it is true, it seems so hard to be able to actually accept everything. How can you possibly succeed at that? I don't expect you to trust that whatever I say is true. On the level of words and thoughts, nothing is true. They cannot express eternal truth. You can only trust your inner guidance. If it wants you to go out in the world and make this better, for yourself and/or for others, to help those in pain, to save the environment, to find your own peace and purpose on the planet, then by all means do that. You cannot serve two masters. Follow the voice you most trust. If you have tried to create heaven on earth, have failed over and over, and feel a bit like Sisyphus[3], then push until the weariness and the hopelessness and the helplessness overwhelm you. Maybe then you will realize that you have no choice but to give it to Spirit, and will find inner strength to do just that. Let Spirit push that rock. Once you have made the decision for Spirit it is merely a question of execution. You pay attention throughout the day and notice where you are having an ego knee-jerk reaction of resistance to something, forgive yourself and give it over to Spirit. The more often you remember to do that, the more automatic it becomes. If you notice that you are still holding resistance, give it over again...and again...and again...as often as necessary. Not only will it get easier but you will feel this gradual sense of love, peace, and joy descending into your experience of the world. There is a tremendous freedom in the realization that the things you thought mattered so much don't matter at all. Peace will replace fear regardless of what is going on about you.

You may still be guided in the moment to react to what is going on around you, to offer support and love. What will be missing is the attachment to the outcome of your actions. Spirit is always leading you down the quickest route home. Follow Spirit's guidance and accept whatever outcome is presented. Always remember that if you are not experiencing peace you are resisting rather than accepting. Give it to Spirit. Claim your birthright, your peace and joy. Spirit holds the keys for you. Listen, trust, surrender. Experience the full Power of God.

Good Now

Sanhia

---

3) In Greek mythology **Sisyphus** was the founder and king of Ephyra (now known as Corinth). Zeus punished him for cheating death twice by being forced to roll an immense boulder up a hill only for it to roll down every time it neared the top, repeating this action for eternity. Through the classical influence on modern culture, tasks that are both laborious and futile are therefore described as **Sisyphean**.

Is compassion an important tool for awakening?

Many people would say that on their list of the qualities of a spiritual person, compassion would be near the top. If I were making the list, there would be no top....or bottom. Actually, there would be no list. To describe a spiritual person would be to describe somebody who does not exist, so the only item on my imaginary list of the qualities of a spiritual person would be non-existence, an awareness that they don't exist as a separate person. But, let us go ahead and look at this term compassion. A common usage of this word is that one feels another's pain, that there is a loving concern for and/or action in support of those who are suffering. This is usually considered to be an admirable thing. I want to remind you that in duality every action engenders its opposite. Compassionate acts are balanced by "inhumane" acts. This is not mentioned to discourage compassion, only as a reminder that the real changes happen on the inside, not in the world.

There is a great confusion around compassion. If you were to say to another that you are sorry for what they have experienced, that it must be painful and difficult for them – the result can be a reinforcing of the "reality" of the pain and suffering for both of you. Instead of focusing on the mind, driven by fear and guilt, as the true creator of the physical illusion, the resulting manifestation in the world is perceived as the cause of the pain. Everything is reversed. The inmates are running the asylum. If compassion is defined as doing the highest thing to support others in being free of pain, we would be helping them to wake up and realize their Divine nature. We would be supporting them in letting go of the illusion, the ego, and the world. The last thing we would want to do would be to agree that they are poor victims and to make the world real for them. The question then becomes one of wondering what the highest action is that you could take in that moment. The first answer to this, if you are human, is you don't have a clue.

You observe only with your senses. You see with eyes that tell you that objects are really there. Your other four senses also reinforce the "reality" of the physical. The only way to come to any knowing is to admit that you don't know anything. You give it to Spirit. Let Spirit guide you.

To begin with, if you are seeing somebody as a victim....stop! That is never compassionate; it is an attack. They are saying they deserve punishment and you are in agreement. The last thing you want is for them to hold on to their victimhood, pain and suffering. That doesn't necessarily mean that you point out how self-destructive they are being. That often won't help them wake up, but may help drive them deeper into helplessness and stimulate them to take a poke at you. No, your first job is to not see them as a victim. If you are perceiving them as such, bring that to Spirit for forgiveness (remember nothing has really happened here, so there is nothing to forgive). Notice that this is the classroom they have been presented with. This is part of their wake up call. Nobody wakes up without facing their fears, without going through painful experiences. If you try to diffuse their painful experience and deny them an opportunity to face their false fear and wake up, how compassionate is that? Not only are you willing for them to stay in hell, but you are offering to accompany them. It is not a choice between reinforcing their suffering or educating them that there is nothing to worry about. The realization for you to have, as a human, is that none of it is your business. It is not for you to figure out how to be compassionate; it is only about how you can wake up. Whose eyes are you looking at all of this through? This is not about their situation; this is all about you. This is your projection. What ego part of you is seeing your projection as real? Are you feeling sorry for the other, and therefore for yourself? Or are you looking through the eyes of Spirit and seeing that none of this is real; it is not really happening. Nothing needs to be changed or fixed or healed. The only job is to stay there with Spirit looking at everything from above the battleground. What you end up doing is of little importance. How you hold what you do is paramount. Let Spirit guide you. Have no attachment to results. Remember, it is none of your business. You are at best an ignorant messenger.

As long as you think it is about them and not about you, you will not hear Spirit. Ego will be your guide. If you think you are doing the compassionate thing, that is just ego telling you how you are special – which keeps you separate from the unconditional love of God which knows no specialness, makes no judgments, sees no differences or separations. An alternative definition of compassion might be to feel Oneness with another. This can only be achieved by eliminating all separation. If you feel that *they* have a problem but you don't, that is separation, not Oneness. Oneness would recognize that what you perceive in another is what is truly in you. If you see another being in pain, it is you who are truly in pain. That is Oneness. If you can take it to the next level and realize that we are all One with God, then none of this pain or separation is real. You can recognize the Oneness you share of being Divine beings who are asleep and believing in the illusion, that you are both in the process of awakening. The true use of compassion would be that realization, the knowing that their pain and your pain are not real, despite the "reality" your physical senses report. So let go of trying to be compassionate and instead try to see the truth. Try to see through Spirit's eyes.

The most important point for you in this discussion is the encouragement to give up the ideal of compassionate behavior, of either being or having a savior. You cannot wake anybody else up. Only Spirit can awaken you. It is hard work letting go of the ego. Nobody can do it for you, nor can you do it for anybody else. Heroics are an ego game. You have but one job and that is to wake up. As an awakened being you fully know that none of this is real, that there is nothing anybody needs to be saved from. Short of that awareness it is a case of the blind leading the blind. Don't be looking for a compassionate savior. You don't need saving. You need to face the truth. If somebody rubs your face in that need, try to be grateful. It was a conscious or, more likely, unconscious act of compassion. It is your classroom.

If you were fully awakened, you would not likely be in a body, nor would you be reading this. Most likely you are looking through ego's eyes. Not to worry. You have noticed what you are doing. Bring it to Spirit to help you forgive and let it go. Let Spirit guide your next step. Maybe Spirit guides you to an act or to words that don't feel compassionate to you. Not feeling compassionate is of the ego. Worrying about how others may perceive and judge you is of the ego. Let it go. The most compassionate action in any moment is the one that most encourages awakening. Remember, you don't have a clue what that action might be. The ego is not to be trusted, but it is the first voice you will likely hear. So, bring it to Spirit. Ask for help in releasing your judgments and in forgiving. Deal within yourself with all of these thoughts of victimhood and victimizers, pain and suffering. That is all yours. It is a heavy load to carry. Spirit will take it off your shoulders. If you succeed in giving it all to Spirit you will look at another and see only a Divine Child of God in the process of awakening. You would see yourself without judgment or guilt. You would surrender to that Oneness and allow yourself to be used without thought of what that should look like. No attachment to the action/ inaction, the reception of the action/inaction, or the end result would register. If that isn't happening just bring everything back to Spirit – over and over. You are already home with God. Your full realization of that is inevitable.

Good Now

Sanhia

What part, if any, should prayer play in my spiritual path?

Prayer is both more and less than what you think it is. That's how it is in duality, folks. There are two sides to every question – and to every answer. The Rolling Stones were quite prophetic when they sang, "You can't always get what you want, but you get what you nee...eed". That is very connected to how prayer works. But, let's start at the beginning. In the beginning you are One with God. At the end you are One with God. You are always One with God. Obviously, we need to find another place to begin. Going a little bit further down the imaginary timeline, we will say that in the beginning of this lifetime you were probably introduced to prayer in some way. Those of you who had any sort of Christian upbringing were likely taught prayers. You were to recite them regularly, especially if you were Catholic. You might say the "Our Father" or the "Hail Mary" or some other prayer you had memorized. Perhaps it was suggested that you pray to God or to Jesus and ask for what you wanted. Maybe you were told that all your prayers would be answered. If you did actually see results, congratulations are in order. If you did feel you had results, it was more likely from a personal request than from a rote prayer; that is, it was from a specific wish from you not from a form letter. These form prayers could not come from the heart; they were more of a duty, a ritual, which if performed correctly might win God's approval, or at least cause him he to throw you a few crumbs. But, prayer does not operate that way.

Let me remind you that God doesn't have a horse in this race. He isn't even watching the race. God is unaware of this fiction you have created. It is not real; it is a dream. When you pray, you are praying to Spirit, who does have a relationship with your separated self and your dream. God doesn't hear your prayers; for Him you are together in heaven and this world is non-existent. Even if you send prayers to God, Spirit receives them. If you sent letters to Santa Claus at the North

Pole, it was Spirit who opened your request. All entreaties go into the same letter box. Spirit hears every prayer and always responds. Always, nothing is ignored. However, as the Stones remind us you will get what you need. If your prayer asks Spirit to do something specific for you which affects the chess pieces on planet earth in order to make things happen the way you would like them to, you might feel that your prayer is not answered. It is not Spirit's job to help you to create heaven on earth. There can be no heaven in duality, and attempts to make heaven happen in the physical help to keep you rooted in the illusion. Spirit's task is to help you wake up from the hell you are in. Therefore, the most powerful and effective prayer is one where you ask Spirit for help in waking up. This might take the form of asking for assistance in transforming fear, releasing judgment, anger, blame, or guilt – asking Spirit to take those things from you. It becomes even more confusing if you ask Spirit to do something for somebody else. Spirit would not likely grant such a specific request for your own problems or dreams, but your friend's "problem" is none of your damn business. One reason that you don't always get what you want is because you don't know what you really want. Most of what you think you want is what your ego desires, but your ego wants to keep you stuck forever in a body in hell. When you are asking to make your world a little more heavenly, you are asking Spirit to make the world real for you so that you can stay asleep. Why would you want Spirit to be an enabler for your ego addiction? Fortunately, Spirit is clear about Its job and will not reinforce your illusions without good cause. Spirit's job may be more to shake you than to placate you. Maybe your problem or perceiving your friend's problem is just what you need to help you to awaken.

When I say that your prayer is always answered, I mean that Spirit gives you exactly what you need, exactly the perfect thing in this moment to help you open your true sight. The clearer you are with your intention to awaken, the more likely Spirit will be in not giving you what you think you want. The truth of what you want is to reclaim your rightful Sonship of unconditional love and innocence. That is your true desire, not the shiny new bicycle (or Mercedes Benz, Janis). If you take this message to heart you will begin to realize that everything that happens in every moment is the answer to your prayers. Whatever is happening is the gift from Spirit that most supports you in this precise moment. This is how it has always been working, but how often have you said no to what comes, expressing your dissatisfaction or even contempt for what is happening? Your mind is constantly asking for more of this and less of that, as if you actually knew what would lead you to infinite bliss. While you are in fear and resistance, Spirit is offering you pure gold. All you have to do is say thank you and roll with it. How easy is that? The most effective prayer, again, is not the one where you direct Spirit in how to change your earthly physical world and experience, but the one where you ask Spirit to please take these blinders away from your eyes and help you to forgive, not take things so seriously, release your attachment to thinking things have to be in a certain way, and let go of fear and guilt. This is what you deeply long for, but don't know how to achieve – so you pray for help from Spirit. If you have no fear, no guilt, no projection, no blame, and no anger – then what is left? Just the real you and your love, that's what you truly desire. Your ego mind may be screaming "bullshit", to not listen to this, that you don't really want to surrender all the nice things in life or not heal your physical ailments. Empty promises, the ego never fully delivers because the illusion and separation can never bring you peace and satisfaction (yes, you can't get no...).

In the duality, in the ego world where you feel like you have to figure out your salvation, this is such an enormous task, and one that you can never succeed at. You never will. There is just frustration. We are back to Sisyphus and the mountain and the huge rock. That's the job. You never get there. You may feel closer one day and then the next you find yourself back at the foot of the mountain. Fortunately, there is no mountain; there is no stone; there is no job for you to do. There is nothing to decide. Receive the gift from Spirit. If there is anything that blocks you from doing that, ask Spirit to lift it away. You don't have to do anything; just ask Spirit to do the heavy lifting. You don't have to earn or deserve anything; you don't have to figure it out. Ask and you shall receive, but ask for what you truly want; don't sell yourself short. But even if you ask for what you don't truly want, you'll find out soon enough because you will likely get something else, or you will actually get just what you asked for and find it brings no lasting satisfaction. What you ask for is not as important as is receiving what you get. If you don't know what to make of what you receive, again ask for support in accepting.

You don't have to figure out what to do with today because you have already prayed for Spirit to bring you what is of value. All you have to do is open your eyes and go with whatever is presented into your moment. You don't have to know why. It doesn't matter. Understanding will come when the time is right. Not understanding makes it no less perfect. You have only one job today and that is to receive what Spirit brings. Your only prayer is that Spirit lifts any resistance from you. You may go through a period of insanity before the resistance lifts. Ego will not let go without a fight. You will only go through that "death" once. The only other choice is to go back to the struggle of living in hell on earth, returning to being Sisyphus in the attempt to reach the unreachable. It has been said many times to "let go and let God". Perhaps it would be more accurate to say "let go and let Spirit". As long as duality exists for you there is truly no space for God, but the linking presence of Spirit is always there. A reason that we talk about the importance of prayer, even though Spirit is always bringing you the perfect thing, is that it can help you overcome your feelings of hopelessness and helplessness to feel that there is someone out there listening and responding to you. Yes, Spirit is supporting you whether you ask or not, but your active involvement nurtures a sense of Oneness and a release from the separation that all humans feel. Beginning to feel that a dialog with Spirit exists is enormously reinforcing. What develops is that you begin to move way beyond ego needs into playfulness with Spirit and the universe. As you welcome what is presented you find what it is that you are going to play with today and it will be fun. Enjoy!

Good Now

Sanhia

How can I deal with my feelings of hopelessness?

Everyone while on their spiritual path experiences moments of hopelessness. It can feel like a terrible thing, something that can never be overcome. It's just too big, too much; it's not possible to ever deal with it. "What do you mean that this world isn't real? It feels so real to me. I don't know how I can ever not take it seriously." We have talked about bringing it to Spirit, and, of course, we always encourage you to do that. But I want to give a little different perspective on hopelessness today. By the time I finish, perhaps you will be viewing hopelessness as a wonderful thing rather than as a curse. Hopelessness is such a gift from Spirit! Thank you Spirit for making me so hopeless!

Let's start by looking at what hope is. Hope is a dream, a wish, an expectation, a desire that somehow the future will be better than the present. We could say that hope is directly connected to the idea of heaven on earth. "Oh! I hope I pass this test. Oh! I hope the weather will be good for our picnic. Oh! I hope I find my perfect partner. Oh! I hope that someday I will wake up." Hope is never about *the now*. It implies separation by its very nature. It is going into the future which is not real. How can you let go of the illusion if you attach yourself to the future? As long as you have hope, you have one foot firmly planted in the future, which is part of the illusion that is not real, that keeps you separated from the experience of your Divinity. As long as you have hope you will find it impossible to let go of the illusion – which ironically leaves you feeling hopeless. As long as you have hope, you want a change in the illusion so that it works better for you. You are taking the world seriously. Even hoping to wake up someday is a separation. The only way to awaken is to be absolutely in *the now*, but the hope to awaken takes you somewhere else. You are not here, now. If you can only awaken in the future and there is no future, how can you ever wake up? That is hope. Hope is an anchor that keeps you rooted in the physical illusion, rooted in duality, rooted in the ups and downs and uncertainties of an ever changing movie that may sometimes feel somewhat heavenly and other times certainly feels hellish. Those are the fruits of hope.

Part of letting go of the ego, part of letting go of the illusion, is to let go of hope. By the way, who do you think is whispering these hopeful thoughts into your ear? Of course! This is the voice of ego which wants to keep you here in the illusion and not in the truth of your mind that knows you are a Divine, innocent Child of God. Ego can even safely have you hope to wake up, because it knows that that hope will keep you asleep. What a wonderful win/win for ego! It gets to pretend it is Spirit while, at the same time, protect its turf. Now you may be starting to see that hopelessness is not something to despair of, but rather something to welcome, to be grateful for. To be hopeless is to let go of any possibility of the illusion ever satisfying you. You can never make the physical be what you want it to be. It's hopeless. "Yeah, can I get an Amen?" whispers Spirit. How wonderful to realize that. So what do you have left when you give up all hope? All that remains is the truth. You are left with just Spirit, with unconditional love, with complete innocence. You are in the eternal now.

If you are walking outside on a beautiful sunny day, the sun's rays shining down on you, feeling warm and comforted and loved – you don't have the thought of hoping the sun will shine today. That would be crazy. The sun is shining. It is equally crazy to say that you hope that God forgives you or you hope that you are innocent. Why would you hope for something that already is? Everything that is true *is*, not because you hope it will be true, but simply because it is true. Hoping can never change the truth. God loves you. You are innocent. You are One with each other. There is nothing to hope for. Everything is already yours that is worth having. This process of waking up is one of giving up hope and accepting what is already here now. Hope is that carrot that is strung out ahead of the donkey. The donkey keeps going for the carrot, but can never reach it. When you give up hope you have nothing left to lose. Instead of hoping for something else, your focus is on fully accepting what Spirit has brought to you in this moment. See the world that Spirit is showing you rather than looking through the eyes of the ego.

As you communicate to Spirit your strong desire to listen to Its voice and to close your ears to the ego's temptations, Spirit will support you in becoming hopeless. The part of you that thinks it still has something to lose, that there is some salvation in the world, will suffer fear, terror, and hopelessness. You must go through this. There is no other way. You only get to determine the speed. Hold on to your hope and the pain will be dragged out and your hands will be bloody. Let go and the suffering is minimized. Be absolutely honest with yourself and look at every aspect of the illusion and ask what you are still afraid to give up or to lose. What is it? Whatever it is, you face that fear and give it to Spirit. The state through which you realize your Divinity is the state where you have nothing to lose. You will try to hold on to any dreams or images, no matter how meager, that you still have any attachment to. It is not unlike staying with an abusive partner – at least things are familiar and maybe someday they will improve. Hope is an abusive partner. The world is an abusive partner. If you are still afraid to lose the little that you have left, you will hold on to it and continue to suffer in the illusion. You will keep yourself separate from true peace, love, and joy.....and God and Spirit. Are you ready to be hopeless? Welcome your hopelessness. Take this as your challenge for this month. Be willing to lose everything in order to realize *Everything*.

Good Now

Sanhia

What is the difference between judgment and discernment?

I have been asked the question of what the difference is between judgment and discernment. What a question! I'm kind of looking forward to hearing the answer to this one. I think you are all pretty clear about judgment, although you may still continue to practice it. Judgment no longer gets many positive reviews in the spiritual press. Jesus said, "Judge not lest ye be judged" and "First take the beam out of your own eye and then you will see clearly to remove the speck out of your brother's eye". Judgment, in truth, is merely projection. You judge in others what you judge in yourself, but don't want to face. Sometimes you do go directly to the source and judge yourself. All judgment comes from guilt and fear. It comes from the insane belief buried deep in your mind – which you don't want to look at or acknowledge – where you believe that you separated from God, deciding that you could do a better job than God. You then created this universe and these bodies to disappear into, to hide from God – to then live with your judgment, self-judgment, and fear of retribution. These are not new subjects; we have talked about this before. It is crucially important to notice where you are holding judgment, whether of another or yourself, and to bring that to Spirit, asking to be able to let it go. It is always helpful to remember that whatever we judge is not real and never happened. This is a dream. You did not separate from God. God loves you unconditionally. You and everyone else are totally innocent. Ask Spirit to remind you of this and to help lift the load off of you.

But we didn't come here today only to talk about judgment. We have another key term here, and that is discernment. Let us see if we can *discern* the difference between the two words. One who was arguing in favor of the importance of discernment might say that it is valuable to be able to look at a situation without judgment, simply noticing what is going on. Perhaps what is noticed is that somebody is doing something that is likely to bring them pain and suffering. Your discerning perception shows that they are choosing this rather than the joy and peace of God. You don't say that the person is bad or wrong for doing as they are doing, for that would be judgment. You simply notice. What might be the value of that? You could support them to make a different choice, helping them to avoid pain and suffering, perhaps, instead finding the forgiveness of God. Well, that sounds pretty good doesn't it? Let's think about this a little bit. If you are discerning that another is not making the best choice in a situation, it would imply that you know what the best choice would be. Hmmm….. That kind of makes you like God, doesn't it? As the man used to say, "If you're so smart, why ain't you rich?" Isn't trying to replace God what got you into this mess to begin with? If you know everything about what's good for everyone else, does that mean you have absolutely no inner suffering or fear of your own, that you are absolutely at peace and at One with God at every moment? Hmmmm….. If you are still in a body, probably not.

It's a slippery slope. It's one of the ego's favorite games. "I'm not judging you; I'm just noticing what you are doing. I'm very sensitive, you know. I just pick things up." One of the first lessons in *A Course in Miracles* says there is no order of difficulty in miracles. Nothing is harder than anything else. There is no order of difference in judgments. No matter how the ego tries to sugarcoat it, each and every discernment is a mild judgment. To think that another is not acting or speaking in the manner that best supports them is a judgment. It's hidden in what feels like love and caring and concern, but it is no less a judgment, still a projection, in truth an act of hate and fear. It is not your job to save anyone else. Your job is to save yourself and even that you cannot do alone. You must humble yourself before Spirit and ask that your guilt be removed and that you see through the all-loving eyes of God. The Will of God may be for you to say something to another person. This comes from your surrender to following your inner guidance, to your commitment to hear and follow the voice of Spirit.

It has nothing to do with your discernment. It is a matter of obedience, not of wisdom. If you feel doubt about whether the voice you hear is Spirit or ego, then hold back. That is called discretion. The first and loudest voice is usually ego. Listen deeply. Breathe. See what is there. Err on the side of discretion. When it becomes clear, when there is no question, when you feel the peace of God – go ahead and act. If you are truly speaking from Spirit you will have no attachment to how your words are received, or to what the listener might think of you. If one of those qualifiers is missing, it is probably still time for discretion. Discernment is the wolf in sheep's clothing.

Let's take this a step further. You all have opinions. You have ideas about how things should be in the world. Perhaps you have political opinions. You think certain types of laws or leaders are better for people and for the world. You have ideas about how people should treat each other. You have thoughts about what is the best food or diet, what music is better, how one should dance. You have thousands of opinions about how things should be, about what is good and beautiful. Those are all judgments, each and every one of them. If you truly want to wake up, you will give away all of your opinions which are expressed in terms of what is good or what is right. In truth those are insane ideas. It is not of value toward your awakening to evaluate what you see (project) in the world. The important question is whether you are viewing what you see through ego's eyes or Spirit's eyes. Any attempt to try to make the world a better place through your opinions and actions serves to demonstrate your belief in the reality of the world and temporarily cements your place here. This, again, is your ego inspired try to replace God through this attempt to create heaven on earth. And, as my favorite question goes, how's that working for you so far? Every opinion you have is a burden. It weighs you down and keeps you from being free. You have no need for opinions, discernments, or judgments. They don't serve you in any way. Let them go.

I am not suggesting that you never make a decision. I am

not saying that you should not have a preference for one food over another when you are hungry. When you are hungry, eat. If you want to hear a certain kind of music, listen to it. This is not a suggestion to not follow your desires while you are in a body. Just don't get hung up in the rightness or wrongness of your desire. And certainly, don't think that because something feels good for you that it should be good for everybody. There is no right diet, right way to breathe, or right sleep cycle. Eating, sleeping, and breathing are neither good nor bad. They are simply necessary while you are in a body, so just do it and get on with what you are here for, which is forgiveness and waking up. I don't want to be accused of beating a dead horse, but right/wrong is duality which is of the ego and the world. The Oneness of God is loving acceptance. The ego's opinions can feel so good in the moment, but beneath that is the need for defense, for separation, for making yourself seem righteous in God's eyes – wanting to throw others to the wolves so that you can be saved. "God take the meat-eaters. Spare me. I don't even eat eggs." Opinions are about separation. They are from the ego. They are what keep you from realizing your Divine innocence, perfection, and Oneness with God. Be a happy idiot. When you think you know something, it is time to give that thought to Spirit. Let go of believing that you know and allow Spirit to show you the way home. You have tried to do this on your own for countless lifetimes. You have had seemingly endless opportunities in this incarnation. It is never too late. Now is the time. Let go and let Spirit guide you.

One last thought, and this may go without saying but I will say it nonetheless. Judgments, discernments, and opinions take you out of *the now*. There can be no judgment without duality. There have to be things to choose between; there have to be past experiences; there needs to be future opportunities. Without duality and time there can be no judgment. There are no two ways about it. When you are in the Divine now, in the holy moment, there can be no discernment, no choice. You look at your brother and see the Son of God. You see your mirror there with absolute love and acceptance. You see only Divinity. If any judgment is there you are not in *the now*, you are off somewhere else, somewhere unreal. Instead you are comparing, analyzing, and thinking. Your Divine mind does not think, it knows. In knowing there are no alternatives; there is simply truth; there is *isness*. If you can think about something, it is an indication that you don't know. Thinking will never bring you to knowingness. You'll never figure it out. In the holy moment at One with Spirit the truth lies. It is revealed: there is no effort on your part. This is a zone without judgment, without guilt. You are simply an innocent, free, and unconditionally loved Child of God with nothing to do and nowhere to go.

Good Now

Sanhia

How do I deal with my fear of death?

There is a popular saying that goes, "There is nothing certain but death and taxes". Within the illusion we would agree that death is certain. Taxes....well....perhaps they are also, unless you can figure out how to avoid them. Just kidding...it is not possible to avoid them all without marooning yourself on a deserted island. We are going to look at death a little differently today. Most of you have a fear of death. I want to question the way that you look upon death and ask you to entertain the possibility that you truly hold more of an attraction toward death than a terror of it. You might be racking your brain right now and come up with the thought that at least those who commit suicide must feel some attraction to death, since they have made that choice. Perhaps you are questioning where the attraction is for those who seem to die from accidents, disease, old age, violence, war, and so on. I want to remind you that all death is suicide. It is all chosen. There are never victims.

So why – let us say you are willing to give me a little rope here to hang myself – would people want to kill themselves? Now we are starting to get somewhere. We will return, as we have done several times over recent messages, to what could be called the "origin story". This is where you had the crazy, mad idea that it would be fun to create an identity, an individuality that was separate from God. This of course was not possible, it was just an idea – it never really happened; it is just a dream you find yourself in the midst of, believing it is real. You have no conscious memory of this creation, but what you thought at the time was that you killed God and took His place. Instead of God being your creator, you held yourself as your own creator of the new individual you, and as the creator of your experience. Now this means that you came into this illusory experience with blood on your hands. You believed that you had killed God. Spirit has a good laugh at this idea; it is a funny concept. However, God is all there is. God is the Creator and Isness of all and could not be destroyed, nor could anything be created outside of Him. But, you convinced yourself that you had actually carried out this violent revolution. You then created these bodies and this physical universe to disappear into. You covered your trail with a figurative branch of leaves to hide your tracks, not just from God, but from yourself. So now you fully believe that you are just these bodies, that you actually are these humans, and that this dream is real. In addition, you covered your tracks so well that you are in denial that you think you killed God. That guilt is just too scary, so you either project it on others (Jesus killers!) or naively go on killing Him (there is no God).

At the same time, deep inside you in your mind that is One with the Mind of God, you know that this murder did not happen. Your true mind knows that you are One with God and that you are Divine; that part of your mind – which we will call Spirit – does guide you and will eventually lead you back home out of the dream. However, the louder part of your mind – which initially came up with this crazy, mad idea and which we call the ego – encourages you to hold guilt over this patricide. "You only exist," says the ego mind, "because you successfully killed God." Your true mind knows that this murder was simply not possible. The ego mind provides the additional fear that you only tried to kill God, but he is still ALIVE! And he is coming after you!! Out of this guilt and fear you have created a body that is not really such a hot item. You may complain about companies that sell products with planned obsolescence, things designed to fail or become out-dated, so that you have to buy a replacement product. That is just the kind of body you came up with. It is designed to break down and die. Bodies are programmed to get sick, broken, old, and finally stop working altogether. Not to speak of the world you set it up to "live" in, which is certainly less than ideal much of the time. The bad news from this ego point of view is that death is certain. But the ego mind has also convinced you that death is necessary in order that you could possibly be forgiven by God. Maybe by losing this "life" you stole from God, He will forgive you. In a more perverse turn, your "death" proves that you are "alive" and have a separate existence. To the ego mind, without death you have no individual life. At any rate the deep fear is that God will get his revenge because He is more powerful than you. And so the insane lead the insane. God has already and has always forgiven you. There was never any judgment to begin with, nothing to forgive. You could not possibly have killed God. He has no part in this nightmare of yours and only sees your Divine presence. The part of you that is in the dream really wants to wake up.

The attraction to death is one part a hope for God's forgiveness and one part a hope for help in waking up. But these are mostly not conscious thoughts. It's also one part desire to get out of the hellhole you have created. Death can appear to be an escape from your pain and suffering. The truth is that the body is not real. There is no such thing as death. Life and death are not opposites. Death does not exist; it is just a part of the illusion. Only life exists. Anything that can die or end or change is not real. It has no life. Again, the body is not real, so it has no life. This event that you call death is something that has never happened and could not ever happen. Only form changes and form is not real. All form is illusory. That's why we call the body and death illusions. You have set up this illusion so that it is necessary to die. In the illusion it may appear that you get another body and play this game again, and again, and again. Meanwhile the truth of you simply is. The human you has two choices. You can listen to Spirit about death or you can listen to ego about death. Ego tells you that death is either something to fear or to welcome, that it is necessary and inevitable. Accompanying the ego picture is the terror of absolute nonexistence, the fear that there is no continuation of you after the body dies. For many humans, that is the belief. That's all folks. Poof! It's over. Finito. End of story. Ego tells you that who you are is your body. From that point of view you begin at birth (or in utero) and then you are busy dying. You are on a trajectory, and the bull's eye is death. This is what happens in the illusion of believing that you have a separate identity. A separate identity means you are separate from God. God is Life, which leaves you with what? Sooner or later the separate identity has to die. The whole idea of having a body is centered on death. Death gives the body meaning. That is why you have an attraction to death. Without death, the body has no meaning. You may have heard people say, or perhaps thought yourself that death is what makes life worth living.

Spirit, on the other hand, reminds you that you are not your body and beyond that, you are not a separate identity. You are One with God. You are One with each other. You are One with Spirit. All that can die is the separate identity, the dream. You cannot die because you are alive. You are created by God in the image of God. You simply are. There is no time; there is no space; there is no physicality. You simply are. Your only job while having the experience of being in a separate body is to wake up to the truth of Who you are. When you fully awaken there is no longer any function in having the illusion of a body. It might look to the world as if you have died, but for your consciousness it is awakening; it is ascension. It is leaving behind the illusion and personal identity, and consciously accepting your true place as the Son – One with God. Each one of you will do this.

Part of the good news is that it makes absolutely no difference if you die, because death is not real, your body is not real. The truth of you always exists. Perhaps part of the illusion seems to be the creation of another body, but that will not be any more real than the one you let go of. The only thing that is certain is that at some point in the illusion your eyes will pop open and you will go, "Holy shit! None of this is real." And you will absolutely know it. You will absolutely know Who you are, that you are innocent and forgiven and unconditionally loved. There is no fear; there is no pain. There is no death. Death is just a part of the classroom that you are in. When you come to an absolute peace with death, neither feeling fear nor attraction, you are free. It doesn't matter anymore. It doesn't matter what happens to you or to anyone else. In the meantime, as you are working with your "death" energy, look around. Notice where you see victimhood connected with death: victims of Corona, victims of pollution, victims of substance abuse, victims of physical violence and war, victims of cancer. Wherever you see this victimhood, recognize it for what it is, that in each case the individual has chosen death – they have an attraction to the death process. If any of this is troubling to you, then you too have a similar attraction. Knowing that, you bring your victimhood and your fear/attraction of/to death to Spirit. You keep bringing it back every time it pops up. You ask to see death and victimhood through Spirit's eyes rather than those of the ego. For those who in the illusion of your life have died...let them go. The truth of them was never who you held them as being, whether it was mother/father, son/daughter, brother/sister, spouse, or friend. That was not who they were; it was a part of the false personal identity of separation. Holding them in that earthly role is holding you in your role as a human, dealing with death, and in pain and suffering with just enough pleasure to keep you hooked into the cycle. On the other hand, as you are able to let go of this fear/attraction relationship with death you will find your time in a body to be increasingly peaceful, loving, and safe. If the meaning of life for humans is eventual death and you have no fear of death, then "life" as you have known it has no meaning. If staying alive no longer matters, how can anything else be of true value? What a step into awakening is provided by the realization that the only reason for anything in your so-called life is to help you wake up.

In conclusion, your job is to heal your issues with death. Deal with the guilt you feel for believing you killed God in order to have life, and come to terms with having hidden that belief. Your job is to remember that life and death are not opposites; they are mutually exclusive. You cannot have them both together. Life is eternal and true. Death is an illusion, having no reality. You do not lose your life when you die because your body is not alive. Your eventual awakening may not mean that you will immediately leave your body to die in the eyes of the world and abandon your separate identity. You may stay in a body for an indefinite period, with the awareness that none of it is real, as Spirit uses you as a pawn in Its plan for waking all of the Sonship. This never means that you ask Spirit for support in guiding another. Such a request can only come from the ego. Healing others is not yours to do. Recognize that your desire to help another is always your call for help and take your cry for help to Spirit. In an awakened state, Spirit will simply use you. This does not come from a place of a separate you knowing what should be said or done. You surrender fully to Spirit and are guided. It's none of your business. Whether you stay in the illusion upon awakening or leave it is also not your call. Your only part as a seemingly separate individual is to wake up. Awake, you can have no thought separate from Spirit. I'll set the alarm for you.

Good Now

Sanhia

Do I have to surrender my personal identity in order to ascend?

In the past few messages we have talked a little about the subject of one's personal identity, the sense of *self*. The questions come flying in, "Sanhia, do you mean that I have to give up my identity, my individuality, my *self* if I want to wake up and to ascend?" First, take a deep breath.....relax..... We will start by taking the "have to" out of the equation. There is no force here, no coercion. You are free to hold on to anything you wish to hold on to. This is not to say that there are not consequences with your choices. Remember that this is an illusion. This world and the identity that you hold are absolutely your creation. Within your dream you are free to create any way that you want. For each and every one of you the day will come when you choose freely to let go of your personal identity, as each of you will wake up to the truth of your innocence and Divinity. Because time is a part of this illusion, how long this will take is just a part of the dream. Time doesn't exist. In awakening, all of this disappears. None of it ever happened. It isn't happening now. This is but a dream and the truth of you is home with God.

Let's return to the beginning, to the crazy, mad idea that you entertained for a moment, but forgot to laugh at. You played with the idea that you could have an identity separate from God, that you could be the creator of yourself. You thought you could choose whatever you wanted, creating your own separate existence. That was the idea, the plan. It was a mad idea, not mad as in angry, but mad as in absolute loony bin crazy. It is simply not possible for you to create yourself. All is created by God in the image of God. There could be nothing existing outside of God. That would be inconceivable, impossible. The only way that you could create this *self*, this individuality – which eventually became a physical universe and bodies – was in your mind, in your dreams. It could exist only as a thought, not as a reality. That is how it stands right now. Your body and this world are just a dream in your mind. You want to project, to pretend that something outside of you has created your *self* and this universe. Then you want to blame God for everything. Why did you create this horrible universe with all of its pain and suffering, and this body which just gets sick and dies? Why, why, why did you do that God? God didn't do that. You did that. Of course, since nothing here is real, you didn't do anything. Perhaps you don't want to face up to blaming God. In that case you merely project all of the problems onto whatever scapegoats you can find: parents, exes, bosses, politicians, the wealthy, the poor, and so on. As long as you live in the world of projection, victimhood, and denial, you will suffer, experiencing pain and discomfort. Finally your physical body dies. You find yourself with another body and another body and....seem to be trapped endlessly in the illusion of time. The only way to wake up from this cycle is to take responsibility, to realize that you are the cause. You are the god of your nightmare. The good news is that it is nothing more than that. It is just a bad dream and you will wake up. And that nightmare will just be gone.

You will each slowly grow tired of the pain and suffering of being human, of having a personal identity. You will grow tired of it. You will ask to be shown something else. You know there must be another way. That opens the door to Spirit to guide you home. Spirit will remind you that you are not a victim to anything, that it is all your creation and you can stop this miscreation anytime you choose to. But, you can't have your cake and eat it too. You can't say that you want to let go of the illusion, but still hold on to being you. You can't let go of the illusion and experience your Oneness with God and at the same time hold on to your personal identity which keeps you feeling separate from God. If you hold on to your individuality you have to keep the whole shooting match along with it. Letting go of the illusion will require relinquishing your individual *self*, because it is part of the illusion. It is not you. It is not the truth of who you are. Part of the good news is that the truth of you is so far above and beyond the limits and poverty inherent in your personal identity, that you would have to be crazy to hold on to your individual *self* when you could be experiencing your Divine nature. That statement is redundant, because holding on to your separated *self* is an act of craziness. It is that mad idea that you could create separately from God that made possible your illusion of an individual *self*.

Let's come back to this idea that you have guilt because you believe that you "killed" God and now He is seeking revenge as we discussed in the previous message. That is the deepest, though usually unconscious, fear that you have, one that perhaps you have done some work with since reading that message. If not, eventually you will face this fear and guilt. Almost as deep and all encompassing, but more conscious for most of you, is the fear that without your personal identity you would not exist. You would simply disappear. You are like the river becoming one with the ocean or the drop of water becoming one with the stream. Does that drop of water cease to exist? It has become part of the oneness of the ocean, no longer having a separate existence. The fear that you hold as an individual is that you don't exist separate from your identity. It is connected to the belief that you are your body, so that when your body dies, that's it. You are gone. But, it is even bigger than that. You might have a trust and faith that when this body dies, you will come back in another body. Perhaps you are able to move into altered states and remember some of these different dreams in different bodies. Your ego may have pride in some of them and there might be speculations about those still to come. All of these thoughts about reincarnation still hold on to the idea of a continuity of the individual *self*. The idea of absolutely surrendering your separate identity is terrifying. That's why it is never forced on anyone. It is not Spirit's job to terrify people. You have enough fear on your plate already. We don't need to add to it. It's fine. Hold on to your personal *self* as long you wish to. Squeeze as much joy and pleasure as you can out of it, midst the tears and fears. It will be fully your choice when the price is no longer worth it for the pleasure that can be obtained. Sooner or later you will make that choice, but it will be your choice.

For those of you who are ready to begin moving in that direction – and I say "begin" because you can't make that jump all at once; it is like leaping over the Grand Canyon; it's too big, too enormous – you will do it step by step. Each time you notice yourself with judgment, anger, victimhood, or guilt – bring that to Spirit. Ask for help recognizing that what you are experiencing is an illusion, that there is nothing to fear, that you are not a victim of anything, that you are the innocent Divine Child of God. Ask for help in remembering all of that and each time you do that you chisel off a little piece of your separate identity. The more you chisel off, the less identity remains, the easier it is to let go of still more, the easier it is to recognize the ego's separation choice and the pain it brings. The more you become aware of the pain of separation as you experience it and the unnecessariness of having that pain – that you are not being forced to suffer, that it always comes from your guilt, from your choice – the easier and easier it becomes to bring each of those moments to Spirit and to release them. That's all you have to do. You don't have to figure out how to let go of your identity. All that is needed is for you to bring each illusion to Spirit as you are aware of it. Spirit will take care of the rest.

One thing that helps hold you in your personal identity is having a sense of importance, believing that you have a significant role to play. It may seem that you are here to help to create heaven on earth in some way – to make the world a better place – or that you are here as a savior to help others; perhaps it is that you have a special gift to share. This is a way your ego tricks you into valuing your personal identity. If you, in separation from God, think that you can help others, you are absolutely hearing the voice of your ego. In separation from

God all you can help others to do is to maintain their belief in their own separation from God. You are helping them to hold on to their pain and suffering. If you think you are doing God's work here, the kindest thing I can think to say is that you don't have a clue. God does not need you; you need God. Save yourself. That is all you can do. If you want to help others, then do whatever you can do to extricate yourself from this hellhole of a nightmare. Wake up! If you are staying here to help others, what you are teaching is martyrdom. If there is any part for you to play in the awakening of your fellow dreamers, it will not happen out of you consciously knowing and choosing the right thing to do or to say to another. It will come through your absolute surrender to Spirit. That means that you give up your personal will, recognizing that your will and God's will are One. You allow God's will to work through you, hearing His guidance. That can be tricky. Your ego can easily convince you that *it* is God speaking, that you are God's favorite, the chosen one who is to act for him. If you have a plan, it is yours: it is of the ego. Spirit will speak through you in the moment. Spirit's use of you will feel spontaneous. You won't think about what you are going to say. It will simply come through. If it is truly of Spirit and not from your separate *self*, you will have no attachment to how it will be received or to what the larger plan is. Your job will be simply to deliver the mail, not to decide on the importance of the contents or how the receiver should act upon opening (or not opening) it. You are just the middle man, a delivery vehicle where you set aside your separate *self* and allow the Oneness of God to speak through you. If you are in doubt about the purity of your transmission, then the ego is likely involved, either in the transmission itself or in casting doubt about your ability to surrender and trust. Let it go and bring your doubt and fear to Spirit and receive whatever comes from that.

I will guarantee you one thing. Letting go of your personal identity and taking on your true identity as the innocent, unconditionally loved Son of God is such a trade up in experience that the difference is immeasurable. It is in the scope of the infinite. Those of you who are in the process of letting go of your ego and of victimhood, of letting go of pain and suffering and guilt are beginning to feel what I am talking about. But you are getting just a taste, just enough that you could never choose to reverse course and go back to just listening to your ego. There are always those days when you feel that you have moved absolutely in retrograde, rather than inching slowly forward. That's okay. When you have clutched onto your personal identity for so long and valued it so highly, it will usually only leave accompanied by much screaming and kicking. This transformation will not take just a few days or even, probably, just a few years. That's okay. It is not your job to be perfect. Remember that nothing that happens here will be remembered. It is not that important. Your only job is to take the next little step. Spirit will take care of the rest.

Good Now

Sanhia

Are love and hate opposites?

One common question when looking at this world of duality, this illusion of opposites, is to ask if hate is the opposite of love. That's a very good question. The answer is that love has no opposite, because it is not a part of the illusion. Love is absolute; it is truth; it is Divine. Love is the true nature of God and the true nature of you. So, you may be wondering, what about this love and hate that people are always talking about? They certainly seem like opposites. Yes, you are right about that because when humans talk about love they are usually not talking about Divine love, which we could call "holy love". Holy love is unconditional. It is not something that can be earned, nor can it be lost. There is nothing you could do to change the unconditional love of God. Nor is there anything you could do to earn that love because you already have it. But in human terms love has many conditions. We will identify this conditional love as "special love". It does have an opposite, which we can call "special hate". Hate is absolutely a part of the illusion. There is no concept of hate in Divinity; it doesn't exist. You could say that special love and special hate are opposite sides of the same coin, heads and tails, good guy and bad guy. They are part of the world of judgment and separation.

Let's explain it like this: In this belief you have that you are separate from God and that God has disowned you, has cast you out, is angry with you and wants to punish you – in this absolute untruth which is nothing more than a projection upon God of your own guilt and self-judgment – no one wants to face that guilt and to feel that badly about themselves. Even those of you who are depressed and self-deprecating are not *that* depressed and *that* self-deprecating. There is no pain that could equal that of fully feeling the imagined separation from God. You don't want to go through that and therefore do not want to take responsibility for having caused that separation. What you do then is to project that pain. When you project it upon another, they are now at fault for your pain and discomfort. That is called special hate. It might be an individual who you see as your enemy. Maybe you blame your mother or your father for your pain and troubles. Perhaps it is your ex who ruined your life. What happens is that through projection you make somebody the bad guy. Sometimes this projection is not so personal; it could be a politician, or a race, or a country, or a religion – but you create multiple evil ones. The, perhaps, unspoken direction you are giving is: "God! Get them. It is their fault, not mine. Look how I suffer at their hands. Punish them. Condemn them to hell. Bring me home with you. I am the innocent victim here."

This creation of enemies and special hate is an ego game. It permits you to not take responsibility and look at your own creation of the illusion with all its pain and suffering. It allows you to hide from your guilt that you separated from God – which you never did – and to pretend that the guilt isn't even there. That all may sound confusing, and it is! There is a double bind. You have guilt over something you never did, but you can't get rid of this guilt because you refuse to even look at it or admit that it exists. How can you forgive yourself for something you never did if you refuse to face the fact that you believe you did it? Your ego convinces you that the way out is to find others to blame. This ruse is destined to fail because they are not at fault either. There is nobody to blame because nothing ever really happened. This is why forgiveness is so crucial. You cannot forgive yourself and blame others at the same time. Forgive them and yourself. Nobody is at fault. There never was a separation from God. God loves everyone unconditionally.

On the other hand, because you don't want to go through life just hating everybody, you create special love. You create those who agree with you. They sympathize with your victimhood – "poor you" – and agree with all of your judgments. These friendships are built upon common enemies. But it can go much further. When you don't believe that you are a good person or loveable, you create these people to come in and tell you how wonderful you are. This especially emerges in special romantic love. Here two people agree to hold each other up on a pedestal. In the end special love cannot work because it is created from fear. No matter how much your partner might tell you that you are loveable, deep down inside you are sure that you are not. You cannot fully trust their love because you don't believe that you deserve it. This means that you don't fully trust your partner either. And that is just the beginning. Special love is always conditional. You love the other because of how they make you feel, so you want them to always continue to make you feel this way. Change is a dangerous thing. Strings are always there. "If you loved me you would....." Each person wants something from the other. At first it is so wonderful to feel wanted, then it slowly dawns on you – at least on a subconscious level – that you are codependent. Without them loving you as you wish to be loved you are not happy. That dependency slowly turns into resentment. What you used to love about your partner now drives you crazy. What used to be cute is now irritating. You rebel against the codependency. Having to be a certain way to keep the other's love makes you a prisoner. You cannot be who you are in the moment, in *the now*. That is special love, which can gradually turn into special hate. They are opposite sides of the same coin. It is possible for two people to hold on to the special love through holding common judgments and enemies and friends, but this is at the cost of denying their Divine selves, being unable to look at their own or their partner's guilt.

When one holds guilt, there can only be special relationships. The purpose of relationships is to project the guilt away either through special love or special hate. Ultimately all special relationships keep you stuck in the circle. The exit from this vicious circle always lies in forgiveness. You can begin by forgiving those for whom you feel special hate. You can only do this by accepting that this is all an illusion, that they have done nothing, that there is nothing to forgive. This illusion is all your creation. They are merely acting out your orders. For those whom you feel special love, set them free. Look at your expectations. What do you want from them? What is their part of the agreement that allows you to continue loving them? Notice also the places where they don't seem to be holding up their end, places where you are already beginning to withhold your special love. Again focus on forgiveness. Bring all of this to Spirit. If you want to wake up, if you want to follow Spirit's guidance which leads you to experience the truth of your Divinity and of the holy love that is you, it is absolutely necessary to give up these special relationships, the special hate *and* the special love.

It is a given that as a human you will have both special love and special hate relationships. That is part of your classroom, part of the battleground. If you did not have those relationships you would not be in a body. If you always saw every human through the unconditionally loving eyes of God – asking nothing of them, not judging them, seeing their Divinity – you would also be holding yourself as Divine. If you were holding yourself in that way, you wouldn't be here – at least not for long. Remember not to judge yourself for having special relationships. They are necessary to your awakening. Notice them and bring them to Spirit. Your intention is always to replace the special relationship with the holy relationship. The holy relationship is one where you have fully forgiven the other for what they have done – or more precisely for what they have not done. It is a knowing that everything in the world is illusion and that the truth of them is Divine. The holy relationship demands nothing on the part of the other. It doesn't even matter if they have intended to cause you pain. They might be filled with judgment about you. Your job is to see them as Divine, though perhaps asleep. You take responsibility for any pain, knowing that only you could create any suffering, out of your own guilt. The other has done you the Divine favor of pointing out that you have guilt so that you can bring it Spirit for release. Through Divine eyes each relationship becomes a holy one. Reciprocation is not required. It is absolutely irrelevant whether the other has any commitment to realizing holy love. What is there is your mirror. If they seem to be denying you unconditional love, that is your creation. That is what you are denying to yourself. This is never about them. It is about you. Go to Spirit. Ask for support in releasing your guilt and accepting your innocence and the full love of God. When you only feel love coming to you from all others, you are realizing holy love. Only you can block holy love and only you can ask for it to fill you.

This does not mean that you need to throw yourself to the wolves by surrounding yourself with those who most challenge your ability to feel holy love. Spirit will bring you the lessons you need to learn. You can even learn these lessons alone by allowing your memories to come in to your mind, looking for where special love or special hate remains. It makes no difference if the specialness feels minor; love is either special or holy. That would be like saying to God, "I don't hate you, but you're not my favorite god." There is no in between. There is the absolute unconditional love of God and there is specialness. This may seem to be an enormous gap and you are likely wondering how to cross it. It will probably not be in one big jump. This is just like we have discussed before when we have talked about choosing to stop listening to ego's voice and instead listening to the quiet gentle voice of Spirit. You begin by noticing when a relationship is expressing either special love or special hate. This is the most important step. Your ego has convinced you forever that there are good people and bad people. It is a big deal just to notice that you are playing that game. You are halfway home. Great job! Congratulate yourself for noticing and bring it to Spirit. Remember the forgiveness work is Spirit's and not yours. Your job is to notice your illusion, bring it to Spirit, and listen for any guidance. You do this over and over. There are no special people, neither especially good nor especially bad. There are only Divine children of God, asleep and in the process of waking up. Again, your job is simple. Notice when you think somebody is special, whether you experience it as special love or special hate. Bring it to Spirit and ask for help in converting the specialness to holiness. There can be no greater trade off for you then exchanging special love for holy love and experiencing the full love of God.

Good Now

Sanhia

If the world is an illusion,
why does it feel so real?

The ego is many things, but one thing that it is not is dumb. Your ego is very clever and incredibly fast. It has convinced you that it is something separate from you, as it has convinced you that you are separate from God. It seems as if what the ego shows you and tells you is not coming from within yourself but is simply obvious truth that the outer world is presenting. The ego convinces you of your victimhood, pain, and suffering, while hiding the truth that everything springs from your own mind. We are not going to go back over the creation story now, though if you wish to revisit it go to *Message 34*. The bottom line of this creation story is that somewhere along the line the ego voice wanted to create a place for you to hide. It had to be a place that was so well hidden that you could not only hide from God, but also from the truth of yourself. Your ego needed to create such a compelling, convincing scene that you could totally believe in it. I am saying that the ego created this, but of course the ego is a part of you. The human mind assumes that only God could have created such an enormous and complicated universe, but it was you, the Divine Son of God, created in God's image, who accomplished this. So through your ego you created this world with its laws that appear to have a consistency about them – although physicists for years have realized that this "consistency" does not hold up when they look at macro and, particularly micro structures. Neither time nor matter are what they appear to be. So ego-you created, or miscreated, this physical earth and placed your Divinity into a fragile, limited body, convincing you that this is the real you. Seemingly unable to hear the still, quiet voice of Spirit within, you live as if this is the truth. And when one suggests to you that the world and your body are not real you pound the tabletop and yell, "That sure feels real! The cold air feels real, and so does water and my thirst, and what about the animals and plants? These rocks and erosion, and our history and evolution, and the love/hate I feel for others – all of this feels so real. How can it not be real?" I can remind you that the last dream you had might have seemed very real as you slept. Now that you are awake do you for a moment seriously believe that your dream actually happened? Perhaps some of you do, but most probably do not. You will have a similar experience as you awaken from this dream of your body in the physical universe.

Let's come back to story of everything seeming so real. The ego did a brilliant job. There is enough beauty here that you can say, "Oh, this is God's creation:" It also has enough destructive qualities, pain, and confusion that you might say, "If this is God's creation, He certainly doesn't seem to like us very much does he?" This generates a great discussion. Is there a God or not? If there is a God, why would he create or allow such pain and suffering? Why would he create war or children starving to death? There must not be a God. Or, perhaps God does exist and He created those things because we are bad and have to learn how to be better. Whether you decide on no God or angry God, you are led into a place of helplessness and hopelessness. Either we are guilty and deserve to be punished or there is no God, no meaning to anything. We live, we die – end of story.

The second part to this is that your ego created your physical body, making it seem so real. You can feel the heart beat and panic when you can't breathe. It seems as if this body is who you are. You are surrounded by other physical bodies and they are they and you are you, and you can't be one with them. It can't happen no matter how much you might try to merge with another. You can have communication and relationship, but you remain separate, unable to bridge the physical chasm between you. Fortunately, you have evolved in your civilization to a point where you have the technology to create scenes on video that also seem so real. When you watch these shows you really believe that these things are happening before your eyes. Even your thinking mind knows that nothing is really happening – that it is all a play; it's all staged. Much of what you see was actually put in to the background by technicians after the scene was shot. It's all fantasy. Yet you still react as if it is actually happening. Your bodies and this world were created in the same way, to appear to be very real. What are you to do with that? Having the awareness that the world is not real, you can bring your experiences to Spirit. You can ask for help in seeing the world through Spirit's eyes rather than the ego's eyes. Gradually this will happen.

In the meantime, the larger part of you believes in the illusion, is convinced of the reality of your body and the physical world. This is the classroom you are to learn in. If you pretend that the world is just an illusion, while actually believing it is real, you are going to have some problems. If you cross the street telling yourself that the cars are just illusions so you don't have to look both ways... there may be a BAM moment! You are not there yet. There is no expectation that you should be there yet. So, you can do several things. First, you accept whatever lesson is being presented to you in this so real-feeling illusion. Remind yourself that it was chosen by Spirit to help you wake up. Your classroom, which might feel more like a battlefield, is there to help you move past the *idea* of the illusion to the full realization of it being illusion. We do not encourage you to pretend that you understand, that you do have an experience of the unreality of your body and the physical before that actually occurs. If there is pain in your suffering, you are being asked to look at something that is uncomfortable. Don't pretend it isn't there. Look at it. Ask Spirit to look at it with you. This discomfort is your belief in your separation from God. It is your guilt. Bring this to Spirit and ask to be able to see the situation through Its Divine eyes. Then let it go.

Constantly have the awareness that what you are seeing or experiencing may not be real. Give up your attachment to how things are working in the world; stop pretending you know how things should or shouldn't be. It is the ego voice that thinks you know. Your ego has an investment in keeping you tied into the illusion. So you are both in the world and not in the world at the same time. You face and fully accept the lessons that are presented to you. You then turn and give whatever pain, guilt, and confusion there is to Spirit, asking for help in seeing it for what it really is. You ask to be able to forgive, which is only possible with the acceptance that there is nothing to forgive. Bit by bit you become aware of the illusion. There is no rush. It is not your job to see through the illusion, to have the realization that the world does not truly exist. Spirit will do that work for you. Your only job is to be aware that any pain or discomfort you feel is always sensed through your ego's eyes. With that awareness, you then bring it to Spirit. Looking through Spirit's eyes, nothing in the world could cause you any distress. You would be filled with love and peace.

As you feel love and peace in your day.....wonderful! If other feelings arise, it is not your job to pretend that all is perfect, that you are more advanced in your process than you are. Notice that you are being presented with a challenge in your classroom. Your guilt is manifesting in form, but you have an opportunity to notice and give it to Spirit rather than crumbling into self-flagellation or finger pointing. This challenge is a great gift of Spirit to assist in your eventual awakening. You are taking seriously something that is actually kind of funny....Divinity pretending to be hapless. Your only job is to notice and then to ask Spirit to help you with seeing the truth, with forgiveness. Either Spirit or ego is active. Which one is it? Notice. If there is anything other than love and peace, it is not your responsibility to see it differently, only to ask for help. Spirit in Its own way and in Its own timing will bring the awakening to you. Gradually, you will find the pain, the fear, and the discomfort melting away, no matter what transpires in the world about you. It is never your job to change what is happening in your classroom. This is not about behaving in a different manner. It is only about noticing and being willing to have Spirit work through you. Everything is happening exactly as it should. No change is needed except the changing of your mind. Change your mind.

Good Now

Sanhia

If the world is an illusion, why does it matter what I do?

That is a very good question, though all questions are very good questions. It sounds as if it might be a question from the ego to try to trip me up, but it isn't really. It is a very profound, important, and deep question. We have been talking about this world being an illusion; that nothing here is real; that nothing is really happening. If that is the case then why should it make any difference at all what somebody does? What difference does it make if you help or hurt others, if you love them or kill them? None of it is real, so there is no consequence for any action because nothing happened. Why not just do whatever brings you the most pleasure in each moment, no matter what the illusionary effect upon another?

Since this is the world of duality there are two answers to this question. The first one is that you are absolutely right. It makes no difference at all what you do. It doesn't matter what happens here. It is inconsequential if you appear to make situations better or worse. You're right. It is not real. Nothing is really happening. The part of you that believes that it does make a difference is trying to do one of two things. First, you may be trying to create a heaven on earth. If that is true with you, I will just say "Good luck with that, love", and suggest you reread this previous message (Message 21: *Can we create heaven on earth?*). Secondly, the whole idea of thinking that anything you do here makes a difference is motivated by an attempt to win the approval and forgiveness of God. The thought is that if you can do the right thing, if you can guess what God wants you to do – which is the entire basis for how the Bible is interpreted – you can get back in God's good graces. Of course the Old Testament shows that if you fail to do this all hell will break loose. You will be punished and probably killed, or worse, if you don't do God's will. This is your ego's teaching about why what you do in a body matters. On that level, on the level of God caring, it doesn't matter. God is not going to love you more or less based on what you do or don't do here. God has no idea that you are even here. This is purely your dream. It is your belief that you have separated from God. He does not have a horse in this race. God loves you unconditionally. You are his beloved only Child and there is nothing you could possibly do to make Him love you more or make Him love you less. That is the end of it. Again, on that level it makes absolutely no difference what you do here.

Now for the long awaited and eagerly anticipated dualistic answer, the other side of the coin. Yes there is a difference here. Here's what the difference is. You don't always want to face it and it doesn't always feel this way, but you are in hell. What you do or don't do here makes no difference to the illusion. It does make a difference to your experience of the illusion. If you treat yourself in a loving way, if you notice where you feel guilt or pain or where you are suffering, and you bring all of that to Spirit, what happens is not that you create heaven on earth, but you create a space of experiencing less and less pain. It's only about you. That might sound selfish to you, but it *is* only about you. Everything else is your creation, your reflection, your mirror. You think there is a world out there to fix, but it is your mind that is creating that world. The only fixing that can be done is in your mind. That adapting means aligning with Spirit instead of with ego. Back to the original question that sounded like an ego trap, well, it can be. The ego may be yelling in your ear that since this is all an illusion and nothing really matters that you have permission to do anything to anybody without consequences. You can do anything and get away with it. That's one way the ego can talk to you. This is a ruse; it's a trick; it's a magic show. Whatever you do to someone else you do to yourself. If you hurt them, you hurt yourself. If you steal from them, you steal from yourself. The only reason to take from another comes from the belief that you don't have enough. If that is your belief, no amount of taking from others will change this conviction. Your lack is in your mind and not in the world. Now, in addition to still not having enough, you are building up more guilt. The part of you that believes you are being judged by God fears that your hand is getting worse and worse. When the game is over you will be slaughtered by God. Remember, this is not about God; it is about you and your experience.

The difference it does make is that if you act from the guidance of ego, your experience in a body is going to be painful. If on the other hand you act on the guidance of Spirit, your experience of being in a body, of being in the illusion, is going to become increasingly pleasant and enjoyable. This is not because the world is likely to change around you, but your way of seeing it will change. It matters to you what you do in the world. If you want to experience the peace and the love that are your birthright, then what you do is to listen to Spirit one hundred percent of the time. You listen to ego zero percent of the time. Now you are laughing! Of course you're at times going to listen to your ego, but hold the intention to always listen to Spirit. When you notice yourself acting from ego – stop! Bring it to Spirit. Beyond that, become proactive. Don't wait until the shit hits the fan before you ask Spirit what to do. It's very hard to hear Spirit when you are in chaos....and you've got shit all over your face. It's very difficult to be aware of Spirit at that time. Get in the habit of talking to Spirit before you get into the deep doo doo. When you wake up in the morning, ask Spirit what He would have you do today. Get into the habit of asking Spirit "What would you have me do?" Listen for the response and then do it. If you can remember that one time a day it is enormous. And then it will be twice a day, three times a day; it will become more and more a constant way of being. As you develop this habit of asking Spirit for guidance and following it, Spirit will communicate to you more and more clearly. Your ability to hear will sharpen. You will develop the capacity to anticipate those moments that would have previously been quite troublesome for you, so that you can ask for help before the flame is ignited. Remember that what you are always asking for is to change your way of thinking and your way of seeing. You want to see everything through Spirit's eyes; you are not asking Spirit to intervene and change the world. Spirit sees the whole picture and is bringing you exactly the world experience you can use in order to awaken. Asking Spirit to interfere implies that you know better how things should be. It goes back to believing your actions make a difference.

So, to return to the question, does it make any difference in this world of illusion what you do? To God, no; to you, yes. Allow yourself to be freed by the first answer we gave. Remind yourself whenever you are feeling guilty about anything you have done or not done, "sins" of commission or "sins" of omission, that it doesn't matter. Your job is not to change your behavior but to change your mind. Ask Spirit to remind you that you are innocent, that there is nothing you need to do or anything you could do that would be wrong. You don't even need to ask Spirit for help. God will not judge you, period. What makes a difference is choosing an action that is aligned with Spirit, not because it is the right thing to do but simply because it is aligned with truth and love and helps bring you the experience of peace. Such alignment can take hours, days, weeks, months, and maybe years off this period of being in hell that you have been experiencing. Both the time and intensity can be reduced. You can feel yourself to be moving off of death row. Ultimately time is an illusion, but while you feel yourself to be here it can feel infinite. It feels like it goes on and on and on, like the only end to it is a graceful death. But even death brings no conclusion, because it, too, is not real. You cannot be killed. You go on. Awake or asleep, you go on. In agony or in peace, you go on. All that is certain is that your pain will not go on forever because forever is eternity and in eternity you are One with God. The illusion has a beginning and an ending. Both have already happened; in fact they never happened at all. All that seems to keep your separate life alive is your belief that it is real. By asking for Spirit's guidance in every moment that you remember to do so, you come closer and closer to realizing a freedom from the prison you have created. The ego mind that created this illusory jail cannot end it. That is why you must ask and listen for Spirit's help.

It is very simple. It is easy. You have the choice to listen to and follow the guidance of Spirit. There is no duality in that there is only one thing to do, one choice to make. The more you do it, the better you get at is; the easier it becomes. The better you get at it, the more you will do it. Everything becomes lighter and easier. The truth is always simple – and beautiful. We are always here at every moment, whispering in your ear. "Come this way. Come this way." All you have to do is to allow yourself to become quiet enough to hear. If there is too much ego chatter and noise, give that to Spirit, and ask again to hear with Spirit's ears and to see through Spirit's eyes. Nothing else. Act from that place with trust and love. And peace.

Good Now

Sanhia

Can you explain more about others being my mirror?

We will start at the beginning here, well not all of the way at the beginning, but at the beginning of the story about mirrors. The idea of mirrors is a very simple one which the psychologist Freud discovered over 100 years ago. It is the idea that when people doesn't wish to look at something in themselves because they have so much judgment about their guilt, they will project it upon others in hopes of making the others guilty and deserving of punishment. This is called scapegoating. It is now the other who is the problem rather than the self. You are off the hook.....except for one thing. The self judgment is still there, though buried into the subconscious. It doesn't go away. Therefore, nothing is really resolved or healed. Let's look at this process. The way that you can identify if someone is acting as a mirror for you, that you are projecting on to them what you don't want to see in yourself, is that you will have some judgment about them. "Whoa!" you exclaim. "I can sometimes see that this projection thing is true, but I am certainly not a mass murderer. Are you saying that I am a mass murderer, but am projecting that on to someone else?" And I reply, "Yes". But this idea of mirror sometimes requires looking a little deeper. First of all, this scapegoating is an attack on others, wanting God to kill them instead of you. That sounds at least like mass attempted murder. More importantly, the guilt that all humans carry and the real belief underlying it all is this idea that you have killed God. There is no truth to this; in fact it is totally insane to think that God could be killed. But you think you destroyed God in order to create an individual self so that you could be the creator of your world. This could give you a separate identity. Of course you didn't kill God. You are off the hook there. You didn't do that, couldn't have done that. Nor did you create a separate identity, couldn't do that either.

A part of you, however, believes that you did all of that. You do not want to look at that part of you. Nothing could be more terrifying. So you project that murdering part of you onto others and you feel like you are off the hook. You are not a murderer like they are. You would never kill someone. You hide from yourself the guilt you have for believing that you killed God. What would the consequence be for *Deocide*? That would have to be swift and severe. In addition to that denial there is a part of you that knows that it is crazy and insane to believe that God could be killed. But, if you wanted to do the deed and failed, that means God is still out there. He knows what was in your heart and He is out to get you. This is another insane idea – that God who is only love could want to hurt his only Son, created in His own image. But, nobody ever accused the ego of being sane, except for the insane.

It is so absolutely believable that there are evil people out there, because in this illusion that the world is real, you are its creator. You don't want to look at your fear, so you create a world of diversion with plenty of targets to play the scapegoat. You have written this entire script and hired actors to play these villainous roles so that you can be innocent and maybe even a savior. In truth, nothing is happening. It is exactly like a movie. There are actors, a script, a director, special effects, and it is being filmed. What is actually happening? Nothing, it is not real. That is the truth of the physical universe. It is simply not real. You may think that I am exaggerating or trying to make some kind of metaphorical point with this. Not at all. I am totally serious, and that is not often true with me. As long as you believe that the world is real you will continue to hide out here and to pretend that you are not responsible for any of it. You will go on finding scapegoats and projecting your guilt and fears upon them. You can do that, as you have been doing, and there is no judgment about it, nothing is actually happening. It is all your drama, having nothing to do with anybody else. It's all in your head. You can do that and suffer the consequences of guilt, fear, and feeling separate from God and from all others until you stop playing that game. The pain is self inflicted and ceases as soon as you stop administering it. Sooner or later you will stop the game. It doesn't matter if it is sooner or later, because time is part of the game; it is not real. When you wake up you will find yourself in timelessness with nothing real around you. You won't take anything in the world seriously. It's a fun place to be.

One of the quickest ways to wake up is to stop projecting, to realize that whenever you judge another in any way whatsoever, it is yourself you are judging. If you don't understand how that can be the case, it is your job to go inside and find the truth. Find your own guilt and self condemnation so that you can forgive yourself and release the lie of your guilt. You can't forgive something you believe is real. You cannot forgive another whom you judge because you really have convinced yourself of the reality and wrongness of what you see them doing. You believe in your righteousness in judging them. End of story as long as you are stuck in that cycle. The first step is to accept that it is yourself you believe is wrong, guilty, and cannot be forgiven. Short of that there is no way out. You can have all of these "wrong" people executed and erased from your illusion, but the guilty one will still walk free. So, more perpetrators must be created in order to maintain your disguise. It is like the zombie movies. You can't kill them; they keep coming back. As you are beginning to have the mental awareness that another is your mirror, even though you may have your doubts or not understand why, you can take that inside of yourself. Ask yourself what it is that is triggering you; what are you judging? Whatever you discover is what you are judging yourself for, what you don't want to look at. Ask Spirit to help you look at that. Look right at it, through your fear. There is a terror here, a dread of being punished for doing this horrible thing. In truth you are innocent and you ask Spirit for support in that vision. It is only when you see the purported guilt as being your own that you are able to let it go, to reclaim your innocence. As you practice doing this, what will begin to awaken in you – likely drop by drop, perhaps in one grand explosion of awareness – is the realization that there is no "other" there. There is no other person doing these things you have been projecting. It's all you; it's all your creation. By doing this internal work you truly see that the world does not exist, it is just something emanating from your mind. You are creating something that you don't want out of something that you don't want to look at, and projecting it into the physical world. At the same time the ego convinces you that you are going to create heaven on earth somehow from your fear-based denial. How crazy is that!

When you take responsibility for your projections and forgive yourself for these judgments, you will stop creating places to blame in the illusion. Finally, all you create in the illusion is forgiveness, love, peace, and support for following Spirit's plan, everything to gain and nothing to lose. The only way to experience a sense of heaven on earth is to create it within you. Absolute self love, forgiveness, and inner peace will lead to a projection of the same. No amount of affirmation, meditation, or wishful thinking will change your mirrors in the world. The only real change you can affect is in changing your mind. That is where your world is created. If you don't face your beliefs and your fears, they will continue to manifest in the world. You are never a victim of the world; you are master of it. It is your creation. Look at your world and see what you are creating. See what you don't want to face in yourself. Face it or continue to run up against it. Stop pretending it is someone else's fault. That is good news. How can you possibly control and change them? You have probably tried. It is so much easier to realize that you have all the power. All you need to do is look within and claim it. Otherwise you will have to kill everyone else, and then there will be more at the door. It's like the five-headed hydra; chop one head off and two more appear. It is so much easier, not to speak of effective, to face your inner demons. You can't change the action on the movie screen; you have to go into the projection room. The projection room is your mind. What happens on the screen/in the world is not real.

This transformation from victim to master has to begin with the intention to do just that. However that intention, in and of itself, is not enough. If you decide to wake up by educating everyone around you as to how an enlightened person should act, you will not wake up. It is not others that need to change; it is you. This does not require one single other person to change their mind. No matter what your intention may be, if you do not face your own fears you will either be in fantasy, hiding from the world, or in frustration. As I have said before, eventually you will wake up, regardless of your intention. If you desire to wake up, but don't find things too horribly bad right now, facing your fears may seem like a less than inviting idea. You won't do it now and that is fine. Those who are willing to take full responsibility and go inside to face their fears, admit their projections, work with forgiveness, give everything to Spirit, and trust Spirit to guide them and to bring the perfect lessons are probably willing to do so because they don't feel they have any other choice. They are experiencing too much pain to keep trying to hold up the illusion. Perhaps they have tried to change the world and have given up in utter frustration. It may take a feeling of having nothing left to lose before you are ready to confront your own mind. Why would you attempt this enormous work if you thought there was any alternative? Facing your fears and confronting the unreality of the universe is a frightful task. It can be done and it eventually will be done, but I won't try to kid you into believing it will be easy. It requires you to face the guilt you have for having created this hell of a world. There is the dark night of the soul to be experienced. There are the forty days in the desert. For many that feels like more than they wish to take on right now. For those who have said "Enough!" there is support as you go through your transformation of awakening. Spirit is always there with you. You are never alone, though you may feel that way. Other humans will likely be of little use for you and will probably act out your projection that you must be nuts. There is no wrong decision here, but if your intention is to face and accept your mirrors and you are willing to stay with it, We are willing to be with you every step of the way.

Good Now

Sanhia

How can I let go of grief?

To begin with, you can never let go of anything by pretending that it's not there. You don't get over grief by acting as if you're not feeling it. It is a very human thing to experience grief, whether it is over the death of a loved one or the loss of something that feels important to you in your life. I encourage you to fully face the grief, to go into the heart of it and feel it totally. Doing the *five-step process* could be helpful here. Only by going into the fear behind the grief can you discover that it doesn't have any true reality. There is a great deal of confusion around emotion, and grief is certainly a strong emotion. There are those who would say that your emotions are what are important, not your mind and what you are thinking. Along these lines, the highest value is in expressing these feelings. There is nothing either good or bad about expressing, but emotional release will never lead to awakening. Emotion is not Divine; it is not real; it is ego based. The emotion that you feel is connected to something that happens outside of you in the world – a person or a pet appears to die, you lose your job, you lose your favorite earring. What the grief is saying is that you believe that what was lost was real. Emotion comes out of belief, or more correctly, out of false belief. There is no other kind of belief, but that is an idea for another message. Emotion is not some pure thing that comes from Spirit though the heart, but a self-sabotage coming from the misuse of your mind. You believe that what happens in the world starts in the world, that you are a victim to it, that it reaches out and affects you. This is not the truth; it is a belief. Belief has no effect upon truth. It cannot change it in any way. When you act as if your beliefs are true you experience emotional responses.

If we come back to this question of how to let go of grief, you can never let go of it if you believe it is real. If you believe that person died and therefore you have a hole in your life that can never be filled, that the loss is irreplaceable, then you will have grief. And though it might subside somewhat over time, it will never fully go away. So what do you do with your grief? Let us go off in another direction. The question you want to ask yourself about your grief or about anything else that seems to be out there in the world, impinging upon you is this: "Is this really true?" I am going to start at a basic level with the question: "What can you absolutely know is true or real?" You find yourself to be in this body and in this world. Do you absolutely know that either is real? As you are looking at this question, you can think about watching a movie. You are aware that what is happening on the screen is not actually real, but emotionally it may feel very real. You may react as if it were actually happening. How do you know that what your thoughts or your senses are telling you, what you perceive going on in the world, is actually happening? Beyond that, how can you know that something your mind tells you happened in the past actually occurred? How can you absolutely know that? Can you fully experience something that you perceive outside of yourself? You can know that you are having the perception, but how can you be sure that your perception is real and true?

While you are thinking about this – and if you seriously take on this line of thought, you will be busy for some time – here is another curveball for you. Who is experiencing this so-called reality? You know that you exist. You know that you are. You know this because there is never a time when you aren't conscious. You are always aware. Can you remember not having awareness? There is a consistent flow through the illusion of time, no matter what happens or where you are, that you are aware of your beingness. There is absolutely no doubt that you are conscious. Can you have the same certainty that the person next to you exists? Can you experience their consciousness? If we were to call your state of consciousness *I Am*, can you know they are having an *I Am* experience? Can you even be sure they are actually there? Can you be absolutely certain that anything outside of your mind exists? You may be thinking that I am asking absolutely crazy, off the wall questions. In the insanity of the dualistic world those are the only kinds of questions I can ask. I challenge you to question everything that you think exists. Ask yourself how you know that something in the world is actually there. As you look at what I am suggesting, and you continue to look at it and to look at it, perhaps your certainty in the illusion will begin to crack. This won't come easily. You have a great deal invested in the illusion being real, in the importance of things existing outside of your beingness. It is a painful and scary thing to let go of. I can guarantee you it is equally as scary to hold on to it. The difference is that the fear never leaves you as long as you grasp on to the world as real, while the other side of letting go leads to a fearless state. Let's look at grief. If you believe in the truth of another's body, then you will experience grief when the body dies. If you only know for certain that you are, what difference does it make what is on your screen? No matter what might appear to happen, you *are*.

Ask yourself that question. Look at everything that you think is true and ask if you really know that it is true. The ego mind will put up a great fight here. You may think, "But wait, I can see it, so it exists". What actually happens with vision? Within the illusion there is light. Something comes into the eye. The image is upside down and your brain makes a correction. You now have a picture, a moving picture. Is your picture the same as another's picture? How could you know? How, for example, could you know that your idea of a color is the same as someone else's? Is the green that you perceive the same as what another claims to see? How could you possibly be sure? Yet you think it is real. And what about a blind person, if they cannot see something is it not there? Virtual reality shows you that you can experience things through your senses that don't exist. There is always at least one step which separates you from an actual experience of the physical. Your mind does not touch, smell, taste, hear, or see anything.

Let's look at this from another perspective. One person looks at another and claims that person is the greatest human alive, while another says the individual is evil incarnate. What is the truth? It is all about perception, not about truth. All your grief, all your emotions emanate from this place of believing that what you perceive is actually true. You have no way of knowing that anything you believe is true. Yet you allow these misperceptions to rule your experience of life. A good rule of thumb is that anything you believe is true is false.

This is what waking up is. This is what enlightenment or ascension is all about. It is becoming fully aware that the only thing you can truly know is that you are. Nothing else can be known to be real or true. The ego voice then comes in to ask if all that is true, then why does the illusion appear to be here. That is a really good question. It probably requires another whole message (Message 43: *If the world is an illusion, why does it feel so real?*) to deal with adequately, but briefly the answer is that you don't know and probably never will. But, what does it matter? If you *are*, which means that you always have been and always will be, and nothing can change that, it can make absolutely no difference what you do or what happens within this illusion. You will still be. Instead of trying to figure out the right thing to do, let yourself flow and play with the game that is here. Just enjoy it. We could say that there is a larger intelligence here, a Divine intelligence if you prefer, that is running the show. Your only job is to trust in the perfection of the show and to flow with it. Nothing could be more perfect than what is presented in each moment. Let's say that someone is removed from your physical perception through the illusion of death. That is perfect! Absolutely perfect! Play with it. Let us hypothesize that some, perhaps all, of the other entities that are out there, that you call human, have the same *I Am* consciousness that you have. Then they too always *are*. Their existence has nothing to do with their bodies. If you perceive them going through a bodily death, they haven't disappeared out of existence. They simply *are*, no matter what is happening in the physical illusion, just as you always *are*. The body is not real. Nothing has been lost with this "death". Nothing real or true could ever be lost. So they are fine? How are you doing? Your thought is that you miss them. Is that really true? How can you miss something that was never really there? You can only miss it if you go into the illusion, which seems to have a past and a future.

In this illusion of time there is an imaginary past where you have memories of this person and an imaginary future where this person will play no part. Meanwhile the only thing that your *I Am* consciousness can be aware of is *the now*, which doesn't include this person. The past is only in your thoughts. All you can experience is *the now*. We are beginning to get a picture of what insanity is. You are looking at what is in front of you and making yourself sad over something that isn't in the picture. You could spend all of eternity concerned with all the things that could be present, but don't appear to be and allowing these perceptions to make you sad or worse. Or..... you can see what is here now and accept it as perfect, with no grief for what is missing or hope for what could be there. It is not a question of what seems to be present being any more real than what doesn't seem to be here, but it is simply what is here for you to play with. If the higher intelligence wanted you to be playing with the one who is "dead", they would still be here in a body. But they are not here. There is something better for you. You are always presented with perfection. Part of this process is to give up this idea of thinking that you know better than the Divine intelligence what you should have in your perception or what is good for you. Is it really true that you know best? How is your track record with that? Have you always been successful in making the choice that has brought you peace, happiness and love? Of course you haven't; you don't have a clue. Everything you believe to be true is false.

Your job is to give up trusting in your perceptions and your beliefs and accept your experience as perfection. Then there can be no experience of grief. Nothing is lost or could be lost. There is only the eternal now. As long as you believe that something real could stop existing, you will have grief. That is absolutely an ego choice. You are welcome to let it go. Be free in *the now*. Accept the blessing that is here instead of mourning for what is not here. Give up everything else. That is just a weight to lug around as you experience emotional suffering. Easy to say, but your work is cut out for you. It's the only game in town.

Good Now

Sanhia

How can I get control over my ego?

Wow, what a fun question this is! There are so many different aspects to it that I hardly know where I want to begin. Let's start with this. We want to talk about the truth of you, which I will call your *I Am* consciousness. We mentioned this in the previous message. *You Are* or, as you would say it, *I Am*. That is the end of the story. *I Am*. It is not "I am spirit" or "I am ego". It is *I Am*. But here you find yourself in this story, this movie, this illusion. You appear to have a body. It looks as if there is a physical planet. You seem to be interacting with other people. There appears to be this ego, this craziness, convincing you that the whole package is true, and, as we talked about last time, you are having a lot of emotional responses to the drama being presented. So, you wonder what you can do to reel in this ego. The shortest, most clear, direct, and honest answer that I can give is that you can do nothing. Trying to do something about the ego is on the same level as trying to create heaven on earth, which is on the same level as rearranging the deck furniture on the Titanic. You are on a fool's errand in which you cannot possibly have any success. You will be wasting energy and ending in more confusion than you began.

Having said that, let's come at this from a totally different point of view. Your mind has a habit of holding onto thoughts or beliefs that are not true. You often begin these thoughts or statements with the words "I am". For example, you might say, "I am depressed". That cannot be a true statement. There is a difference between your Divine *I Am* that always *is* and this illusory physical self, that we could call your "*me*", which experiences all of this fear, doubt, and guilt in the world. Your me and the events it encounters are all temporary, while the truth is always true. When you find yourself feeling depressed you can say to yourself, "I am noticing that my *me* is feeling a little depressed right now". This is a far different statement than saying to yourself "I am depressed" which suggests a permanent and unchangeable truth of who you are. Instead, you acknowledge that this little *me* is experiencing depression. Interesting! All you do is notice. The process of waking up involves the realization that your *me* is not real and what it is experiencing is of no lasting importance. Your job is to develop your awareness of what your *me* is doing.

The process can happen something like this. You have, or more correctly You Are, a Divine *I Am*. When we have spoken of taking things to Spirit we could also describe it as taking things to your Divine *I Am*. As a visual, you can picture yourself high above the playing field, the game, the battlefield, the physical plane. You are looking down on your little *me*. Oh poor little *me*, depressed, angry, jealous, horny, happy, sad, head-over-heels in love, heartbroken and so on. All that this awareness amounts to is that you are separating your true self from your *me*. You look down and observe your *me*, not with the idea of changing its thoughts or actions, simply being aware that this is not the truth of you. Your *I Am* is just watching and noticing what your *me* is going through right now. If you try to change your *me*, that is if you try to control your ego, you will fail. You are then making the experience of your *me* real. You are giving it an importance and an existence that it doesn't have. That is a big one to get over, because your *me* thinks that *everything* that happens to it is so important. But the experiences have no meaning beyond being the description of your self-created prison. Your job is not to stop feeling whatever your *me* is going through, but to simply notice what is going on from a detached separate space, from your *I Am*. You might lovingly notice without judgment or guilt, "Oh isn't my little *me* cute". That is called being aware.

As you are able to simply be aware, the behavior will begin to dissipate. You have likely heard before that what you resist persists. Your attempts to bring about change are only empowering and encouraging the craziness of the ego to continue. When the behavior is given no attention, it has no further reason to hang around. So, it is not about controlling the ego; it is about ignoring it and instead focusing on your *I Am*, which doesn't have a horse in the ego game race. Of course, ignoring does not mean sticking your head in the sand, pretending you don't see what your *me* is doing. Notice everything, but don't identify with it. Give it no juice. That little *me* is not You. Of course, you will forget to step back at times. You will find yourself again caught up in the ego games. This is not because you can't control the ego; it is because the ego still has control of you. This is not a fight over who has control. The ego will win every fight. All you need to do, as often as you can remember to, is to become aware of the situation. Separate out and rise above to your *I Am* and watch the spectacle taking place. "There I go again."

One of the most persistent *me* fears is around death. It might look like your fear of losing somebody close to you, or the reaction to just that having happened (as we talked about in the last message), but it is always the fear of your own death. Your awareness job is to notice yourself having that fear. The *I am* does not know death. It is not real. *I am* is only life, consciousness, and awareness. Death is the perfect vehicle for your *me* to ride in and for your *I Am* to look down upon, observing yourself dealing with your fear. When your fear of death dissolves, which it will do if you persist in watching it in awareness without judgment from your *I Am*, you will for the first time realize life. Your ego mind thinks life is all of the things that are not real, all the dramas and emotions.

Your ego mind looks at the possibility of awakening and asks what is left when all it values disappears. If the drama is gone, what remains? There is no good answer to that question. The *I Am* is what is left when all that is not real is gone. The best I can do is to tell you what the "*I Am*" is not. *I Am* not depression. *I Am* not sadness. *I Am* not fear. *I Am* not hate. *I Am* not anger. *I Am* not jealousy. *I Am* not boredom. *I Am* not death. We could say that everything that you do not want, everything that causes pain and suffering is a part of what *I Am* not. *I Am* also not special love, heaven on earth, or any idea you have ever had. The only way for you to realize who You are is to jettison everything that you are not. *I Am* is what is left. What I can tell you is that while you are in this awareness process of separating your *I Am* from your *me*, watching and slowly allowing those behaviors to dissipate – not by trying to change anything but just by noticing – you will begin to have less of your *me* operating. You will experience less depression, fear, jealousy, worry, and so on. You will experience yourself as living more and more in *the now*. In this disappearing act will be the guilt about what you have or have not done and the fear about what might happen. Fewer thoughts will run through your mind about what you should be doing, to be replaced by thoughts of what you could be doing. In *the now* there exist none of the emotions we have been talking about. In *the now* there is guidance available from a Divine intelligence that is directing everything, perfectly.

This is what happens when you move to the *I Am* consciousness and simply observe. Your *I Am* does not pretend to know everything, or perhaps even anything. It simply is. So, gradually, bit by bit, your little *me* begins to exist just in *the now*. The separation between your *I Am* and your *me* slowly dissolves. You realize that whatever is supposed to happen in this illusion is exactly what *is* happening. There will not be a thought that things should be any different than they are. You will simply know how to react to whatever presents itself. You will be guided. That's all there is: no drama, no confusion, no fear, no past, no future. So, returning one last time to the opening question, there is nothing to control. It's about letting go of control and replacing that need with awareness, noticing how your *me* is acting and reacting. There is no battle. You get to sit back and observe the absolute insanity of the ego world. You will grow to appreciate the humor in this absolute insanity. It is permitted to laugh. Sit back and enjoy the show.

Good Now

Sanhia

Sanhia, how can we trust that the things you are telling us are true?

Wow, that is a question that gets right down to the nub! How can you trust that anything you are reading or hearing from me, or from any spiritual teacher or book, or from your own mind is true? Scary! What if you act as if something is true and it turns out to be a false teaching? Now you may have wasted your entire life or at least destroyed major parts of it for no reason, losing along the way the other opportunities that might have presented themselves. Life as you know it is over. As you may have noticed, there is usually a short answer to the question. The short one is that you can't. As Bob Dylan said, "Don't follow leaders; watch your parking meters". You absolutely cannot trust anything or anyone. The second short answer is that whatever you may think the truth is – you are wrong. Is it the truth that whatever you think is wrong? No, wrong again. Boy this is fun. We are, nonetheless, winding our way toward where we want to go. I will continue by jumping in with both feet, which is quite a feat because I have no feet, by saying that there is only one truth. That truth is *I Am*. I could also say *You Are*, but I won't because it is not for me to speak for you. I have no idea if you are. You are free to declare the one truth for yourself, *I Am*. As you think about that you can ask yourself if there is any way it can be refuted. Can you say I am not? Can you say that you have no awareness, no consciousness? You might think that your awareness is only connected to this physical body and its brain. In that case, when the body dies, which by all evidence will be the case, you will not be any more. Maybe that is true. I guess you will have to kill yourself to find out if there is still an *I Am*. Or, you can start with the truth of your *I Am-ness* as a working basis for looking at everything else you think is true or that you think is false.

We call this considering of something as true or untrue – belief. The thing that separates *I Am* from all the other beliefs we are going into is that you do absolutely experience your being-ness. There is no time when you don't experience your being-ness. A hypothesis for you to test out for yourself is that any qualification you might add to *I Am* is not true. Again, I am not telling you that everything else is false; I am asking you to check it out for yourself. The hypothesis is that any qualification you might put on anything in the world around you is false. That is what I suggest you test for yourself. You will likely find yourself in one of three places right now as you read this. One place is that you are holding the thought, "Sanhia, you are so full of shit. I can smell you from here." From this position you believe that there are obviously diseases like Corona, extreme weather, falling rocks, and all other types of things that are dangerous to humans. You can provide endless items to add to this list of things you know are true. A second position you might take is that this is an interesting way to look at existence and you might want to think about it some more and see what you can make of it. In the third position you might think I am correct with my hypothesis, but you still experience your body as very real and have physical and emotional reactions to things going on in the world. It makes absolutely no difference where you place yourself on this spectrum. I could care less. It doesn't matter. All three points come from a place of being asleep and not awake. The question you could ask yourself is, "Am I content with my state of slumber?"

If your answer to the slumber question is that you would like to wake up, the question now becomes one of what you need to do to shake yourself awake. It is likely that if you are still opening these messages you have some level of desire to wake up. On the other hand, maybe you are just fooling yourself. Maybe you like being asleep and it is just a fun game to entertain thoughts about non-duality, but you don't really take them seriously. That's fine. As we said, none of these ideas are true. *I Am* is all that is true. But if you are saying to yourself that you really want to wake up, then my work is done. My only job was to rattle your cage a little, to offer you the possibility to make that decision for yourself, or not. I cannot tell you what to do. It is absolutely your job, your responsibility to follow the road to truth. Nobody can do that for you, nor can you do it for anyone else. But, you ask, can't you even give us a hint? Well, if you twist my arm – which I also don't have, I am unarmed – I will say a few things, but don't write them down in stone. Don't make commandments out of them or a Bible or a religion. These are only general guidelines; your truest direction will come from a voice inside of you that will set your course if you allow it to. It will not come from a voice outside of you – hello, that's me. You can listen to me until the cows come home, as they say, and you will still be fast asleep. You might laugh a bit because I can be amusing, but you'll be laughing in your sleep, which might be less objectionable than snoring. If you want to fully awaken, the ball is in your court. You make that happen.

Okay, here are some of the promised hints. First of all, keep in mind that whatever you think is true, beyond *I Am*, requires deep examination. Look at it and look at it and....okay, you've got it. Question yourself about it. Ask it questions about itself. Do this in writing if you choose, or maybe speaking out loud. Stay with it until you either can prove it to be true or until you realize it was just an illusion; it is not really true. This truth is to be beyond the shadow of a doubt. It is to rely on no outside "experts" for validation. This can be aided by asking yourself how you can be sure that any "expert" is right. Most of what you believe is something that somebody taught you. How likely is it that one would open their eyes one day, look around, and out of the clear blue say that there is a pandemic around and it would be a good idea to take a vaccination? That is probably not an idea that comes to one through an inner guidance. These ideas of pandemics, disease, vaccinations, and death are all ideas you were taught. Perhaps the "authorities" that you give power to in your life said these things: doctors, scientists, media, governments, or friends.

How do you know absolutely that any part of what you "know" is accurate? If you actually look and look and question everything until you have irrefutable proof for yourself that a belief or statement is true, you will end up finding only untruth. If you commit to follow each trail to its bloody end, I guarantee you will go through terror, fear, and pain on every level. All your comfort areas will disappear. You will find yourself alone. Even your friends who feel like spiritual buddies will not be there with or for you. The cozy, warm beliefs you shared will not stand the test of truth and your co-conspirators will not be willing to walk this path of blowing up truths with you. You will find yourself separating from them and nearly all of society. Perhaps, if you are really serious about your pursuit of truth you will eventually find others who are similarly drawn. This will likely only happen when you have already done the heavy lifting and no longer require outside life support. If you are hoping in any way that your salvation will come from some place outside of you – like the second coming of Jesus, aliens from more advanced planets, or a master teacher – you will simply fall back into deep slumber. If you hold the belief in a savior, look deeply into it until you see your way through. You will have to kill the Buddha. As long as your actions are based on beliefs of how the universe is, you will remain asleep to the truth. On the other hand, if you grab that bull of "truth" by the horns and don't let go until you are aware of the untruth, these beliefs will one after another fall away until all that is certain is *I Am*.

When everything but *I Am* is gone there will remain an inner voice which guides you in each moment. You will be aware of a Oneness and a perfection, that there is nothing that needs to change. You will accept your role in the human drama and carry it out without question and without attachment to results. You will simply love the game. Now, perhaps some of you are thinking that these last sentences sound like beliefs. Wonderful! You are on the road to truth realization. I agree with you absolutely, *absopositivily*. There is no way to jump directly into the awakened state to see if this will be your experience. All you can do is to unwind the untruths to see what remains. Holding these thoughts as beliefs while you are still sleeping will leave you still asleep. I am simply suggesting that as you release all the false beliefs you have and go to your inner core, your Is-ness, your *I Am*; your experience may be something like that. But it is practice, not belief that will take you there. Look at everything. Question everything. Doubt everything, including all that I say to you. Believe nothing. Doesn't that sound like fun?

As we let this entertaining discourse draw to an end, I want to again remind you that the words I am speaking to you or that you are reading are never the truth. I can only hint, and talk around the truth, and sometimes speak out of both sides of my mouth, even though I don't actually have a mouth. I have said in the past that you are not really in charge of anything, that Spirit is in charge of everything and that all will happen at the perfect time. I still hold with that as I ask you what choice you are going to make here. Mostly, those who feel like they are making the choice to absolutely and fearlessly face the truth are not doing so because they got out of bed one day and said that it seemed like the time for truth realization. More likely they got out of bed (or couldn't) and realized there was no other choice. "The world is hopeless and useless, and so am I. I have to do something to end this misery." That's a common beginning. There is a saying that when the student is ready the teacher will appear. I'm going to make a slight modification and say that when the student is ready the shit will hit the fan. That is when the student chooses to act. Yes, perhaps a teacher appears at that moment, but it is not the teacher that is important. All depends on the actions of the student. It is all connected. There is a Oneness and a perfection as you let go of what is not true and allow your inner guidance to lead you to the truth of *I Am*. You will find yourself acting in the world in a way that impacts others. You will do this, not because you know the truth, but because there is a perfect plan we are all a part of. When you are truth realized, you would never choose any other course than the one being presented to you. Your part in the perfect plan today might be to continue to play the loyal opposition, holding on to your "truths" and thinking everything else is bullshit. Everything has its purpose. Maybe your perfect place is to suspect there is no truth in your beliefs but you aren't ready to act on it. Perfect – that is Spirit's plan for you today. When it is time for you to wake, it will feel like you have no choice. Spirit will provide a swift kick in the ass and you are off to the races.

What is true is true. No amount of belief can make anything true or untrue. What is true is *I Am*. The rest of it is all illusion, nothing but smoke and mirrors. Within that dream you will awaken. It can be no other way. You will never accept this truth until you follow every untruth to its logical end and destruction. How long it will take for you to choose this makes no difference. Your level of intelligence makes no difference. Your spiritual discipline makes no difference. When the moment comes, it will happen. Is that time now? There is no correct answer to that question. You may make a start and be satisfied with whatever distance you come toward letting go, telling yourself that you are through for now. You may say that you are not ready now and then find things happening in your life that make any other choice impossible. As I said, my only job is to rattle your cage a little, to shake things up. Maybe something falls on your head or your toe stimulating you to take some sort of action. Maybe not. Maybe you are just left with the thought that Sanhia is full of it. I certainly am. *I Am*.

Good Now

Sanhia

Can you give a few more hints on how to go about finding the truth?

In the previous message we talked about what you can trust and about finding the truth. I gave you some hints as to how to go about finding the absolute truth. As I say this, I want to remind you that this is a work you must do yourself. I cannot hold your hand through your internal investigation, nor can anyone else. It is your job to do, or not. But, I have been asked if I can't, please, give just a few more hints to help guide the way. I'm a nice guy, so I say, "Sure, I can do that." I want to begin by suggesting that it is not so much a search for the truth as a dedication to realizing untruth. When you finish the job of untruth realization all that can remain, if you have done a good job, is truth. You find truth through the process of elimination, the releasing of untruths. The hints I will give to you are designed to help you do just that.

Probably the biggest thing that gets in the way of releasing untruths is they seem to be connected with things that you want to be present in your life. You have resistance to seeing the untruth because it might require letting go of something you would rather hold on to, something that provides some comfort in the midst of your pain. Your ego is never going to make it easy to wake up. Because you are giving importance to these things, the illusion becomes more important than the truth. The illusion is built upon untruths. Let's look at what some of these things might be.

We could start by listing three categories of untruth encouragers found in the illusion. The first one we will simply call stuff. Think about how much of your time and energy goes into dealing with your stuff, your material possessions. The time you spend dealing with your stuff is time you are not spending with untruth realization. It's a diversion. You think about stuff you have right now. You think about stuff you want to have. Maybe you think about stuff you used to have. There are numerous ways that you have to deal with your stuff. Stuff breaks down. Your stuff stops working. Spirit has brought in planned obsolescence so stuff breaks down faster and faster. Now you have to deal with fixing it or having somebody else do that for you. Maybe it's time to buy newer stuff. In the meantime you have to figure out how to live your life without that particular stuff. Maybe, you decide one day that you need the latest model of your stuff, because yours is outdated and not good enough anymore. When you get new stuff you have to figure out how to operate it. All your stuff requires attention. It may need cleaning, maintenance, and protection against the elements and from theft. You worry about your stuff. You alter your behavior for your stuff. So much of your energy, your time, and your mind are devoted to handling your stuff. If you want to be dedicated to untruth realization, that will require plenty of space in your life. Having less stuff can free up this time. This can be part of your process. When you realize that a piece of your stuff is demanding a lot of time or is adding to the stress in your life, you can look at the truth of your need for the object. Follow that line of thinking all the way to the end. I am not suggesting you live your life as an ascetic monk with no stuff. I am not telling you not to do that either. If you really wish to wake up, to release the untruths that you believe in, you will not be able to avoid looking at the addictions you have to the stuff in your life. You will also find yourself dealing with the fear that you might lose any or all of your stuff.

The second category is people. Do I want you to let go of all the people in your life? I neither suggest adding or subtracting people from your life, but untruth realization will require you to examine the attachments you have to your relationships. Like your stuff, your relationships require maintenance and time. How do you alter your behavior because of the people around you? This is a profound question to pursue. You will find it nearly impossible to realize untruths while hoping to obtain approval or agreement from friends, family, and other cohorts.. How much of what you choose to do, how much of how you spend your time is determined by what the people around you seem to want from you (realizing that this is often your projection)? The implication may be that if you are really my friend or if you really loved me.....you would do what I ask of you. Do you fill your life with people so you don't have to look at your mind? Is it a way of keeping busy? Is it your fear of being alone? This aloneness is exactly what is required of you to have the space for untruth realization. If you really wish to let go of untruths, it can only be accomplished by going deep within your own mind. Talking to or being with others will not help; that can only stand in your way. Part of your process will be dealing with the fear that you might lose any or all relationships.

If you truly focus on truth/untruth it will come ahead of the people, the friends, the family, the stuff, the money..... everything. This is some serious shit we're talking about. Again, it's fine if you admit to yourself that you are not ready for that kind of commitment. It's okay to just play around with these ideas without jumping off the cliff. But, I am talking to those of you who do want to get that serious. Let's talk about the third category.....goals. What goals do you have for your life? What do you hope to achieve? What do you want to have success with? What do you wish to accomplish? What do you want to be known for? What experiences do you wish to have? What do you hope to realize? All of these goals stand in the way of your untruth realization.....unless your goal is untruth realization. There is a saying attributed to Jesus that I'm almost embarrassed to repeat here because it is often used. However, it is used so often because it resounds of truth. Here we go, "You can only serve one master". You can serve the illusion or you can serve the truth. The illusion is not true. Yes, you seem to be living with it and need to deal with and find your peace with it, but it is not true. If you want to know the truth, the focus cannot be on the illusion. You can only serve one of these. They are mutually exclusive. Pick one or the other. If you choose truth, then stuff, people, and goals go out the window, down the toilet, or wherever you get rid of things. Am I suggesting you have to get rid of absolutely everything? Take one thing at a time and look at it. Find the truth or untruth about it. You cannot be in a body without stuff, people, and goals. The question is one of function. Are they there to serve your awakening, or are they there to try to make the illusion more fun and to shield you from the harsh glow of truth?

What happens as you release the excess stuff, people, and goals from your life is you clear the decks so that you deal with what really matters, untruth realization. The process is very simple. Whatever thought or feeling comes to you, ask yourself if it is really true. Follow your thoughts about this down the rat hole and through the maze until you find its untruth. If you haven't found the untruth, you haven't followed far enough. Perhaps it's time to make a minor revision in the saying, "Find the truth and it will set you free" to "Find the untruth and it will set you free". These thoughts and feelings that arise are likely to be connected to the stuff, people, and goals that you are in the process of relinquishing. Let's say thoughts arise about your car. It is not the car that is the issue; it is the thoughts and feelings you have about the vehicle. What is the purpose of your car? Let's play with this a little. Does your car make you feel better about yourself? Will others think better about you because of the car you have (or worse)? Is that really true? Does it really matter? Does the possession of an object change who you are? If you didn't have that car, would you be someone else? Who are you? Is who you are affected by how others think about you? Do they have the power to affect the truth of you? Who would you be if you didn't (or did) have a car? Would your experience of the illusion change with a change of vehicles? What is necessary in order for you to maintain your existence in the illusion, for example, getting food, doing the work you are here to do, meeting with the people that it is important to get together with? How would this affect all the different things you do while in a body? How important is each of them? What absolutely needs to be done? If a car is found to be necessary to continue your untruth realization, what kind of car will suit you? These answers are not outside; they are within you. Nobody can tell you what kind of car will satisfy your needs; at best they can project what they believe would suit them. We have just scratched the surface of all the possible roads this car question might lead you down. On the one hand you can look at the amount of your energy that is consumed by your mode of transportation while on the other hand ask why any of that matters. As you investigate fully you will come face to face with looking at the actual importance of everything you have held to be of value. If the bottom line is that only untruth realization is important, how will this piece of stuff help you get there? Where is it in the way and where does it support? You will only know these answers through relentless self examination.

This is only one of a multitude of possessions that you might have. This process of untruth realization will take you quite a while. If you seriously look for your answers, you won't have so much time to spend with other people and you probably wouldn't provide the best company. You won't have time to be dealing with all of your stuff. You won't be able to accomplish your goats while trying to figure out if they are worth reaching or even having. This is why Jesus is also quoted as saying that, "It is easier for a camel to go through the eye of a needle than for a rich man to enter the kingdom of heaven". You can only serve one master. If riches are important to you, you will hold to them rather than surrender them for the truth within you. You cannot pay attention to your stuff and to the people who look after your stuff and still have enough time to follow your thoughts all of the way to the end. That will be even less likely if you suspect that untruth realization will lead you to give up all attachments to your stuff. There is nothing evil in stuff; it is only the addiction to it that causes a problem. Does more stuff really give you power? Does it free you? Do your relationships support you in untruth realization or do they enable you to hold on to prejudice and victimhood? When you are afraid of the truth, you attract those equally committed to untruth to join together in protecting your right to ignorance, to spiritual childhood. No matter how many goals you reach, you will never feel you are fully a success. What success brings is an emptiness that can only be filled by striving for another goal. Accumulating money or stuff leaves you still wanting more. There is never enough of anything in the illusion to fully satisfy you. No matter how many friends you might feel you have, you know inside that they don't love the real you. It's all conditional and you have to maintain a façade just to hold onto what you don't even really have. Stuff, people, and goals are drugs. They are addictions. A drug can be used in an appropriate way to support you in untruth realization, but addiction never does that. You can serve untruth realization or your addiction, but not both.

This is where the pedal hits the metal. The more dedication you have to untruth realization/truth realization, the more time and energy you will focus there and the less important the addictions will be in your day to day life. Everyone hopes to be able to have their cake and eat it too, but it doesn't work that way. I'm here to rain on your parade. There isn't room to hold on to the illusion and grasp for the truth simultaneously. There is a moment where you will have to let go of the illusion but will not have yet fully grasped the truth. The bottom falls out from beneath you. There is nothing left to hold on to. This has been called the dark night of the soul. I wish I could tell you differently, that your transition to truth will be a smooth ride. Everyone fears facing this abyss. Addiction feels like a safer, more comfortable place. This is part of the package. In the illusion you believe you need to fulfill the three categories to be happy, but they will never bring you there. They can't because they are not built upon truth. Only untruth realization can bring you what you desire to experience. If you maintain your commitment, you will move through the dark night into real freedom. You will know when it is time for you to make the choice for untruth realization. Maybe it's not meant for this trip. Eventually you will find yourself there. Bon voyage.

Good Now

Sanhia

Should we still be doing the forgiveness process?

I know how some of you react when you hear fingernails being drawn along a blackboard. The sensation is immediate and leaves you shuddering. If I were capable of having such a reaction, which of course I'm not, it would be triggered every time somebody said the word *should*. The answer to any question that begins with *should* is no. There is nothing that anybody should be doing. We would want to rephrase today's question into something that allows me some scope of answers. You could say, "Sanhia, you haven't talked about forgiveness for a while. You've been speaking of *I Am*, that we don't know anything, and searching for untruth. We were just kind of wondering if it is still a valuable thing to be focusing on forgiveness as a healing technique." That is phrased in such a better way, that is, if I believed in better or worse, that would definitely be better. Underneath it all with this question – and I am not singling out the person asking the question, it is simply a human ego thing – is the desire to check to see if you are doing it right. This is looking outside of yourself for validation. I want you to know that if your intention is to awaken, there is no wrong way to go about it. If your intention is not to awaken, it matters not what spiritual path you follow, you will not get there. The road that you will be traveling is already tough enough. Without intention, you will stop somewhere along the way and call it a day (or a life). Now, coming back to the question, the short answer is "of course". Forgiveness is always a good idea. Forgiveness is based on the truth that you are not a victim of anyone, including yourself. Since nothing has happened to you from the outside, who do you have to forgive? The only true forgiveness comes from the realization that there is absolutely nothing to forgive. If you think there *is* something to forgive, it doesn't matter how hard you work at it, you'll never reach forgiveness. The thought deep down inside is that they are guilty, guilty, guilty, and in need of punishment. That is your deepest thought about yourself. You are guilty and need to be punished. Yes, forgiveness is always an excellent choice, and would you like fries with that?

Having said this, forgiveness is a very hard thing to do because most of you, no matter how hard you try to convince yourselves otherwise, don't buy the truth of non-victimhood. A little inner voice whispers "bullshit" every time you claim you are not a victim. There are few satisfactions within the prison of the illusion that can equal that of seeing the "guilty" punished. It is so nice to see it happen to somebody else instead of to you. That's a lot to give up. It takes a lot of courage to accept that you can only be doing these things to yourself and that it is all about your imagined separation from Divinity. So again, the shorter answer is of course, keep on keeping on. But there is a longer answer. There might be an easier way to be successful than working directly with forgiveness. I am not saying to forget forgiveness and seek vengeance for all of your "enemies". I'm not suggesting you start your own little inquisition. It's not time to reinstitute the rack and the thumbscrews. When you find yourself judging, being a victim, or lacking forgiveness, it is always a good idea to notice that and to choose differently. What I am saying is that if you think that truly forgiving is a hard thing to do, I am here to say that it is even harder than you think it is. Absolute forgiveness is a very advanced thought. You can repeat over and over to yourself that everyone is innocent, but that won't make you believe it or quiet the little inner "bullshit" voice.

It might be an easier and a more direct route for you to take the happy idiot approach. By that I mean that you acknowledge that you don't know anything. If your mind is going in a direction of judgment, the questions become: "Is my judgment really true? Am I really a victim of that person? Does that person really have power over me? Where did they get that power? How did that happen? Can I take it back? Did I give it to them? Were they just born holding power over me?

Is all of this really true? Is that person as selfish as my mind is saying? What does selfish mean? If I give up everything in the world to pursue truth, is that selfish?" If you follow your lines of thinking, as I am modeling here, when you are in the judgmental process – rather than jumping to the end of the line and pretending that you know there is nothing to judge – you have a chance of changing your mind. Right now you haven't earned that. You still believe in guilt and punishment, right and wrong.

Rather than sticking your head in the sand and pretending you are judgment free, look hard and deep at your thoughts. Is there anything wrong with affirming innocence and freedom from guilt? Of course there isn't. But is it really true for you? Spoiler alert: if you are even having these thoughts it is not true for you. Are they absolutely innocent? Are you not a victim? Don't look away. Keep investigating the truth in these thoughts. How enormous is it to give up victimhood? You will have looked at all the places where you feel yourself to be a victim, whether of another person, of nature, of your own body, of disease, of governments, or of the economy. You will have to follow many of these threads before you can unravel the untruth of victimhood. And this is just one aspect of judgment. Perhaps you are judging yourself and others for one of the "the seven deadly sins".[4] This is an enormous work and it is one you must do if you wish to wake up. Hearing me say it or reading it in *A Course in Miracles* isn't enough. You have to do the heavy lifting. You have to analyze every last thought that comes into your mind for its veracity. Let your mind follow these thoughts wherever they might take you. Wherever your mind finally rests, is it resting on the truth or do you need to go deeper? You may be wondering if your mind will ever get to rest. When you reach the truth you will be able to rest in the

4) **The seven deadly sins** in Roman Catholic theology, the seven vices that spur other sins and further immoral behavior. are (1) vainglory, or pride, (2) greed, or covetousness, (3) lust, or inordinate or illicit sexual desire, (4) envy, (5) gluttony, which is usually understood to include drunkenness, (6) wrath, or anger, and (7) sloth.

truth forever. At a certain point of following your thoughts, the remainder may just tumble of their own weight to join the debris of untruth you have realized. As we mentioned in the last message, you arrive at truth by eliminating all of the untruths until only truth remains.

It might not be easy for you to follow your mind, to stay with it, when you have been acting as if and believing that an untruth was true. What you will find if you stay with the process is that you know less and less every day. Getting smarter means unlearning untruths. Knowing more requires knowing less. Piling up more untruths cannot lead to wisdom. It is said that you shouldn't believe half of what you read or hear. The wise person knows which half is which. The wisest person knows that the true half is infinitely smaller than the untruth portion. When you reach the point of absolutely knowing that a thought of judgment or victimhood is not true, how could you possibly still hold on to that thinking? So maybe the quickest and most direct way to release judgments is to go directly into the untrue beliefs you are holding. Then the judgment will fall away of its own weight. Without untruths there is nothing left to support judgment. The lack of forgiveness has been propped up by false beliefs.

A "should" question will never lead you to truth. Chase it down and find what isn't true about it. As you are following the strands you may realize that you don't do some things because you should, but because you want to. There is no "should" about breathing, you desperately want that next breath. Check out your "shoulds" and see if they are actually desires. Forgiveness is a wonderful concept and to whatever degree you are able to embrace it this is a great guide for you. However, if you desire to be fully successful at forgiving, look at the untruths you are holding. This includes any beliefs you have that you do things because you should do them rather than because you want to do them. Untruth realization is the easy way to forgiveness. You have enough of a challenge without making it any harder on yourself. You have your work cut out for you. If you haven't arrived at the place where you realize the untruth of any belief or thought, you have another *think* coming. Have fun with that!

Good Now

Sanhia

Is there a difference between awakening and ascension?

This question has come up recently. We have been using the term *awakening* quite a bit of late. People are wondering if that word means the same thing as *ascension*. Are the terms interchangeable? I can understand the confusion, and it is time to clear things up. Not only will we clarify the information, but we will give you some valuable insights that I have not previously presented. Now it is time for you to receive them. We dealt with this question some years ago using still different terminology and I highly recommend that you read that message (Book I: Message 80: *What is the difference between ascension and enlightenment?*) as it provides good information on this subject without specifically focusing on most of what I have to say now. So, with no further ado, let's speak of awakening and ascension. In that previous message we used the term *enlightenment*. We'll deal with that word right now so that our focus can be limited to the two terms in the title. *Enlightenment* and *awakening* are synonyms. They have the same general meaning as I use them. You are welcome to substitute the word *enlightenment* any time I say *awakening*, but I will only use the latter term for the rest of this message.

Now, let's go back to the beginning. In this process of dealing with the subject of pure non-duality – the realization that any time we are dealing with opposites we are dealing with illusion, with things that are not real in that they do not pass the test of foreverness – we are dealing with questions of truth or untruth. In truth there is Oneness. Of course it goes without saying – though I am saying it anyway and have said it before – we are using words here and words never express the truth. They are by nature dualistic because your reasoning mind can only work in the realm of separation. When we speak of Spirit and ego, we are speaking dualistically as if these are two different things that truly exist, when in truth only Spirit exists. Spirit is connected to the Divine and ego is not. This process that we are talking about in using the terms *awakening* and *ascension* has two steps. This is the new information for you, or at least for most of you. The first step is what we have often been dealing with in these messages. That is the letting go of the ego. This process is what we have been calling awakening. When you are awakened you are in an ego-free state. This means that you have no attachments; you no longer hold people or things as special; you have no personal goals; you have no horse in the race – whatever happens is perfect. What you do is to simply listen to your inner guidance, to Spirit, and follow it in absolute trust and love without a need for understanding. When the ego is dropped there is no judgment, no competition, and no right and wrong; there is only love.

Let's go deeper into what this ego-free state is like. I won't cover all of the many questions you might have about it, so feel free to send any that linger with you to Michael and we will visit them in future messages. When you are in this awakened state there is nothing that limits you. This physical illusion is now your playground instead of your classroom. You know that whatever happens is perfect, so the thought of anything possibly being upsetting to you is insanity. It does not compute. It will not happen. You know that everything that does happen is on purpose and as it should be. Your part is to play your role, following your guidance, doing something that will be a joy for you. You know what to do because you feel guided. You are being told what to do, but there is no separation between you and the guiding Spirit. Your wills are One. That is non-dualistic. There is no limit to the possibilities of what different services you may be asked to perform. You might be teaching others through your words, written or spoken. You might be led to artistic expressions. You might be building things or growing things. Again, there are no limits to what you may be inspired to, other than you will be filled with love and joy in the doing. Results will not matter; only the doing itself has value for you.

You may be wondering how long this ego-free state goes on for. The answer to that is up to the Divine. We will say that as you are performing the services that Spirit is asking of you, which you are doing with love and joy, you are still aware of yourself. You notice the world. You have consciousness, even though the ego has disappeared. There is the observer and the observed. You are in an in-between state. Perhaps we could say that you are not ruled by dualism, yet you do not have the full experience of Oneness. It is not possible to have a self and to be One at the same time, so your non-dualism cannot be pure. You are still experiencing separation from God. The longer you are in this state of egoless self, the more you will feel the separation blurring. As you do all of these Spirit inspired things you will gradually realize there is less that you are motivated to do in the illusion. Ultimately, you come to the second step which is the letting go of the self. When this occurs you no longer have an identity; you no longer have consciousness. There is no you remaining that can observe. You are One with all, One with God. There is no longer a physical experience, a body.

There is an important understanding that accompanies the two step ascension process of first dropping the ego, and second dropping the self. Some of you have been afraid to drop the ego because you thought that ascension was in one step. You feared that dropping the ego meant you would immediately – poof! – leave your body, the world, everything! But that is not the case. When you awaken, everything is still there, except the ego. You are now experiencing the illusion without an ego. That's it! Then you will have a long run – or a short run, depending on what Spirit has in mind for you – of playing with the illusion from an egoless perspective until you are complete with that. You cannot be forced into letting go of the self, nor can you force it to happen. You will stay and play in the illusion until you have had your fill. What we call ascension is the point where you willingly and through the grace of God let go of the self. Then the illusion absolutely disappears. There is no separate consciousness, and you are One with God. Of course the truth is that you are already One with God, even as you are experiencing the illusion of a separate self and an ego, but that hasn't been a part of your conscious awareness.

In the awakened level of letting go of the ego, you know that it is all an illusion so you are able to play in it without attachment to anything. In the second level, or ascension, there is no more you. You have let go of the self, of consciousness of any separate awareness. Both of these ascension steps happen with the grace of God. Your ego will not choose to let itself go, so you ask Spirit to do that for you. You, therefore, cannot control the timing, though you can maintain a clear focus and continually face the untruths you are holding. Your awakened self also cannot decide to let go of itself because that would be an act of consciousness. Only Divine energy can dissolve that illusion of separation to allow the self to be submerged into the Oneness. It is analogous to falling asleep. You cannot will yourself into sleep. The more you try to sleep, the more you will remain awake. Sleep comes when you let go, which allows it to happen. When you have left the ego, your awakened self may still have a lot to do. Let it run its course. Your ascension occurs when the self has nothing left to do and can let go, simultaneously free of any need to stay or to leave. When this happens, we call it "by the grace of God". This was demonstrated by Jesus. This was not demonstrated by the Buddha, though he did demonstrate awakening.

We have today, and in all of the messages, talked about the egoless experience, how to achieve it and what it is like. To talk about the self-less experience is not possible. There is nothing I could say that would give you the remotest feeling for what the Divine experience is, not even a sniff. I have given the following analogy before. It has been said that the human mind only uses five per cent of its potential. What would the experience of using the full potential be? The awakened egoless self has a similar relationship with the experience of the

Divine. Notice we're not even bringing the ego consciousness level into this equation. And in saying that the awakened self experiences only 5 percent of the ecstasy of Divinity, we are being very generous. When the self has a "divine" experience, this a projection of the self, not a true experience of the Divine. The most glorious earthly experience with perfect weather, fantastic nature, smells, sights, sounds, loving people, and the feeling of a divine connection with God would, from the Divine perspective, be a descent into hell. The highest dualistic heaven would be experienced as hell by the Divine. So much for your ego attempts to create heaven on earth.

For most of you reading this, the information about leaving the self is academic. Your work is in leaving the ego. If there is anyone in the audience who is egoless, your job is to enjoy creating in that place as long as you are so inspired. Leaving the self is not a focus of any importance. Back to the rest of you, there will likely be a gradual transition where you are less and less influenced by your ego and more and more listening to the guidance of Spirit. If you still can get upset, there is work remaining. Again the final letting go of ego is through grace, not your efforts. It is not earned, but there is clear intention. For all there is never a rush. Everything happens in Divine time and order. Go set your alarms for awakening, but without selecting a time.

Good Now

Sanhia

Will you speak to us again about the Coronavirus?

It is time to revisit our friend the Coronavirus. It has been nearly two years since I last devoted messages to this subject. I encourage you to go back and read these two: Message 32: *What is the meaning of the Coronavirus?* and Message 33: *How long will the Coronavirus last?* As we mentioned back then, this is a wonderful opportunity that Spirit has presented to all of you to notice whether you are choosing love or fear, to see if you are listening to the voice of Spirit within you or to the voice of ego. We'll start by reminding you that the world is an illusion that is not real; nothing that happens there has any lasting importance. It is all part of a dream, or a nightmare – depending on your personal experience of the moment.

Having reminded you of that, I am going to diverge for a bit from where I normally go when I speak of the illusion.

While you are in a body as a human it feels very real; it is your classroom for waking up. When you are in that unawakened state you are in the realm of the ego – and if you have any issue whatsoever with what is going on with Corona or Covid-19, you can be certain that *is* the state you are in. There exists what can be labeled as truth and falseness within the illusion. These of course are the two sides of the coin of duality. Even though it ultimately makes no difference, while you are in the illusion there is a value in noticing the distinction between truth and untruth. For example, if you walk outside on a clear blue sunshiny summer day and somebody tells you to prepare for the blizzard that will be here any minute, will you say to yourself that you had better go back inside and put on your warm winter clothes to be ready for this avalanche of freezing weather? Now, that's a little crazy isn't it? What you would likely do would be to use all of your senses and some rational thinking, perhaps checking the weather on your phone, and come to the conclusion that that person was not telling you the truth. You don't cancel your picnic, put your snow tires on the car, or swear at god for wrecking your plans. If you did act on the lie, you would experience some difficulty navigating through the day. There is a difference between truth and untruth in the illusion. How can you tell the difference? You use the same techniques of untruth realization we have mentioned to help you awaken from the dream. The process is one of accepting nothing as the truth that you hear or observe from the outside world. Instead you ask yourself if it is really true. You investigate, follow threads, and persevere until it is proved or disproved. Often the place where this investigation breaks down is in the presence of fear and terror. Here humans tend to become paralyzed, not trusting anything and looking outside of the self for protection.

This is exactly what we observe happening in this age of Corona. I am going to lay out before you a few of the untruths about Corona/Covid-19 and then we'll go on to more "important" topics that relate to the awakening process. Many of you are accepting things as true that are absolutely false. Each of these things can be proven by you as false by doing a little research. You don't have to take my word for it, in fact, please don't. Do your own untruth realization. The things I will share are not wild theories from half-crazed conspiracy nuts, but carefully researched information from experts, including scientists, doctors, and economists. To begin with, there is no pandemic. That is an untruth. By any acceptable definition of a pandemic (before the WHO changed its definition last year) a pandemic is not happening. Is there a virus on the loose? Yes, of course, but a virus is not a pandemic. Flu viruses come through with great regularity. Some are worse than others, but they are not pandemics. Pandemics bring about a large number of excess deaths over the statistical norms. This has not happened over the past two years. Why are we being told that this horrible thing is happening that requires us to totally alter our lifestyles and to curtail freedom for people, both in mobility and healthcare choices? That is a good question. That is a question that I encourage you to explore at great depth for yourself. Our suggestion is that the ultimate reason for this "plandemic" stems from those who wish to have control over the planet. Now let's take a step backwards. Why has there been no reasoned, calm discussion in society or in the media about this virus, about what it is, about how best to treat it? If you have not asked yourself those questions, why haven't you? Why has there been only one voice, one opinion to be heard and to be taken seriously? Why was there not a debate to look at the reasons for and possible effectiveness of actions such as lockdowns, social distancing, masks, and treatment? Why has there been no public forum? Why is it that any voices that disagreed with the "party line" have not been allowed a place in the mass media and, in fact, have been ridiculed and their proponents labeled as lying, dangerous, and destructive conspiracy nuts? Why has this happened? As I am bringing up these various questions, I remind you that you can easily do your own research and see what you find. See how you react as you hear or read the words of these reasoned, educated voices who have quite different points of view about all the actions that have been ordered by fiat, without democratic participation.

The voice that has been declared as the only acceptable one has stated that everyone should be vaccinated two, three, maybe four, and probably eventually more times. There are three very good reasons why this is not a viable solution for handling this virus. **The first** is that the vaccine is neither safe nor effective. For a vaccine to be trusted to be safe or effective requires a minimum of three years of testing; some experts would say as many as ten years. This amount of time is necessary in order to trace the side effects and to check out long term effectiveness. Yet, in six to eight months these vaccines were produced. Where is the testing being done? It's being done on those who are taking the vaccine. You are all guinea pigs. This, in and of itself, is illegal by international law. Some vaccine developers who are not in the employment of the companies selling you these products are in serious disagreement with their use. There are severe potential side effects, so it is better if the vaccine is used only by those who are most at risk. It is probably not a good idea for those who have little risk of Covid-19-related death to take the vaccine. **Secondly**, the Corona virus is not deadly. What about all the Covid-19 deaths that are being reported? These people are not dying from the virus; they are dying from preexisting conditions that are being aggravated by the virus. Why are these conditions not being treated, rather than fighting the virus? Some doctors are having great success in approaching the situation in that manner. The official line however, discourages any other approach than that all must be vaccinated. Treatment programs are not to be considered. Many are dying because their symptoms are not being treated in the best possible manner. The result is that more "Covid-19 deaths" are reported and the reason given is because some are resisting vaccination, even when the majority of new infections are among the already vaccinated. **Thirdly,** most of the weapons being recommended and used are wrong-minded and doomed to fail. You cannot hide from a virus through lockdowns or social distancing. The virus is in no hurry and will wait you out. Masks are of little help because viruses are too small to be contained by them. They do allow you to re-breathe the waste air your body wants to release and limit the amount of oxygen that can get to your cells; so there is a definite downside.

If following the ordained guidelines is not an advisable approach, then what? The first line of defense is to have a healthy immune system. That can take some time to build if you have not been conscious of taking good care of yourself. The next best line of defense is to get the virus and receive excellent care from day one. You will likely survive if you are not one of those highly at risk people. Once you have recovered you likely have lifetime immunity, not only from the strand you caught, but from all the variants that might mutate. Vaccines try to mimic the effects of this natural immunity with limited success. As they are providing you only partial immunity, they bring with them serious potential side effects, have limited effectiveness over time, are much less likely to have any effectiveness with the variant strands, and hamper your immune system from developing. There are reports that the vaccine may have even more sinister long term effects. I encourage you to do the research.

Lockdowns are an effective way to keep people from comparing notes, but they also have a negative effect on economics, similar to what happened with the banking crisis. People living on the edge lose their houses or are evicted. Jobs are lost. Small businesses go under. The corporations roll on (continuing to eat each other up), and pick up the remains of the dispossessed for pennies on the dollar. Lockdowns also are physically, emotionally, and psychologically destructive. The cumulative effect of lockdowns is to prolong the time life of the virus. Like all of the other "protections", they primarily do the job of distracting your attention from the truth. "Pay no attention to the man behind the curtain". Another major result is accomplished by the age-old technique of "divide and conquer". People are being encouraged to blame each other. It is all the fault of those who refuse to vaccinate, or our rights and freedoms are being threatened by ___________ (fill in the blank).

The pharmaceutical companies were financed by governments to develop vaccines that were then rubber stamped as safe and effective. The companies have the perfect product. They were paid to develop it, get to keep all the profits (immense), are granted absolute freedom from liability, and have governments pressuring and even forcing people to use their goods. Not a bad deal. The "plandemic" benefactors are willing to share the profits with the drug companies, but they actually have bigger fish to fry. They want all citizens to need to have vaccine passports. Those who don't will have their rights and freedoms severely curtailed. The requirements for holding on to your card will continue to escalate until every aspect of your life is controlled. Are you beginning to wish you had read the fine print? If you think that your passport is giving you freedom, it is time to think again. Freedom cannot be given. It is something that you must take for yourself. The first step is to start doing your own thinking. Today they come after the "anti-vaxxers"; tomorrow they may come after you. Many of you decry the absolute lack of freedom in China today. You might be looking at your future. Why is all of this not being discussed on every street corner, in every newspaper and magazine, on every news show? With many experts trying to explain what is going on, how do you come to be so ill-informed? Your first line of community protection and communication has been compromised. There is no more free press. All mass communication is controlled by a surprisingly small group of people. It doesn't matter if it's Fox News or CNBC or public television. It doesn't matter if it is the Chicago Tribune or the New York Times. Nothing is allowed to be printed or said that doesn't pass muster with those who have an interest in having a pandemic and you becoming vaccinated. Again, please feel free to trace down the ownership of all the major corporations in the world. Do the research yourself. Find out what is true and what isn't. Before taking any action, however, I suggest you read the second half of the message.

Now that I have perhaps filled you with fear and anger (possibly directed at the bearer of the "bad news"), let's take an enormous step back from all of this and look at the spiritual aspects.

When you accept anything as the truth, whether from me, from the media, from the government, from the World Health Organization, or from any outside source you are listening to the voice of ego. You are giving your power away. You have become a victim. You are living in fear. Nobody can awaken by following the mass consciousness. If you want to remain asleep, sleep away. If you are choosing to awaken you act not from fear, but from love. You listen to the gentle voice of Spirit, not the threats and warnings of the ego. If you are deciding whether or not to get a vaccine, you don't do that from fear but from clear guidance. Spirit has the perfect plan for you. That plan might include you getting Covid-19. That plan might include guidance for staying healthy. If you choose the vaccine out of fear, that fear will continue to rule your life. The vaccine will bring no true, lasting peace or sense of safety (witness those who have been vaccinated, but still fear the unvaccinated). Some of you claim to have no fear of the virus, but believe you have taken the shot for other people. Perhaps it was due to pressure from a fearful family member, or from not wanting to get sick and add to the overtaxed hospital situation, or simply not wanting to be responsible for passing the disease on to another, particularly the elderly. These are all voices of the ego. Spirit never asks you to sacrifice anything. Sacrifice comes from the assumption that you know better than God, that you know what is good for other people. As I have reminded you many times before, you are doing well if you can figure out what is best for you, let alone for another. How do you find out what is best for you? You listen to Spirit; you go to the place that is beyond fear, and you trust what is brought to you. Spirit will take care of others. What you are calling "doing for others" is always fear based. Look at the fear. Own it and don't hide behind "sacrificing". The ego is very skilled at co-opting "spiritual" language. It will talk about "solidarity" and "selfishness" when trying to convince one to be vaccinated. The ego accuses you of endangering others by refusing the needle. It plays on your guilt. The big ego lie is that Jesus sacrificed himself for us. We were so bad that he had to give his life to save us. Rather than seeing the truth of the Spiritual gift of his awakening and ascension – of his modeling for us the potential for what we would all choose someday – the ego offers us a model of pain and sacrifice. Coming into the physical world against your wishes and living as a human would be a sacrifice. Going back home is a dream that we all share, whether we are aware of it or not. If you truly want to do for others, the only path for you is through waking up.

You may now be going into reaction thinking "Oh my God! What have I done? I never should have taken that vaccine!" Perhaps you are concerned about the ongoing negative health effects it will have for you. The fear is that this step is irreversible and you will be punished for your stupidity. However, the vaccine has no power. Neither do those who wish to control the world. The power is in you. There is no action that you could ever take that could not be changed. Everything going on in the world is a part of your classroom for awakening. When you have awakened, all previous choices and actions will make absolutely no difference. Bring your fears about your choices to Spirit. Look at each fear until you find the untruth in it. I want to mention here that you might be one who chose not to get the vaccine, but also did so out of fear. Perhaps there was fear of death or disability from the vaccine. You, too, have your work cut out for you. This Corona situation is an enormous gift for everyone. It is turning up the heat. It is pressing you to choose love or fear. There is hardly an in-between place to hide out in anymore. It is almost impossible to go on with "business as usual". There may never again be a time of "business as usual" for you in this body. You may have only the choice to wake up *or* to become a part of the new world order, which will control every aspect of your life. Fortunately the choice is entirely up to you. In truth, there is no difference between the new world order and the old world order. If you have not chosen to wake up, your life has always been directed by fear. The only difference is that now it is much harder to avoid noticing how *everything* is run by fear. It is never too late to make the choice. When you choose to leave the ego behind and to dwell in the eternal now, time will stop being a factor. The choice is going to become quite clear now; be a part of the new world order or wake up, noticing that the emperor has no clothes.

You will no longer believe the mass consciousness and the mass media, but will find the truth inside of you, along with Spirit. That is the only place where freedom exists. It will require brutal honesty on your part to confront every untruth, but freedom is never bought by fear-based actions. That makes you a prisoner of your fear. There is a part of you that believes that freedom means being the decider of everything in your life in the illusion: where you will go, what you will do, and when you will do it. Now come all of these regulations affecting travel, shopping, workplaces, entertainment, meetings, and more. Terror comes in over how to maintain or regain your freedom. This is an ego fear-based response. Spirit is bringing you the perfect thing. If Spirit is restricting your travel, there is a reason to stay home, or at least nearby. As you become aware of the lies that you have been told by the health authorities and the human damage that is and will continue occurring because of vaccinations, passports, lockdowns, masks, and so on – your job is to not go into anger, blame, and attack against them. Remember that all of those who want to manipulate the system for their own benefit or agenda, as well as those who cooperate out of fear, are asleep humans, unaware of what they are doing and even that they are asleep. They are all operating out of fear and terror. Any attack upon them is projection on your part. Your job is to take responsibility for your reactions, to work with forgiveness, and to bring it all to Spirit. Remember, *none* of this is real! If Spirit has presented you with extra time by limiting your choices, use this time to wake up. You are a victim to nobody and to nothing. Your fear and anger are all truly aimed at yourself. Face them and see through them to the truth. Accept Spirit's gifts to you and use them.

The "plandemic" is a mass call to awakening. There is no difference between accepting the mass consciousness belief in this being a pandemic with all the trimmings, and the mass consciousness sayings that you don't deserve happiness or love or that there is evil in the world which must be fought. They are all the same. There is no difference between the belief that there is not enough to go around or the idea that you have to work hard to survive, and the acceptance of the doublespeak about the pandemic. It makes no difference if mass consciousness thoughts have been passed down through the ages or seem to be the creation of a modern day cabal. When you give your power away to what seems to be a truth outside of you, therefore placing yourself into a victim role, it is never the truth. Keep looking until you find the truth and that *will* set you free. This will never come about through taking actions in the world, because the world is not holding you prisoner. Getting the vaccine will not set you free from anything. If you are guided there by Spirit, by all means go. Go fearlessly without expectations or attachment, without the thought that the guidance is for anyone but you. Either way, Spirit has your best interests at heart. Death is not real.

Good Now

Sanhia

Biography

Michael Hersey has been working personally with his own ascension process since the early '70s. He was guided to study numerology and then to establish a practice in 1979. Michael also developed a workshop program which supported others to give up their fears about money and do the work they came here to do. He began channeling ascended master Sanhia in 1985, and has channeled for numerous groups and individuals throughout the United States and Sweden. Since 2013 he has co-led Spiritual Alchemy groups with his partner Ulla Lindgren. The focus of all the work is on realizing personal Divinity. Michael is also the author of the books *Ascension Numerology: A Love Letter from your Higher Self* and *God Blesses You: Ascension Messages from Sanhia.*

The five-step process

1 Define the area in your life that is causing you emotional, spiritual, mental, and/or physical pain. This will be referred to as your "old story". State it succinctly in, preferably, a single sentence. Saying it out loud is good. Your "old story" is what your brain-mind thinks is true. Sometimes you are carrying uncomfortable energy in your body, but don't know what "old story" it is connected to. In such cases your "old story" is that you have this pain in your body. Then go on to the second step.

2 Focus on where you feel the discomfort in your body when you think of your "old story". Close your eyes, relax, breathe slowly and deeply, and turn off your brain-mind. You can do this by imagining you have a switch on the side of your head. See yourself flipping it to the off position. Now, watch the discomfort from your belly-mind. Do not judge, label, or try to get rid of the feeling. Simply accept it, let it be, and let it do whatever it wishes to do. Become one with the sensation and embrace it with love. Stay with the energy until you notice the nature of it changing. When the feeling becomes calm, perhaps warmer and lighter; move the energy to your heart chakra. Then, on your exhales, see it move slowly out of your heart chakra through a laser-like beam out into the universe. Continue breathing until the energy is largely dissipated.

3 Take full responsibility for having created your "old story", knowing that as you are a Divine being it could be no other way. Speaking it out loud is good. Even though you may not yet understand why, remind yourself that the creation came out of love, choosing the best way for you to realize your Divinity.

4 From the depth of your heart hear your new story. State it positively and in the present tense. Don't require any individual to play a role in your story. If you want another person to be involved, describe the role without naming the actor. Trust Spirit to find the one who will fit. Your job is to express your story. Spirit's job is to bring it into your life. State this new story succinctly in, preferably, a single sentence. Saying it out loud is good. It should fill you with feelings of love, peace, and joy. If it doesn't, find a way to restate until it does.

5 You aren't always able to get to the deepest level of your story at once. Therefore, your "old story" could come back at some point in the future. If it does, congratulate yourself for noticing and as soon as possible begin the *five-step process* over again. Know that the energy that has been transformed from fear into love is permanent, while your pain is finite. Eventually there will be no reason for repetition.

You can listen to a recording which leads you through the *five-step process* on our website:

www.channelswithoutborders.com/5-step-process/

Acknowledgements

This book would not have been possible in its present form without the contributions of Ulla Lindgren. I considered listing her as co-author, but she said that the original text all comes from Sanhia or from me. Nevertheless, not one word made it into print without Ulla's consideration. For one whom English is a second tongue – and who claims to not be very proficient at it – she has an amazing feel and command of the language and its subtleties. Ulla's contributions included word choice, sentence structure, ruthless slashing of unnecessary text, and – above all – consistency to Sanhia's ascension message. She also was at least an equal partner in choices for the cover, layout, and font.

I learned a lot more about how the co-creation process works with Sanhia. It would be so nice if he just dictated in word perfect form as many others do through their channels. But no, Sanhia wants me to be more involved with the process, as it is a part of his training for me. After recording an interview with Sanhia, which takes twenty-five to forty minutes, I spend a half day transcribing it into the format that becomes the monthly message. Then, Ulla and I go over it together. Sometimes that goes quite smoothly. Other times it becomes quite a vehicle for working out the spiritual issues in our relationship. Sanhia is always there to give us a loving push into our process. I can say that the final result that comes out of all of that matches the growth that we each experience alone and as a couple.

Working, perhaps playing is a more accurate term, with Marie Örnesved is always a joy for us. Marie is above all in her professionalism and efficiency, but at the same time is open to whatever intuitive guidance she receives as we create the book. Not only does she freely offer whatever insights come to her, and defends them vigorously – she also lovingly defers to us to make the final call. Marie will spare no effort to make every nuance of the book live up to the highest standard. She had a hand in many of the stylistic decisions we made. We feel gifted to be working with Marie and LightSpira.

Stella Hansen has again offered incredible support as our editor. Stella offered years ago to donate her services in editing the monthly messages (which were replete with irritating miscues), as her eagle eye always noticed small (and some not so small) errors. She not only catches the repeated or misspelled words, the missing or misplaced comma, and punctuation errors in general, but also contributes meaningful questions about the content and lets me know when a concept has not been clearly explained. Her years of work with Sanhia are of great value to us (and to her, I think). Thanks also to different readers who have offered suggestions for topics. The : groups have generated wonderful subjects for messages in the past few years through their questions to Sanhia and his responses.

Finally I want to give thanks to Spirit for guidance, to *A Course in Miracles* for daily inspiration, other authors too numerous to mention here, and, of course, to Sanhia. One of Sanhia's trainings for me throughout my life has involved leading me to different books. He wants this information in my conscious mind so he can better play with it, but I'm the big winner. I get to play with the ideas, too. He wants me to say that his job with the messages is the easiest of all, talking for a half hour once a month about the subject that holds the greatest passion for him – ascension. He says that he left all the heavy lifting to me, and to Ulla. I am grateful for the workout.

Book: Ascension Numerology

Ascension Numerology brings ancient wisdom into the 21st century by presenting a strong focus on your spiritual intention, particularly through the Ascension Number. It introduces key concepts such as the *"Love Letter from Your Higher Self"*, and the message that you are the creator of your life. You have been planning this adventure for a long time. During the pre-planning you set things up to encourage the likelihood of you realizing your ascension. This information is available to you through your numerology chart. New insights await long-time students of numerology, while new students will find simplicity and clarity guiding them into an intuitive grasp of their charts. And all readers are empowered to go deeper on their own with this cutting edge book. A new dimension is the use of multiple color graphic representations to speak directly to your right brain. This book is fun!

You can find out more about *Ascension Numerology* at:

www.channelswithoutborders.com/ascension-numerology-book/

or order it from your favorite online bookstore.

Book: God Blesses You
Ascension Messages from Sanhia

Ascension is the experience of your Divinity. It is the full conscious realization that you are the creator of everything in your world. You cannot be a victim. You always exist. Nothing outside of love is real. You are One with God and with Spirit. The possibility of realizing your ascension is the major reason for your present incarnation.

The channeled messages in this book come from the ascended master Sanhia. They hold a particular power coming from one who has realized his own Divinity. Sanhia's expressed purpose is to support you who are on the ascension path. This collection can serve as a workbook to support you in understanding your Divine nature and allowing Spirit to direct your life. It can also help you decide if ascension is your path in this incarnation. The messages are organized under a variety of themes to allow you to focus deeply on one aspect at a time. They are designed to be read and reread to help you widen your understanding as you work with the content. The wisdom is profound.

You can find out more about *God Blesses You* at:

www.channelswithoutborders.com/
god-blesses-you-ascension-messages-from-sanhia-book/

or order it from your favorite online bookstore.

making **messages** from
loving hearts

available to a **global** audience

cocreators @lightspira.com
www.lightspira.com